# SMALL BUSINESS LEGAL GUIDE

# ENTREPRENEUR MAGAZINE
## Small Business Legal Guide

Barbara C. S. Shea, Esq.

with Jennifer Haupt

John Wiley & Sons, Inc.

New York • Chichester • Brisbane • Toronto • Singapore

To my grandfathers, creators of their own small business, who showed me that it is not money and formal education, but imagination, vision, determination, and natural intelligence in action that are the building blocks of success.

B.C.S.S.

To my husband, Eric, and my children, Andrew and Justin. Without their support, love, and an occasional kick in the pants, I could not have completed this project and maintained a modicum of sanity.

J.H.

This text is printed on acid-free paper.

Copyright © 1995 by Barbara C. S. Shea
Published by John Wiley & Sons, Inc.

This publication is designed to provide accurate and authoritative information in regard to the subject matter covered. It is sold with the understanding that the publisher is not engaged in rendering legal, accounting, or other professional services. If legal advice or other expert assistance is required, the services of a competent professional person should be sought.

ISBN 0-471-11950-4 (cloth)
ISBN 0-471-11951-2 (ppb)

Printed in the United States of America

10   9   8   7   6   5

# PREFACE

We are happy you have decided to purchase this book as a primer covering the basics of the law. Welcome to the fraternity of "can-do" people; that growing number of folks like you who are eager to learn, empower themselves, gain control of their wallets, and flourish as small business owners and entrepreneurs. This legal guide is meant to take the mystery out of the law that governs commercial enterprises in the United States, a nation conceived by immigrants with an entrepreneurial spirit.

Few small business owners have a legal background and most are neither inclined nor able to hire costly legal talent. And, even though lawyers rarely come with a price tag of $750 per hour and up (as was reported about some of O. J. Simpson's defense team), law firm associates can be charged out at as much as $200 per hour and partners often times command upward of $250 per hour—fees far beyond what many small business owners can afford or are willing to pay as a "cost of doing business."

Nonetheless, a small business owner must deal with many legal issues, questions, and challenges on a daily, weekly, monthly, and yearly basis (remember, the tax man cloaked in IRS law comes twice a year for many small corporate entrepreneurs). Every entrepreneur must realistically factor into any business plan a line item for legal costs. (And yes, you do have a line item veto as President and Chief Executive Officer of your own business! One of the perks.)

*The Small Business Legal Guide* will help you in the following ways:

- It will make you aware of the major legal issues and laws affecting every small business owner.
- It will help you educate yourself about the legal realities impacting your particular business.
- It aids you in developing a plan for your business that factors in all relevant legal considerations.

- It teaches you how to save yourself legal, financial, and emotional costs by using Court Coach methods and philosophies.

We hope that you will become as fascinated with the law as many others who have taken an active role in learning how to perform certain legal tasks and, most significantly, *how to think like a lawyer*.

Keep in mind that all of the special features of this book are intended to help you handle your legal affairs and solve your legal problems—but it's *not* intended to *replace* your lawyer or teach you how to *be* a lawyer. Use the book as a *guide* to doing some of the legal legwork and reducing your legal costs. Nothing in this book is meant as legal advice. Read this book for legal information only.

# ACKNOWLEDGMENTS

To Jennifer, my "Sleepless in Seattle" colleague and co-author extra-ordinaire.

To my office colleagues, Debbie Douglas, Alicia Sullivan, Terry Wettergreen, and Ellen Essman, who put up with my time-outs to write this book, supported my efforts, edited, organized, faxed, phoned, and filed . . . . all in a joint effort to finish this book on time.

To my children, Cynthia, Sally, Tommy, and Cara, for their advice and support along the way.

To my friends on the cheering squad, Joyce, Rae Elizabeth, Joan, Sara, Chad, Molly, Catherine, and Debbie. Thanks for the encouragement.

To Ruth Mills, editor par excellence, for guiding us from start to finish; to John Mahaney, the original editor; and to the staff at Publications Development, especially Nancy Marcus Land, who guided the production process . . . Thank you.

And to the readers, I share this family motto: "Hitch your wagon to a star—you won't fall far behind." (And remember, you are the star.)

# CONTENTS

# INTRODUCTION

Many entrepreneurs who undertake a business venture are surprised by the amount of legal work they encounter. Myriad legal documents must be drafted, evaluated, and filed to launch, run, or dismantle a small business. And, legal entanglements and conflicts in and out of the business venture pop up frequently—disputes with vendors, employees, and customers, any one of which can quickly turn into a lawsuit.

To attack the varied legalities associated with operating a business *without the proper knowledge* may mean losing more than money. You can lose valuable time, good employees, peace of mind, and even your freedom if you run afoul of the criminal law. And, while self-representation *(pro se)* is flourishing among small business owners, the results are not always positive. Approaching your legal realities with the mindset of a lawyer—being able to think like a lawyer—is a major advantage you will gain from reading this book. You will gain further advantage by your acquired familiarity with legal terms and other knowledge gleaned from this handy legal resource.

We will suggest ways to work with your attorney to save you and your business from skyrocketing legal costs. You will either be able to work comfortably and confidently on your own (pro se) or in a collegial relationship with your lawyer. In this way, you will avoid getting in the position in which so many small business owners find themselves—feeling inept, intimidated, and angry about legal realities.

All too often, a small business owner comes away from the legal table paying a lawyer a large sum of money and is less than satisfied with the outcome, not to mention the significant dent in the business ledger. For those folks who feel that high legal costs are de rigueur for setting up, operating, and dismantling a small business, we beg to differ. The *Small Business Legal Guide* will show you that you have many creative options in how much legal work you want to take on yourself and how much you want to turn over to an attorney—from handing over your entire case to going it pro se.

As you read this book, keep in mind that it's all about showing you the legal options. We will open many legal windows for you, but don't feel compelled to jump out of any if you are uncertain about the availability of a safe landing. The ultimate choice is up to you, and even if you decide to hand over your entire caseload to an attorney, at least you will know what she or he is talking about and doing on your behalf. You will be better equipped to understand what services you are paying for; in short, you'll be a more informed consumer.

Also keep in mind that our purpose is not to give you a condensed law school experience and teach you everything there is to know about business law. Rather, we want to arm you with sufficient knowledge to research the laws that apply to your business, to handle many of your own legal affairs, and/or to work more efficiently with a lawyer. Our goal is for you to learn how to maintain control of the legal and personal processes involved with setting up, running, and eventually dissolving a small business.

The methodology and approach to solving legal problems in this book follows an innovative approach to the law, called *Court Coach.*® This legal program was developed by one of the authors, Barbara C. S. Shea, out of her own personal experience as a lawyer, mother of four children, former writer/editor, and community volunteer, combined with her professional expertise in the counseling and legal arenas. Since 1990, a wide variety of clients have utilized the Court Coach® program.

Integral to the Court Coach® philosophy is:

- The attitude that the client is not just a case or legal file, but a person who happens to have a legal problem and has come for help.
- The belief that attorneys are members of a "helping profession," much the same as a therapist, psychiatrist, nurse, or doctor.
- The expectation that clients will:
  —Save money.
  —Receive "digestible," understandable legal advice.

—Be treated with respect.

—Learn from this experience about the law, the legal process, negotiating skills, and themselves.

Court Coach® and the *Small Business Legal Guide* are based on the "unbundling" of legal services.

## HOW "UNBUNDLED" LEGAL SERVICES CAN REDUCE LEGAL COSTS

According to Los Angeles family law attorney and mediator, Forrest S. Mosten, the guru and current leading legal advocate of the "unbundling" concept, this term refers to allowing the client to choose whichever portion of the full packet of legal services the client wants. Further, the client may also specify the depth and extent of the individual service. The full package of services in traditional legal representation usually requires the following activities on the part of the attorney.

1. Gathering facts.
2. Advising the client.
3. Discovering facts of the opposing party.
4. Researching the law.
5. Drafting correspondence and documents.
6. Negotiating in court.
7. Representing the client in court.

Practically speaking, unbundling simply means that the client is free to purchase a little piece of the package—just a consultation or a second opinion or a short telephone answer. Or, the client may want representation if the business dispute goes to court but may also want to handle the court filings, discovery, and negotiations without a lawyer.

Under the Court Coach® concept, the lawyer works with the client on a partnership basis, overseeing all the client's work product and deciding, with the client's input and consent, which tasks the client can handle adequately and which tasks are best left to the attorney. If necessary an attorney also will be willing to get involved in the legal issue at almost any place along the road.

The *Small Business Legal Guide* helps you in the same way: it describes how you, the entrepreneur, can do much of the legwork required in handling your legal affairs and problems—thereby reducing the cost of just turning over a problem to a lawyer.

## HOW THE *SMALL BUSINESS LEGAL GUIDE* HELPS YOU CUT YOUR LEGAL COSTS

The *Small Business Legal Guide* is based on the Court Coach® philosophy and guidelines, and it will help you win the small business legal game by cutting your expenditures of time, energy, emotions—not to mention finances—in dealing with the law.

Our goals for this book are to teach you:

1. To think critically and analyze situations like a lawyer.
2. To determine what options are available in various legal situations, how to optimize those options, and what work can be handled safely *without* a lawyer.
3. To organize your business with the purpose of hiring a mentor/coach, as opposed to handing over the entire legal workload; to find the "right" lawyer; and to work with your lawyer productively (with inside tips about how to become your lawyer's favorite client).
4. To speak, write, and negotiate like a lawyer—on the phone, in a letter, at an informal hearing, or at a full-fledged legal proceeding.
5. To represent yourself in specific legal proceedings commonly encountered by small business owners, including Small Claims Court and administrative proceedings outside the courtroom.
6. To research the law using law libraries and use the resources that legal professionals rely on.
7. To develop a legal vocabulary and a comfort level using legal terms in written and spoken communications.

While understanding the law is certainly important, another skill that lawyers have—and you will learn—is how to take in the whole picture and grasp all the realities impacting your situation. Good lawyers not only have control of the legal facts and laws, but also are able to read the emotional reactions of the other players and are keenly aware of the political realities of the legal situation.

## THE IDEAS SOUND GREAT, BUT IS THE BOOK USER FRIENDLY?

This is an excellent question. You certainly don't want to purchase another book that's going to serve the sole purpose of warming your bookshelves because it is too difficult to access information quickly.

We know you want to devote the bare minimum of time to reading when what you really want to be doing is running your business. Hence, our resolve is to make this book simple to follow.

Here's how the book works: There are three parts, covering your legal concerns as a small business owner:

1. Setting up a small business.
2. Running a small business.
3. Planning for and dismantling a small business.

## The Anatomy of a Chapter

Each chapter is divided into the following easy-to-read sections:

- *The body of the chapter.* The meat and potatoes.
- *Know your key terms.* A short glossary of legal terms to help you comprehend the chapter material.
- *Basic legal research.* A bibliography of legal books and periodicals.
- *Key resources.* People, places, and things to make dealing with the legalities of small business life even easier still.
- *Court Coach®* *suggests.* Practical ideas, inside tips, and creative strategies relating to the specific topics discussed in that chapter. These are taken directly from the Court Coach® program.

### The Body of the Chapter

The bulk of each chapter gives the legal basics—essential information about incorporation, taxes, or whatever subject is under discussion. There are many, many legal rules and precedents for situations you'll encounter as a small business owner. Yet, there are no pat answers. The reason: The law is generic, applicable to all, but each situation presents a different set of unique facts and circumstances.

Consequently, when you apply the generic law to the specifics of any given situation, naturally you come up with many different conclusions. And that's what makes horse races, gang! That's also why juries sometimes have a difficult time applying the generic law to a compelling, heart-wrenching set of facts and sending certain defendants to prison (but that's another story). Or, as lawyers say: Difficult cases make for tough decisions.

*This book is not meant to make any legal decisions for you, or provide legal advice.* This book is a *source* of legal information. We'll supply you with the legal guidelines that can serve as a foundation for many of your business decisions. We'll help you weigh your options, by discussing the pros and cons when appropriate, so that you can make informed decisions about how to set up, run, and dismantle your business.

### Know Your Key Legal Terms

Although you're not a lawyer and may have little cognizance or use for legal jargon, knowledge is empowerment, and so this section will review key terms used in the chapter. We are not trying to give you legal definitions of these terms, but plain English, commonsense translations to demystify these terms of art. If you are interested in the full legal definitions, *Black's Law Dictionary* (West Publishing) is an excellent resource; it's big enough to be a doorstop but is the ultimate resource for legal definitions. (This is what lawyers use instead of Webster's.)

### Basic Legal Research

You don't want, and we couldn't possibly give you, all the information to be had on every topic covered in this book—that's not our goal as writers, nor yours as a reader. The Basic Legal Research section is a guide to other publications and sources (generally found in most law libraries or large bookstores unless otherwise stated), that will give you a better understanding of the laws discussed in a given chapter. So whet your appetite on the legal topics that pertain to your stage of the game in developing a small business, and follow the suggestions for further legal research in this section to really develop your expertise and confidence.

Researching the law is easier than you may think once you get the hang of it. That's because the law is precise in detail, highly structured, and has been recorded methodically and chronologically. You can conduct a search either manually with law books or on a computer using legal software programs. Using either method, you can find any case recorded and all of the following information about any case:

- The names of the plaintiff and defendant.
- The court in which the case was tried.
- The year in which the case was tried.
- The cause of action (why the case was filed).
- The major issues in the case.
- The facts on which the court's decision or verdict was based.
- The court's decision (the rule of the case), which sets a precedent for future similar cases.

- *Dictum,* which is a judicial aside that does not "count" as a precedent but provides a guideline in dictating the court's thinking on a side issue.
- Other courts following this precedent.

### Key Resources

Here's where you'll find other sources of knowledge on the topics covered in each chapter. While "book smarts" are great, it also helps to speak with real live people so we have tried to include the phone numbers of various helpful agencies whenever possible. This section lists local agencies that can provide brochures, pamphlets, and other materials; sometimes there are even personnel who will answer your questions on the telephone.

Unless otherwise stated, you can find the phone numbers and addresses of state, regional, and other local agencies in the government listings in the front of your phone book (usually, the blue pages).

### Court Coach® Suggests

Many legal guides for small businesses tell you what the law is. Our goal is to make your legal life easier by explaining simply and clearly how you, as a nonlawyer, can use the law with confidence. This section will give practical tips you probably won't find anywhere else for applying the law to various aspects of your business operations. Drawing on Barbara Shea's years of experience as the founder of Court Coach® and Jennifer Haupt's background as an experienced business writer, we share with you our combined perspective honed from our own unique experiences with the trials and tribulations of small business law.

Please do not go into court or an attorney's office and quote these suggestions as legal advice. Regard each of them as more like a dictum, from *obiter dictum,* Latin for "a remark along the way." Or, as Henry Campbell Blackwell (author of *Black's Law Dictionary*) defines dictum: "any statement of the law enunciated . . . merely by way of illustration, argument, analogy, or suggestion."

In short, keep in mind that all of the special features of this book are intended to help you handle your legal affairs and solve your legal problems—but it's *not* intended to *replace* your lawyer or teach you how to *be* a lawyer. Use the book as a *guide* to doing some of the legal legwork and reducing your legal costs.

# Part I

# SETTING UP
# A SMALL BUSINESS

# 1

# SETTING UP YOUR BUSINESS TO AVOID LEGAL PITFALLS

## AN OUNCE OF PREVENTION IS WORTH SEVERAL POUNDS OF LEGAL CURE

When opening or buying a small business, there are many issues to consider (some of which we'll discuss in the following chapters of this book) and decisions to make. That frightening and inexplicable thing called "the law" may be the last thing you want to think about and on the bottom of your "to do" list. But, believe it or not, one of the first things you need to turn your attention to is the law. Why should you think about lawyers, legal fees, and litigation before the paint's even dried on your "Open for Business" sign?

This chapter will answer that question. And, it will give you a bird's eye view of preventive law, a concept at the cutting edge of delivering legal services to the public. As you'll see in digesting this chapter, spending a modicum of extra time and money for the proper legal precautions when you set up your business operations will save you major headaches in the long run. The goal of this chapter is to help you avoid legal pitfalls and hefty legal fees by:

- *Factoring legal fees into your budget as a cost of doing business.* Legal fees are a necessity of setting up and running a business, so you might as well live in reality and calculate these fees into your overall budget.
- *Choosing the right kind of attorney to suit your business needs.* A simple one-person shop will need considerably less legal consultation than a more complicated corporation involving a handful of officers plus employees. We'll go over the different kinds of legal consultation that are available so you can match up your business with the right legal partner.
- *Developing a good working relationship with your attorney.*

## FACTORING LEGAL FEES INTO YOUR BUDGET AS A COST OF DOING BUSINESS

A major pitfall of small business owners with limited funds is the omission of legal fees from their start-up costs and operating budgets. "I don't plan on getting into any legal trouble, so I don't need to worry about legal costs" is a foolish rationalization. We have some sage words of advice for folks of this ilk: Wake up and smell the coffee; the time to think about legal costs is *before* trouble brews!

In view of the multitude of laws impacting every business, large and small legal costs in running even the smallest business can be substantial if you rely simply on traditional legal representation. We will describe optional services and new ways to work with traditional lawyers to cut your legal costs. Also throughout the book, the legal information provided will alert you personally to potential trouble spots, so that you will consistently be able to avoid legal disputes, mistakes, and bad business judgment due to misinformation or lack of information about the law. When you consider the constantly changing nature of federal and state law, as the political stage shifts between Democrat and Republican agendas (and egos), you can easily see why just staying current and on top of legal requirements is a business necessity.

Factoring legal costs into any business plan is not necessarily a complicated process, but it is somewhat amorphous. It is not possible to draw up a "laundry list" of legal costs that apply to *all* small businesses since they will depend on the nature of your business as well as its structure, size, form, and your style.

As you peruse this book, keep potential legal expenditures in mind (or, better yet, write them down), so that you, with your attorney, can estimate the actual costs.

## The Organizational Form of Your Business: Sole Proprietorship, Partnership, or Corporation

As you'll see when reading Chapters 2 through 4, which discuss the three organizational forms that small businesses can take (sole proprietorship, partnership, and incorporation), your legal costs will first depend on the complexity of your business organization. Note that legal costs include fees and out-of-pocket expenses. Your attorney will charge you per billable hour for legal services rendered on your behalf. Additionally, you need to include out-of-pocket expenses billed through your attorney's office, or that you incur on your own, such as filing fees, copying costs, phone bills, faxes, and the like.

Setting up a sole proprietorship will involve the least legal expertise, as this is a simple process with little paperwork. Setting up a partnership will require negotiations between partners, the hammering out of the partnership agreement, and various other legal documents along the way. Incorporation is the most complicated form of business organization because the business is treated as a separate entity, legally responsible for all of its own actions, and must conform with state law and possibly federal law depending on the nature (e.g., securities) and structure (e.g., franchise) of the business.

## The Process of Setting Up Your Business

It's easy to see that if you're buying a well-established business, with its operational procedures intact, you'll incur considerably less legal costs than if you're starting a business from scratch. But look to net costs, as you may also incur liabilities and debts, and there may be litigation in process or pending, or even threatened but not disclosed to you. So, be sure to ask these questions when acquiring an established business:

- What are your legal costs per month, per year?
- Are any lawsuits pending, or waiting in the wings?

The bottom line: The more complicated the issues, the costlier your legal bill will be.

## The Industry Your Business Is In

Even if you plan on opening a one-person shop, which seems like a simple, straightforward endeavor, many regulations may be applicable in your chosen industry.

Let's say, for example, that you want to open a catering service/sandwich shop that will consist of you making soup and sandwiches behind a counter. Sounds simple enough, but a host of health, safety, environmental, and zoning regulations may apply. And what if you want to hire an assistant? There will be even more regulations to consider.

## ASSESSING YOUR OPTIONS FOR LEGAL SERVICES

Now that you have an idea how to start calculating your legal expenses, the next step is to acquaint yourself with legal service options and the options that are available to you locally (although with the explosion in telecommunications, the definition of local has greatly expanded). In the legal profession, your lawyer must be licensed to practice in your state. Lawyers can be licensed in more than one state and will inscribe the states in which they are licensed on their letterhead. Also a law firm can have offices in more than one state and even more than one country. You may actually save dollars hiring a more expensive lawyer who will be a part of a larger network.

### General Practice Attorneys

If you consult your local bar association, yellow pages, chamber of commerce, favorite networking group, or your compatriots in business, undoubtedly you will come up with the names of a handful of local lawyers in "general practice." These attorneys, like medical general practitioners, offer a broad range of legal services, and ordinarily specialize in several areas of law.

A "jack-of-all-law" may seem to be just the ticket for getting an overview of your wide variety of legal obligations as a small business owner. The downside of general practice is that your needs may require more time than the lawyer can commit to one client, or the lawyer may not have the special expertise you need.

The ticket is a general practice attorney specializing in business law, commercial law, litigation, and corporate or corporation law. Beware of attorneys, especially solos, whose practices seem to be all over the map, advertising specialties in 10 or more unrelated areas of the law.

### General Practice Law Firms

A general practice law firm is composed of many attorneys who specialize in different areas. This means that, in a legal pinch, more than one lawyer can attend to your needs. Another plus is that if you don't like one lawyer, you can have another lawyer work on your file right in the same firm; you don't have to switch to another firm.

## Alternative Law Practices

*Court Coach*® is an example of an alternative law practice (see the Introduction for an explanation of the Court Coach® program), as are the other successful practices described in this chapter, such as *Lawyers on Duty* and *Divorce Helpline* and *TeleLawyer* in California.

Other alternative legal services are popping up throughout the country as well, but we must offer you a significant word of extreme caution: Make absolutely certain that "alternative" does not translate to nonlawyer or paralegal. Trust us, just as you want a great nanny for your new baby, you only want the real thing for your fledgling enterprise: a bona fide attorney with a law degree (J.D.), a license to practice in your state, and malpractice insurance. *Ask* the lawyer you are hiring these questions:

- Where and when did you graduate from law school?
- Where are you licensed to practice, and for how long?
- In what courts are you licensed to practice?
- Do you have malpractice insurance in place now?

For a list of attorneys with thriving alternative legal practices, see Appendix I.

## Legal Clinics

The nation's first private legal clinic, the Legal Clinic of Jacoby & Meyers, was started in 1972, then known as Meyers, Jacoby, & Mosten. Since then there has been a proliferation of these high-volume law offices, which usually operate as a chain. The attraction is that these firms charge substantially less than prestigious law firms. Make sure you check out both the clinic and attorney who will handle your case if you go this route. Has the attorney handled cases such as yours before? And, most importantly, what were the results?

## Prepaid Legal Plans

This is a fairly new alternative; it has cropped up during the past 10 years or so and is enjoying quite a bit of popularity. These plans, which vary a great deal in cost and coverage, are marketed to the general public through large banks, credit card companies, and retailers.

Again, you get what you pay for. Annual fees range between $100 and $200, which covers limited services including telephone consultations, letter writing, will preparation, and review of brief legal documents (less than 6 pages). Any more complicated services will cost you extra. Hourly fees are usually around $50, which is well below the market rate for experienced attorneys in most cities.

## Paralegals, Independent and Otherwise

Paralegals are definitely a viable option as well. While paralegals are more popular now than in the past, they are better trained in some states than others. They can be a great resource for gathering information and organizing data, but there are severe limitations.

Paralegals cannot practice law or give you legal advice. They do not have the decision-making experience of attorneys, nor do they have the extensive law school training in legal reasoning or courtroom experience. If you want to use an independent paralegal, consider this option in conjunction with employing a *licensed* practicing attorney, *with malpractice insurance in place*, and you may have the best of both worlds. If the attorney is not willing to work with you on this basis, just go down the street and find another who will, or call Court Coach® (203-838-7001) and for a small fee we will help to find a lawyer who will unbundle services.

Paralegals and legal interns (usually lawyers in training) are a common staple of and the backbone of many lawyers and firms. You would want a medical doctor on your case as well as the lab technician, and that is what you get in this approach.

## DEVELOP A WIN-WIN PARTNERSHIP WITH YOUR ATTORNEY: HOW TO BECOME YOUR ATTORNEY'S FAVORITE CLIENT

"Muzzle your attorney," advises David R. Evanson in an article in *Entrepreneur* magazine (March 1995) on the secrets of buying a business. Evanson maintains that too many people let their outside advisors make the important decisions when buying a business and concludes with an admonition about the expense of allowing a law firm (or accounting firm) to perform the "due diligence." Evanson suggests that the law firm be involved only after a letter of intent is signed. In other words, do the legal footwork yourself.

Talk about risky business! Do not muzzle your attorney. Have your legal advisor jump aboard *before* you have dug up all the facts. We suggest involving your attorney, and accountant if necessary, from the get-go. We advise you to make them an integral part of your excitement, enthusiasm, and entrepreneurial energy. (*Note:* This applies to any business transaction on which you embark, not just buying a business.)

Which is not to say that you shouldn't do some of the legwork yourself. *Au contraire!* We believe that, absolutely, you should be involved as much as your skills, time, energy, and interest allow. Use your attorney's interest and expertise from the beginning because she or he can help you identify major issues and problem areas, advise you on exactly what due diligence you need to do, and ascertain what you can handle well on your own.

## Court Coach® Tips for Becoming Your Attorney's Favorite Client

While attorneys try to remain unbiased, both in and out of court, it's only human nature to go the extra mile for people who do the same for you (the law of human nature). It wouldn't hurt to learn some client etiquette to promote a relationship based on mutual respect. Consider the following:

- Share your dream.
- Treat your attorney with respect.
- Discuss problems or concerns *ab initio* (from the beginning) and keep an open line of communication. If you speak up right away about dissatisfactions, you will not reach a breaking point.
- Say thank-you. Write a thank-you note to recognize a job well done or say so right away.
- If you make a mistake, admit it. If the attorney makes a mistake, inquire. Accept apologies graciously.
- Recognize that you are human and that your attorney is, too. Have a good laugh together, every once in a while.
- Respect boundaries. Don't expect more from your attorney than your attorney can deliver, professionally and personally.

Just make sure that you apprise your attorney of your activities. One of the most enjoyable aspects of practicing law is being involved in something creative, innovative, and positive. It's rewarding (dare we say even "fun") for professionals to help a client realize a dream.

## What to Expect from Any Attorney—Beyond the Technicalities

In return for your show of respect for the attorney, you also have a right to expect more than a robotic performance of legal functions. In other words, there's some etiquette for attorneys dealing with clients too.

The American Bar Association Rules of Professional Conduct provide:

> In representing a client, a lawyer shall exercise independent professional judgment and render candid advice. In rendering advice, a lawyer may refer not only to law but to other considerations such as moral, economic, social, and political factors, that may be relevant to the client's situation. (Model Code of Professional Conduct, Rule 2.1, 1994)

### KNOW YOUR KEY TERMS

- *Due diligence.* Black defines this as a standard by which you measure the amount of care you "do" an activity with when you give it the attentiveness or care that a reasonable, prudent person would give in the circumstances. In the range of diligence from the slightest momentary thought to the most vigilant anxiety, you give what is "due" depending on the relative facts of the case.

- *Unbundling.* In taking apart the tasks that make up the complete bundle of a service, the client contracts for "pieces of the service," rather than the total package. If you were to apply this concept to a beauty parlor, the client might wash their hair ahead of time and the hairdresser might only cut their hair—and not blow-dry it.

### BASIC LEGAL RESEARCH

- *Preventive Law Bibliography.* For a bibliography of publications on preventive law, write to the National Center for Preventive Law, 1900 Olive Street, Denver, CO 80220.
- *Preventive Law,* by Louis M. Brown. The bible of preventive law.

## KEY RESOURCES

- *Client interest groups.* Client interest groups are active on both the national and local level. One group, the National Legal Consumer Resource Center, P. O. Box 340, Gloucester, VA 23061, publishes a monthly newsletter, conduct studies, and lobbies on behalf of legal clients.
- *Help Abolish Legal Tyranny (HALT).* This organization, 1319 F Street Northwest, Washington, DC 20004, is a lobbyist group supporting clients' rights.
- *The American Bar Association Standing Committee on the Delivery of Legal Services.* This is the arm of the ABA concerned with alternative legal services. Contact: William E. Hornsby, Jr., Staff Counsel, 510 Fairbanks Court, Chicago, IL 60611-3314, (312) 988-5761.

## COURT COACH® SUGGESTS

1. *The trend among U.S. Supreme Court cases is to support entrepreneurial and consumer-oriented marketing of professional services.* This means those TV ads for lawyers won't be going away anytime soon. See *Bates* v. *State Bar of Ariz.*, 433 U.S. 350 (1977) (holding blanket bans on lawyer advertising unconstitutional); *Edenfield* v. *Fane*, 113 S.Ct. 1792 (1993) (permitting a Florida certified public accountant to personally solicit clients).
2. *While we don't recommend replacing an attorney with "fill-in-the-blank" legal forms, it may be worth your while to invest in a legal software package of documents to familiarize yourself with the information your attorney will require of you.* The ever-growing market of software packages with legal business documents on disk offers a variety of options. For example, Excelsior-Legal Software publishes *Document Assembly Software,* 20 separate libraries of common legal documents for New York State (16 for other states). Expert Software publishes the popular *Do-It-Yourself Lawyer,* which has information to help you fill out eight different legal documents. Other legal document software packages to check out include *It's Legal* (Parsons Technology), *Personal Attorney* (Managing Your Money), and *Law Desk* (Lawyers Cooperative Publishing).

# 2

# FORMS OF ORGANIZATION: CREATING A BUSINESS THAT FITS YOUR STYLE

## CONGRATULATIONS, YOU'RE AN ENTREPRENEUR

An entrepreneur is anyone who has the intelligence and courage to transform a viable business plan into a moneymaking reality. Entrepreneurs come in all shapes and bank account sizes, from the neighborhood kids hawking lemonade in their front yard on a hot summer day to software billionaires Paul Allen and Bill Gates, who made computers accessible to the masses by inventing DOS and continue to invest in expansion of the information superhighway.

Once you've crossed the line from dreamer to entrepreneur by making the decision to green-light your business plan, the next step is to establish your business in the eyes of the law. There are three standard legal forms of business ownership: sole proprietorship, partnership, and incorporation.

Sole proprietorship is the simplest, cheapest, and most popular structure for small businesses, you name yourself as the exclusive owner of the enterprise. Most small business owners start out as sole proprietors before deciding to take on partners or expending into a full-blown corporation.

If two or more people are going to share the finances and/or workload, then you should either establish a partnership or a corporation. A partnership establishes legal guidelines for sharing the financial profits and losses, and managing the operational aspects of the business. Setting up a business in corporate form, while more expensive and complicated than a partnership, also disengages the business owners' legal and financial status from that of the business.

## THE PROS AND CONS OF SOLE PROPRIETORSHIP

Entrepreneurs are typically independent and self-motivated, so it's not surprising that most choose to open shop as sole proprietors. While being solely responsible for a business can be the most rewarding form of ownership, it can also be the most stressful. Basically, you and your business are one and the same. If your business makes a profit, you reap the benefits. If it fails, you fail alone.

One of the chief advantages of sole proprietorship is that it's quick, easy, and inexpensive to hang out your shingle (see Chapter 3). No special contracts or agreements need to be drawn up, as with a partnership or corporation.

Also, tax advantages are a great sole proprietorship perk. The tax-reporting procedure is easy enough for many to tackle without an accountant. For legal purposes, the individual owner and the business are one and the same, so your annual federal tax return will be the same familiar Form 1040 that you filed as an employee. The only difference is that you'll now need to attach Schedule C, which states your profit or loss for the year, and Form 4562, a record of your company's property and its value. Chapter 10 will provide more detailed information on taxes.

Since all income generated from the business is reported as personal income, you are allowed to take any business deductions and financial losses personally as well—which can add up to big tax savings. If you are a sole proprietor, you are also permitted to take on a personal basis certain investment tax credits available to stimulate business start-ups and expansion.

Being the master of your own fate is a powerful plus for sole proprietors, but sometimes fate refuses to be mastered. A debilitating illness or accident could render your business extremely vulnerable if nobody else is trained to step in and temporarily oversee your responsibilities. Consequently, you may need to absorb the extra expense of disability insurance and/or overhead insurance (discussed further in Chapter 6). In addition, one can be an awfully lonely number when trying to secure credit or a commercial loan from a bank. Lenders are much freer with their money when a company comprises more than one owner who can contribute to paying the debt.

The major disadvantage of sole proprietorship comes in the form of unlimited personal liability. This means that a legal suit precipitated by a disgruntled customer or unpaid creditor could cost you not only your business but your house, your car, your bank accounts, and other personal assets as well (depending on your state's bankruptcy rules and regulations). Personal liability insurance and an umbrella policy can be purchased to alleviate some of the stress associated with unlimited liability (see Chapter 6).

For example, let's say Gump's Gourmet Chocolates runs a modest operation and lands an uncommonly large order to supply Bubba's House of Shrimp with confections for the restaurant's Mardi Gras extravaganza. Despite the best intentions, the Gump factory simply doesn't have the capacity to produce the goods on time and Bubba sues to recoup his losses. Since Gump is a sole proprietor, his personal assets—the home his mother left him, his solid gold Ping-Pong trophies, and his personal bank accounts—as well as his business assets, are subject to liquidation to compensate Bubba.

## THE PROS AND CONS OF PARTNERSHIPS

Sole proprietorship isn't for everyone: Some people simply function better and enjoy their work more as part of a team. A general partnership is formed when two or more people legally own a business, sharing the profits, financial commitment, workload, and liability risks. Often, once a business begins to expand and become more complicated, proprietors decide that two or more heads, and bank accounts, are better than one.

By far, the hardest part of forming a partnership is finding a partner, or partners, who will bring new and complementary skills, sufficient capital, and/or new clients to the business. But partnerships should not be entered into lightly, nor should you be too dazzled by the potential partner's resources. Why? Because running a small business means that you'll probably be spending more waking hours with your partner than your spouse. The same principles that sustain a healthy marriage can, and must, be applied to your relationship with a partner:

trust, communication, a shared vision, and a commitment to hard work for a common goal.

Creating a partnership becomes slightly more complicated than establishing a sole proprietorship, although the costs involved can still be kept to a minimum. Taxes also become a bit more complicated when a partnership is involved (see Chapter 3).

The obvious advantages of creating a partnership are, first, widening your circle of resources—skills, finances, and clients. Second, the more partners you have, the more capital you can amass to fund your company. Third, each person's network of business, social, and personal contacts can expand your customer base exponentially. Additionally, there's power in numbers when seeking credit or a loan.

Pooling acquired and innate skills is a great motivating force in bringing partners onboard. One person may be a whiz with numbers, while another is a born salesperson or marketing/public relations pro. Some people are natural rainmakers, and attracting new clients is second nature to them. If you are not, then a partner may really help. The trick is to "know thyself" and accurately assess the real skills of potential partners to assemble a complementary team that meets your business's specific requirements.

Unlimited liability is the same looming problem for general partnerships as sole proprietorships. Each partner in a general partnership is personally liable for all business transactions and subject to the risk of losing personal assets as well as partnership assets if the business folds or a catastrophic legal judgment is awarded to a creditor. It's obvious, then, that partners must be chosen with great care since each general partner has the power to bind any other partner to liability. You can avoid unlimited liability is by declaring yourself a limited partner, which means you will contribute to the business financially but absolve yourself of any responsibilities for the day-to-day operations and company management. A new development in the law is limited liability partnerships (LLPs).

The biggest difficulty partnerships encounter, especially when one or more partners are accustomed to working solo, is that of personality conflicts. While Jekyll and Hyde may bring different skills to the enterprise, their very differences may chafe too much for working comfort. Some partners start out as close friends and wind up destroying the friendship and the business. The awful truth is that no matter how well you may think you know someone, you don't really know the person until you get married or become business partners! Consequently, we recommend that if you start out as a sole proprietor and decide to take on partners, keep control of at least 51 percent of the company.

## THE PROS AND CONS OF CORPORATIONS

If you absolutely had to have a boss, wouldn't it be great if you could create an invisible one who would be legally responsible for your mistakes but let you take all the credit and profit obtained from successes? Well, that's the simple definition of a corporation. Incorporating your business legally makes it an entity separate from you and any of its other owners. This invisible entity, always referred to legally as "it," becomes your boss and you become an officer and/or stockholder.

In the eyes of the law, a corporation is, in effect, a person with all the rights afforded citizens under the Bill of Rights, except the right against self-incrimination provided for in the Fifth Amendment. It can also be charged with almost any crime where the punishment is monetary restitution.

Once you establish a corporation (incorporate), the company is now an "Inc." and becomes liable for its debts, not you personally. If the corporation is found liable for any judgments from a suit or the company folds and creditors are left unpaid, the owners can only lose their financial interests in the business, not their personal assets. However, if the corporation is not set up properly, run according to the statutory requirements, or is guilty of fraud or criminal activity, or is a sham corporation, attempts can be made to pierce the corporate veil and hold individuals personally liable (see Chapter 4).

Corporations generally have an easier time than sole proprietors or partners in obtaining loans and investment capital because they are seen as more stable business operations. And the real beauty is that you can borrow money without putting your own assets in jeopardy, although many lending institutions require collateral or personal guarantees of debt as a precautionary measure.

While a corporate structure has some wonderful advantages for rapidly expanding businesses, particularly taxwise, it may not be something to jump into when you're fresh out of the starting gate. Incorporating saves you liability headaches, but there are other tradeoffs to be considered. Corporations are subject to additional state and federal taxes, bookkeeping becomes more complex and expensive, and then there are the legal fees and complexities involved with setting up and running a corporation (see Chapter 4). And you can always incorporate down the road.

Also, if you don't like to be bogged down with rules and regulations, you may want to think twice before incorporating since corporations are closely regulated by the state in which they are incorporated. This means your business operations are governed by your state's statutes on corporations, which must be stringently complied with;

whereas with a sole proprietorship or partnership, there is usually no official registration with and oversight by the state. A corporation is required to establish bylaws, hold stockholders' meetings and keep records on an ongoing basis (the office of the secretary of state in most states will supply forms you can fill out, or you can purchase a corporate kit at a stationery store). You'll also need to file an annual or biannual declaration of stockholders and directors' meeting and report. Failure to file this report can, among other things, result in fines and penalties, and the possibility of being automatically dissolved.

Income taxes also become more complicated because as a legal person, the general corporation—unlike a partnership or sole proprietorship— must file a separate tax form. However, you can get around this requirement if the company qualifies for S corporation status with the Internal Revenue Service (see Chapter 4). If your business is incorporated, your taxes are bound to be substantially higher as a corporate president than as a small business owner. A corporation's profits are taxed twice, once as the separate entity of the corporation and once again as income distributed to shareholders. As a shareholder and employee, you are liable for income tax on your salary and also on your share of the distributed profits. Although corporations accrue some significant additional tax breaks, they lose the ability that sole proprietorships and partnerships have to write off business losses and expenses as a personal expense to the owner.

## Limited Liability Corporation

The newest option is the limited liability corporation (LLC), depending on the state in which your business is operating. This partnership-corporation hybrid qualifies for the same tax benefits as a partnership and simultaneously has the limited liability of a corporation.

---

**KNOW YOUR KEY TERMS**

---

- *Entrepreneur.* Anyone who launches a commercial venture, no matter how small or large, with the intention of turning a profit.
- *Sole proprietorship.* For all legal purposes, an owner and business that are one and the same. One individual owns the business, taking personal responsibility for all debts, profits, and transactions associated with the business.

- *Partnership.* Sharing the financial and operational obligations of a company with one or more persons. Akin to establishing a business marriage—complete with prenuptial agreement, vows of commitment, and the possibility of dissolution.
- *Corporation.* A company that legally becomes a separate entity, an "it." It, rather than the owner(s) personally, is responsible for business debts and business transactions.
- *Limited liability corporation.* An arrangement that allows you to have your "corporate cake and eat it, too." It is a partnership-corporation hybrid with the tax benefits of a partnership and the liability protection of a corporation.

## BASIC LEGAL RESEARCH

- *Law libraries (local courthouse, law school, or community library).* Most people don't know that the local courthouse has a law library open to the public, not just lawyers. This is the first place to start researching the legal requirements of setting up your business (see Appendix L for information about law libraries).
- *State statutes governing business enterprises.* These statutes, which differ from state to state, can be found in the law library. They reflect the requirements your legislators have voted on over the years regulating how a business must operate in your state.
- *Uniform Partnership Act.* Every state except Louisiana has adopted this federal act governing partnerships in one form or another. Look up this document in the law library and check out what provisions your state has allowed for.
- *State licensing boards.* You need to find out whether you need a special license, and if so, you must decipher the requirements of your profession's state licensing board. For example, some states require you to have a license to be a psychotherapist or masseuse and some don't. Phone numbers for state licensing boards are found in the blue pages under Government Offices—State.
- *Law publications (available in specialized bookstores or your local law school).* The Nutshell series of West Publishing Company are small, inexpensive paperbacks available in most libraries that can provide you with everything you need to know about specific areas of the law. *Corporations in a Nutshell,* by Roger Bernhardt (West Publishing) is a good source, as is Selected

Corporation and Partnership Statutes, Regulations and Forms (West Publishing). Law review articles and other legal articles can be researched in the *Periodical Guide to Legal Publication.* Write to the law review (a legal publication published by a law school) or magazine if the article is not available in your law library.

- *Your local bookstore.* Books such as *Entrepreneurship,* by James W. Halloran (McGraw-Hill) and *The Legal Guide for Starting and Running a Small Business,* by Fred S. Steingold (Nolo Press) can supplement what you learn in this book about the different forms of business organization.

## KEY RESOURCES

- *The U.S. Small Business Administration's SCORE/ACE chapters.* Local SBAs, listed under U.S. Government offices in the blue pages of your phone book, recruit retired and active executives to volunteer to help small businesses off the ground. These folks are great sources of advice about the form of organization that meets your specific business needs as most have "been there."
- *State government economic development offices.* A terrific resource, found under state offices in the blue pages, which your taxes have already paid for. If they don't have what you need, they can point you in the right direction.
- *Seminars/Lectures.* Check out adult education programs, libraries, community bulletin boards, and newspapers for free programs geared toward entrepreneurs and small business owners.
- *Entrepreneurial or finance institutes at universities and colleges.* Excellent business programs and courses are available—whether you want to receive credit or not (see Appendix B).

## COURT COACH® SUGGESTS

1. *Understand the basics before approaching an attorney.* You are already on the right track by reading this book. Consult some of the other resources previously listed as well. You can save on time spent in an attorney's office, and therefore money, by doing your homework.

2. *Join professional and civic groups.* Local professionals are a wonderful—maybe the best—source of business information and expertise, and they are your potential clients and referral sources. Examples of networking organizations to consider joining include Women in Management, Toastmasters International, the Rotary Club, Kiwanis, your local alumni chapters, and civic groups such as the League of Women Voters, the Junior League, and the local chamber of commerce.

3. *Go public.* Get out of the office and circulate among your neighbors and local merchants. Remember that you are an advertisement for your business—being warm and cordial to everyone you come in contact with is a must for entrepreneurs. Your rude behavior scares off potential customers, namely everyone in your community.

4. *"No man is an island."* Interview professionals you need to support your business—secretaries, bookkeepers, accountants, lawyers, real estate brokers, financial planners. Talk to several people in each profession about their business expectations and what they charge. This can be a useful tool in looking at the big picture of your business costs. When you're actually ready to hire employees, you've already started the screening process. Start small but make sure you have enough expertise to start your business off right.

5. *"Spend good money after good."* Money spent on professional advice, as opposed to having a professional do all your work for you, is always money well spent. Go into all interviews well prepared with written questions and focus on having all your questions answered.

6. *Think big, but start small.* The primary reason that small businesses fail in the first year is financial troubles due to being overly ambitious. There's nothing wrong with having monumental dreams and expecting your business to be a huge success—someday. The key is to start small, investing only what you can afford without jeopardizing all your personal financial stability. That way, it's not the end of the world if your business goes belly up. You still have the resources to sustain your quality of life (food, shelter, and clothing), and start again.

7. *Build slowly and methodically, based on a solid business plan, so that you don't inadvertently shoot your business in the foot.* After your business has proven itself and is making a profit (which can take years), you may want to start investing more vigorously in a growth plan. A well thought-out business plan will help you stay on track and achieve the long-term results you want.

# 3

# SETTING UP A SOLE PROPRIETORSHIP OR PARTNERSHIP

We discussed the pros and cons of sole proprietorship and partnerships in Chapter 2. Now it's time to get into the nitty-gritty of setting up each of these forms of organization.

## SETTING UP A SOLE PROPRIETORSHIP

Basically, once you decide to open a business on your own—no matter how big or small—you become a sole proprietor. Having your business legally recognized as a sole proprietorship is as easy as "one-two-three" (sometimes four):

1. *Apply for a business license in the community where your business is located.* While states differ on the licenses various occupations require, a business license from the city or county clerk in which your company is located is usually mandatory. The cost for this is but a few dollars and the process is easy—just fill out a form at your town or city hall, and the license is usually

granted immediately (see Chapter 8 for specific information about licenses and permits).

2. *If you choose to operate your business under a trade name instead of your own name, you must file a "Certificate of Doing Business Under an Assumed Name" form with the city or county clerk.* Some states also require that you publish a fictitious name statement in the local newspaper to identify who is responsible for the activities of your business. All these licenses involve little time and expense

3. *If you are employing others, apply for an employer identification number from the IRS.* If you don't have any employees, your Social Security number is your tax identification number. Any business employing workers in a manufacturing operation must also register with the Labor Commission through the Department of Labor.

4. *Other professional licenses.* Depending on your profession, you may or may not be required to have a professional license. Check with the state licensing boards of your profession and the state statute governing your profession (see Chapter 8).

## There's No Place Like "Home" for Fledgling Sole Proprietors

Many unseasoned entrepreneurs prefer to test out their wings in the comfort, privacy, and relatively inexpensive surroundings of their own home before investing in office space and expensive furnishings. Just because your basement or kitchen table doubles as your office, though, you're running an "official" business in the eyes of the law—and your neighbors. You still have to comply with municipal laws and zoning ordinances, state laws, federal regulations, and may need business permits, registrations and licenses just like the "suites" downtown.

The most important thing you need to find out when considering a home-based business is, Is it legal to operate a business from your home? Zoning ordinances regulate which areas in the city are designated as residential, commercial, industrial, and agricultural. Chances are good that your home is zoned for residential use, which may greatly restrict what you can and can't do in the privacy of your own home-based business. Check with your city or county planning department, building inspector or zoning administration to determine the zoning classification and concomitant restrictions for your property. The following are some examples of the zoning restrictions you may face:

- Restrictions limiting increases in vehicular traffic.
- Restrictions on use or size of outside signs or advertising.
- Restrictions on street parking.
- Limitations on employees.
- Limitations on the amount of floor space used for a business.
- Restrictions on the storage of materials.

Many home-based entrepreneurs who don't have a parade of customers and employees coming and going simply ignore the zoning laws, but we don't recommend that route, especially if you are investing dollars into printed stationery, business cards, and other nonrefundable items. If a disgruntled neighbor, customer, or employee reports you to the authorities for a zoning violation, your business could be shut down temporarily or permanently. Here are some legal ways to negotiate your way around the zoning problem:

- *Apply for a use permit.* This allows you to use your home as a business, even if you live in a designated residential area. You need to let the authorities at the city zoning board examine your business plan and facilities (a somewhat scary thought). (You can find them under city government offices in your phone book's blue pages.)
- *Apply for a variance.* You can request a waiver of zoning restrictions from the local zoning board.
- *Take action to amend local zoning ordinances.* Some ordinances are extremely outdated—some were written back in Civil War times to protect neighborhoods from the smokestacks of the Industrial Revolution—and others simply don't take into consideration the growing number of small home-based businesses. If there's an ordinance you can justifiably see doing away with, remember that there's power in numbers and join together with other home-based entrepreneurs in your neighborhood to create change.

Besides city ordinances, you also have to make sure there aren't any restrictions in your property deed, or lease agreement if you are renting. And, sometimes homeowners' associations and condominium associations include restrictions on homes being used for business purposes.

And then there are the state laws and federal regulations that restrict the type of work that can be done in private homes. These laws were primarily passed in the late 1930s to protect women and children from unfair labor practices. For example, Illinois forbids the manufacturing of metal springs at home. Several states do not allow women's clothing to be made in private homes. To find out about laws in your state, consult with an attorney or your local small business association.

After you've figured out all the ordinances, restrictions, and regulations that apply to you and your business, you're ready to fill out the appropriate paperwork for establishing a sole proprietorship and get to work!

## SETTING UP A GENERAL PARTNERSHIP

Like sole proprietorships, and unlike corporations, general partnerships require no permission from the state to legally exist. However, most states have adopted the Uniform Partnership Act (UPA), which sets forth the law governing partnerships. Your business is legally a partnership once a "partnership agreement"—oral, written, or implied—is accepted by all joint owners, two or more. While a written document is not mandatory, it is a business imperative to have a concrete outline of the company goals and responsibilities of each owner. Besides being an important reference when partners need to refresh their memory or when a dispute breaks out, it is critical to pursue legal remedies for breach or fraud, or to dissolve.

To take this thought a step further, a "prepartnership agreement," or "letter of intent," is used to record discussions and decisions taking place prior to formally drafting a partnership agreement. Let's say, for example, that you are intent on opening a restaurant and your old college roommate is considering becoming a joint owner. During the course of your discussions, you discover that your former roommate has had a divorce, and has substantial financial commitments to his former wife and children. The two of you become aware of the financial risk you are both taking investing in this new venture.

The following sections describe the steps typically involved with establishing a partnership.

### Preliminary Documents: Prepartnership Agreements, Letters of Intent, and Nondisclosure Forms

These preliminary documents are useful primarily to recap any informal discussions and decisions the partners-to-be have had or made as a precursor to establishing a partnership agreement. Figure 3–1 shows a sample letter of intent, which may also serve as a prepartnership

**Figure 3–1**   Sample Letter of Intent: Prepartnership Agreement

John Smith, President
Smith's Furniture Shop
12 Wood Street
Rowayton, CT

Dear Mr. Smith:

Thanks for meeting with me last week. As we discussed, I am interested in joining forces with you to open a new furniture shop in Darien, Jones' Furnishings. To recap our meeting, here are the terms of partnership that we discussed:

1. The partnership of Smith and Jones would do business as Jones' Furnishing.
2. Both parties would be equal partners, sharing the profits and debts on a 50/50 basis. Profits shall be distributed on a monthly basis.
3. Ms. Jones would be responsible for managing the daily operations of said business.
4. Both parties would make an initial investment of $100,000 to lease a storefront on Main Street in Darien, and pay for inventory, fixtures, and other start-up costs.
5. The partnership shall commence on June 1, 1998, and the partnership shall last until it is dissolved by all the partners, or a partner leaves for any reason.

There are many other details that need to be resolved before I have my attorney draw up a partnership agreement, but I believe these are all of the terms that we discussed in our meeting last week. Please let me know, in writing, if these terms are agreeable to you, as well as if I left anything out.

I look forward to speaking with you soon.

Sincerely,

Sue Jones
President
Jones Furnishings

agreement. This agreement is a wonderful tool that lets you know early on in the game whether you and your partner(s) are on the same page and can work together; and it demonstrates the level of commitment each party brings to the joint enterprise. Each person must sign on the dotted line, and with timelines incorporated therein, it requires each party to "move" in this initial phase and fulfill preliminary commitments. If there is a breach by failure to perform, there is no need to proceed further and waste time, energy, and money on a business relationship that will not work. What you cannot accomplish at the outset with enthusiasm running high, you cannot accomplish further down the pike either.

The nondisclosure form is used to legally swear a new partner to secrecy (see Figure 3–2). For example, if you decide to bring a partner onboard to help finance and manage your expanding baking enterprise, "Grandma's Goodies," the last thing you want is for your new partner to use *your* family's secret recipes to win a bake-off contest, or start up a competition with "Grandpa's Favorites."

## Develop a Partnership Agreement

The partnership agreement establishes ground rules for your business relationship. This agreement should cover the division of labor, profits, decision-making power, management duties, and the rules for expansion and dissolution of the partnership. Figure 3–3 shows a sample partnership agreement.

**Figure 3–2**    Sample Nondisclosure Form for Partners

---

The undersigned partner in the venture Grandma's Goodies (the "Company") hereby promises to keep the Company's business secrets, including but not limited to customer, supplier, logistical, financial, research, and development information, confidential and not to disclose the Company's business secrets to any third party during and after the term of the partnership agreement.

If for any reason any part of this promise is void for any reason, the undersigned accepts that the partnership may be severed without affecting the validity or enforceability of any other parts of the partnership agreement.

Signed, sealed, and delivered on  __(date)__  in the presence of:

_____(signature of witness)_____          _____(witness name, typed)_____

_____(signature of partner)_____          _____(partner's name, typed)_____

---

**Figure 3–3**   Sample Partnership Agreement

This partnership agreement is made between the following partners:

(1) _____

(2) _____

(3) _____

## 1. PARTNERSHIP NAME AND BUSINESS

1.01   The Partners agree to carry on a business pertaining to \_\_(type of business)\_\_ , as partners under the name _____ (the "Partnership"). No person shall be introduced as a Partner and no other business shall be carried on by the Partnership without written consent of all the Partners.

1.02   The principal place of business of the Partnership is _____ (address) _____ .

## 2. TERM OF PARTNERSHIP

2.01   The Partnership begins on \_\_\_\_\_(date)\_\_\_ , and shall be terminated in accordance with this agreement.

## 3. PARTNERSHIP SHARES AND CAPITAL

3.01   The Partners shall participate in the assets, liabilities, profits, and losses of the Partnership in the following percentages of Partnership Shares:

| (name of Partner) | – | % |
|---|---|---|
| (name of Partner) | – | % |
| (name of Partner) | – | % |

Total shares = 100%

3.02   The Partners shall contribute a total of $\_\_\_\_\_ in cash, in proportion to their respective Partnership Shares, to the start-up capital of the Partnership by no later than \_\_(date)\_\_ .

3.03   If further capital is required to carry on the Partnership business, the Partners shall contribute it as required in proportion to their respective Partnership Shares.

3.04   No interest accrues on a Partner's capital contributions to the Partnership in proportion to his Partnership Share. However, if a Partner makes an actual payment or advance for the purpose of the Partnership beyond his Partnership Share, he is entitled to \_\_\_\_\_% per annum interest from the Partnership on the Additional Advance until refunded by the Partnership.

## 4. BANKING ARRANGEMENTS AND FINANCIAL RECORDS

4.01   The Partners shall maintain full and proper accounts of the Partnership business at all times. These records shall be accessible to each of the Partners at any time upon request.

*(Continued)*

**Figure 3–3**    *(continued)*

4.02    The Partners shall maintain a bank account in the name of the Partnership business on which checks may be drawn only on the signature of at least <u>(number)</u> of the Partners.

## 5. PARTNERS' ACCOUNTS AND SALARIES

5.01    The financial records of the Partnership shall include separate income and capital accounts for each Partner.

5.02    No Partner shall receive a salary for services rendered to the Partnership but the profit or loss of the Partnership business shall be periodically allocated among the Partners' separate income accounts and each of the Partners may, from time to time, withdraw against a credit balance in his income account.

5.03    The capital accounts of the Partners shall be maintained in proportion to their respective Partnership Shares.

5.04    No Partner shall draw down his capital account without the previous written consent of the other Partners. If a Partner draws down his capital account below his Partnership Share, he shall bring it up to his Partnership Share on the demand of any of the Partners.

## 6. MANAGEMENT OF PARTNERSHIP BUSINESS

6.01    Each Partner may take part in the management of the Partnership business.

6.02    Any difference arising in the ordinary course of carrying on the Partnership business shall be decided by the Partners having a majority of the Partnership Shares.

## 7. PARTNERS' DUTIES AND RESTRICTIONS

7.01    Each Partner shall devolve substantially all of his ordinary working time to carrying on the business of the Partnership.

7.02    Each Partner shall at all times punctually pay and discharge his separate debts and liabilities and shall keep harmless the property and assets of the Partnership and the other Partners from those separate debts and liabilities and, if necessary, shall promptly indemnify the other Partners for their share of any actual payment or discharge of his separate debts and liabilities by the Partnership.

7.03    No Partner shall assign or encumber his share or interest in the Partnership without the previous written consent of the other Partners.

7.04    No Partner shall bind the Partnership or the other Partners for anything outside the ordinary course of carrying on the Partnership business.

## 8. FISCAL YEAR END

8.01    The fiscal year end of the Partnership shall be on ____<u>(month and day)</u>____ of each year.

**Figure 3–3** *(continued)*

9. TERMINATION OF PARTNERSHIP

9.01  The Partnership may be dissolved at any time during the joint lives of the Partners by a Partner giving notice in writing to the other Partners of his intention to dissolve the Partnership, in which case the Partnership is dissolved as from the date mentioned in the notice as the date of dissolution, or, if no date of dissolution is mentioned, as from the date of communication of the notice.

9.02  The Partnership shall be dissolved upon the death or insolvency of any of the Partners or on any of the Partners becoming mentally incompetent as found by a court of law.

9.03  Upon dissolution of the Partnership, subject to any contrary agreement binding the former Partners and their estates and after making any necessary adjustments in accordance with generally accepted accounting principles to allow for any debit balances in the Partners' separate capital accounts, the Partnership business shall be promptly liquidated and applied in the following order:

a.  to pay the debts and liabilities of the Partnership;

b.  to refund any outstanding Additional Advances, together with accrued interest;

c.  to distribution of the credit balances of the Partners' separate income accounts;

d.  to distribution of the credit balances of the Partner's capital accounts;

e.  to distribution of any residue to the Partners in proportion to their respective Partnership Shares.

10. ARBITRATION OF DISPUTES

10.01  Any dispute between the Partners arising out of or related to this agreement and any amendments to it, whether before or after dissolution of the Partnership, shall be settled by arbitration in accordance with the rules of the American Arbitration Association in force at the time and judgment on the arbitration award may be entered in any court of competent jurisdiction.

11. MISCELLANEOUS

11.01  In this agreement, the singular includes the plural and the masculine includes feminine and neuter and vice versa unless the context otherwise requires.

11.02  The capitalized headings in this agreement are only for convenience of reference and do not form part of or affect the interpretation of this agreement.

11.03  If any provision or part of any provision in this agreement is void for any reason, it shall be severed without affecting the validity of the balance of the agreement.

11.04  Time is of the essence of this agreement.

*(Continued)*

**Figure 3-3**   *(continued)*

---

11.05   The terms of this agreement may only be amended in writing dated and signed by all the Partners.

11.06   This agreement binds and benefits the Partners and their respective heirs, executors, administrators, personal representatives, successors, and assigns.

11.07   This agreement is governed by the laws of the State of (state name where Partnership will be operating).

Executed under seal on _____(date)_____ .


Signed, sealed, and delivered in the presence of:


_____,   _____
(signature of witness)     (signature of Partner)


_____,   _____
(signature of witness)     (signature of Partner)


_____,   _____
(signature of witness)     (signature of Partner)

---

Some typical elements of the partnership agreement are:

- Date of the formation of the partnership.
- The business's official name and address.
- Names and addresses of all partners.
- Statement of business purpose.
- Compliance of the business with application laws and rules.
- Duration of partnership.
- Financial contributions of each partner.
- Decision-making powers and managerial responsibilities.
- Managerial meetings; how often, when, and where they will occur.
- Designation of company officers.
- Division of labor.
- Distribution of profits and losses, including salaries.
- Business expenses.
- Bank accounts.

- Accounting policies.
- Policy regarding admission of new partners and departure of established partners.
- Distribution of asset at the time of dissolution.
- Settlement provisions in the event of death or disability of a partner to ensure that the business will survive.
- Procedure for arbitrating disputes and laws that will apply.
- Use of property.
- Dealings with affiliates of partners (partners' family members or any representatives of partner who are designated to carry out their business affairs).
- Annual reports and statements.
- Tax matters.
- Powers of attorney.

## Register Your Business

It is necessary to register your business as a partnership with the Internal Revenue Service to receive a partnership identification number. The partnership must file a separate income tax return detailing profits or losses (see Chapter 10). This tax return must also include a balance sheet outlining assets, liabilities, and partners' equity (how much money each partner has invested in the company).

## Operating under a Trade Name

A "Certificate of Conducting Business as Partners" is needed if you operate under a trade name. As with a sole proprietorship, some states also require that you publish a fictitious name statement in local newspapers.

## SETTING UP A LIMITED PARTNERSHIP

Now that you've got sole proprietorship and general partnership down pat, let's throw another common form of organization into the mix: a limited partnership. This can be a very useful thing to know about if you have a general partnership and are interested in raising money, but not in having other partners put their two cents' worth into how you run your business.

Here's how a limited partnership evolves: In the beginning, there must be one or more general partners who share the same fiscal and managerial (including liability). You then have the option of selling "limited partnership interests" in your business to raise capital. The limited partner(s) pay a set amount for the rights to a given percentage of your company's profits for a specified number of years. Obviously, the more a limited partner pays into your business, the higher percentage of the profits he or she will be entitled to.

Limited partners are solely concerned with the financial end of your business and have no say in how the business is managed on a day-to-day basis. As a result, limited partners also have no liability for the debts of the partnership other than the amount of money they initially invest.

A major difference in setting up a limited partnership and a general partnership is that you must file a certificate of limited partnership with the secretary of state for your state. While general partnerships are not required to register with the state, limited partnerships are.

## UPA and RUPA

No, these are not cheerleaders, but the Uniform Partnership Act adopted in 1914 and its progeny, Revised (UPA) were recently completed and are up for adoption in 49 states. You need to check with your individual state about the status of its partnership law. Most significant among the proposed changes under RUPA are:

- Breakups do not require a dissolution in every case and can be subject to a mandatory buyout of the departing partner's interest.
- Establishes and defines the scope of the partners' duties of care and loyalty and the obligation of good faith and fair dealing.
- Abolishes the confusing concept of property ownership under a tenancy in partnership.
- Clarifies the rules on the nature and transfer of partnership property to better facilitate transactions.
- Clarifies the rights and remedies of creditors.

## LIMITED LIABILITY CORPORATION

The newest option is the limited liability corporation (LLC), depending on the state in which your business is operating. This partnership-corporation hybrid qualifies for the same tax benefits as a partnership and simultaneously has the limited liability of a corporation (see Chapter 4 for more on LLCs).

## KNOW YOUR KEY TERMS

- *Sole proprietorship.* A business with a single owner.
- *General partnership.* Two (or more) owners who jointly share the financial and operational responsibilities of a business.
- *Limited partnership.* A partnership agreement wherein one (or more) general partner(s) take on a limited partner who has a financial interest in the partnership but doesn't take part in the daily operations. The limited partner has the perk of limited liability.
- *Prepartnership agreement.* A written record of decisions and discussions that take place prior to and during the course of forming a partnership.
- *Partnership agreement.* A written contract between partners outlining the specific financial and operational terms of the partnership.
- *Uniform Partnership Act.* A federal act, adopted in 49 states, that provides the rules governing partnerships. The revised version (RUPA) is up for adoption for the first time in 80 years.

## BASIC LEGAL RESEARCH

- *Tax law.* A copy of the tax laws applicable to sole proprietorships and partnerships can be obtained from the IRS. This is a key reference that you should study and refer to often. We will present more information about taxes in Chapter 10.
- *Municipal and zoning laws.* These can be found in any law library and are especially important to utilize if you're running a home-based business and don't want to antagonize your neighbors unintentionally or jeopardize your home-based status. Chapter 7 provides more information on permits.
- *Small Time Operator,* by Bernard Kamaroff (Bell Springs Press). This is a good primer on how to start and operate a small sole proprietorship.
- *The Partnership Book,* by Denis Clifford and Ralph Warner (Nolo Press). A to Z on the basics.

## KEY RESOURCES

- *State and city departments of commerce.* These offices can help you figure out which state licenses your chosen profession or business requires, if any. Often, a pamphlet has been prepared as well.
- *State departments of economic development.* Check to find out what federal licensing requirements your business is subject to.
- *State licensing boards of your chosen profession.* Most professions have a State Licensing Board, with regulations varying slightly from state to state for each profession.
- *State departments of labor.* If you're employing workers, check with them for registration requirements and worker's compensation regulations.

## COURT COACH® SUGGESTS

1. *When starting out, save money with a proprietorship.* For economic reasons, many entrepreneurs get their feet wet by embarking on a proprietorship before investing time and money in a more complicated business setup. No special contracts or agreements need to be drawn up, as with a partnership or corporation, so you'll save on legal fees. And the tax forms a sole proprietor must fill out aren't much more complicated than those you filled out as an employee.
2. *Take the time to draft and sign a partnership agreement before you go into business.* In your enthusiasm to get your business off the drawing board and to a flying start, you may want to skip this sometimes tedious step. Do it anyway.
3. *Always consult an attorney to review your partnership agreement.* Although it's not necessary to hire an attorney to develop the substance of your agreement with your partners, a legal eye can make sure that you've covered all the necessary bases.
4. *As Socrates advised: "Know thyself."* If you are a visionary, unyieldingly independent, or like your solitude, going solo is definitely right for you. Many people take on partners out of fear that they can't make it on their own and live to regret it.
5. *So, pick your partners with extreme caution.* It's much easier to get "married" than to get "divorced." In the event that you want to end your partnership, you'll have to have the financial

wherewithal to buy your partner out, or wait until you can find a replacement partner for an existing business, or agree to dissolution jointly, which may be a real problem!

6. *Another consideration: The law governing partnerships can and does change.* A new Uniform Partnership Act (RUPA) has been approved and is expected to be adopted by half of the states in 1995. It includes four sets of rules that must be followed by all partnerships. So you may have to change your partnership agreement to comply.

# 4

# THE ABCs OF BECOMING AN "INC."

## TO INCORPORATE OR NOT TO INCORPORATE, THAT IS THE QUESTION

As we have progressed from the cave to the boardroom, from barter to trade, society has created more and more sophisticated structures to accomplish the business of doing business. Corporations first existed in the Roman empire, where citizens were permitted to form private clubs, or collegia, for certain nonprofit purposes. From guilds to regulated companies, later Europeans then took this ancient Roman concept and applied it to trade, permitting incorporation for profit.

By 1860, corporations were commonly recognized in Europe as a means of exempting shareholders from liability, since they sometimes had little knowledge of a trade company's actual business transactions. The famous novelist Sir Walter Scott, for example, spent years writing novels, not for his own benefit solely but to pay off the debts of a publishing firm that had published his works.

Besides limiting liability, incorporation provides a big incentive in the form of significant tax breaks. While limited liability and tax havens are powerful aphrodisiacs for small business owners, and while there is security, more credibility for your company, and prestige associated with an Inc. tagline, there is a downside as well.

It may not be wise or economical to jump right into incorporating your company. A start-up business must focus on keeping expenses to a minimum. Filing fees and initial taxes to incorporate vary from state to state, but can run as high as $1,000, as in California. Corporations must also pay yearly or biennial recording fees as well. Plus there's the cost of hiring an attorney to make sure your paperwork is on target, and a bookkeeper or accountant to manage your corporate accounts and to make certain you're square with the IRS.

Also, in return for the liability protection afforded by corporate status, a small incorporated business owner also gives up a certain amount of freedom and laissez-faire. Documents must be filed with the state and annual meetings must be held. Every time a major decision is required, the corporation is required to act by drafting a corporate resolution and filing it in the corporate records. If you want to do business in another state, by filing paperwork with the state's secretary of state, your corporation will be granted "foreign corporation" status. As Leona Helmsley, among others taught us, as a corporate officer, you have the added responsibility for keeping corporate expenses completely separate from your personal expenses.

If you decide not to incorporate, or not to incorporate just yet, you can still protect yourself with extra personal liability insurance or an umbrella policy until your company is established and on a fast track to expansion. Another option to consider is the newest trend, the limited liability corporation (LLC), now allowed in certain states.

## THE ABCs OF INCORPORATING

Becoming an Inc. is more complicated than setting up a sole proprietorship or partnership. But it is definitely doable.

## Preincorporation Agreement: Solve Problems before They Arise

Forming a corporation with others brings up some of the same potential miscommunication problems encountered by those attempting to form a partnership. Both situations entail joining forces with other individuals who come with their own unique vision and expectations (obviously, if you are incorporating alone, this agreement is not necessary). Thus, although not legally required, a preincorporation agreement can be a great aid in making sure everyone is on the same page.

This agreement outlines the terms of the business proposition and the responsibilities of each party involved. The time required and the cost of preparing a preincorporation agreement, usually with a lawyer's assistance, is small compared with the cost of litigation if the corporation fails to materialize and someone sues (but see Court Coach® Suggests at the end of this chapter for tips on saving attorney dollars). A preincorporation agreement should include:

- The company name and mission statement.
- The financial obligations of each shareholder, including stock purchases and other long-term and short-term investments.
- Job titles and descriptions of the offices each person will hold (president, vice-president, secretary, treasurer).
- Compensation, including salary and bonus opportunities, and benefits such as insurance, pension plans, paid family leave, and vacation.
- Ownership of property, which may include furniture, office/ business equipment, art, and anything else on the company premises that is not purchased with the corporation's capital.
- Lease agreements setting forth the terms of the initial commercial lease of the premises, telephone, and office equipment.

## Making Your Corporation Legal

Once everyone involved with incorporating the company has agreed to and has a clear understanding of the business's purpose, the finances from capitalization through short and long-term growth and return on investment, and the organizational structure, you are ready to start filing papers to make the whole thing legal. The office of the secretary of state will usually supply you with the required forms and sometimes with an incorporation outfit to walk you through the process (or you can order a corporation kit at a stationery store or through a mail order company for about $70).

Corporations are regulated by state laws, which differ from state to state, but the basic steps in creating a corporation are similar. (*Note:* In this context, "similar" does not mean "the same." You *must* check your state's incorporation statute to see what specific requirements you need to fulfill in your particular state.)

The incorporator(s) complete the paperwork and get the ball rolling by lending their names and signatures to the incorporating documents. The initial directors are appointed by the incorporators and afterward, incorporators can step out of the picture or continue as officers and/or shareholders. After all the documents are filled out properly and later filed with the state, an organizational meeting must be held wherein the officers and permanent directors are elected, bylaws are adopted, and you're in business!

If you're thinking this all sounds too complicated, despair not! Review the Legal Primer in Appendix L, which explains how to conduct legal research and provides step-by-step instructions for finding your state statutes on incorporating.

The following subsections described are the typical process of incorporation.

### Reserving Your Corporation's Name

Naming your baby is not only fun, it's important. You do this by making a simple telephone call to the office of secretary of state (or corporate commissioner's office), where the name of your corporation will be approved after it has been verified that no other corporation within the state is already using the same name. Also, most states have statutes regarding the wording of a corporate name—what's allowed and what's not (see Chapter 9 on name selection).

### Prepare and File the Articles, or Certificate, of Incorporation (Charter)

This form, which you receive from the secretary of state or will find in your corporation kit, registers your corporation with the state, and is an official record of your business's name and location, corporate purpose, shares of stock, and capitalization (see Figure 4–1 for sample Articles of Incorporation). After you've mailed back this document (or returned it in person) to the secretary of state or corporate commissioner, the state will review and approve your request, and issue a Certificate of Incorporation that comes back to you in the mail with an official state imprimatur or stamp of approval.

Because the corporation can only legally perform acts authorized in this charter, the tricky part of completing the Articles of Incorporation is drafting the statement of purpose, that is, why the corporation exists. To cover yourself legally, the statement of purpose should include the specific purpose of your corporation, such as "to operate a retail hardware business," followed by a very broad grant of power, such as "and to engage in any other lawful act or activity or business which corporations organized to provide *(name the service)* according to *(name the state statute and include et seq.)* are authorized to perform and provide."

The Articles of Incorporation identify the key players in your company: the company president, and one or more other officers, in most instances. (The forms themselves may indicate what your state requires.) Next, the registered agent for the corporation, the person authorized to receive official notices and legal papers, must also be

**Figure 4–1**   Sample Articles of Incorporation

1. The name of this corporation is _____.
2. The purpose of this corporation is to engage in any lawful act or activity for which a corporation may be organized under the General Corporation Law of California other than the banking business, the trust company business, or the practice of a profession permitted to be incorporated by the California Corporation Code.
3. The state in which this corporation will officially do business and operate is _____.
4. The address at which the corporation will do business is _____
_____.
5. The name and address of the corporation's initial agent for the service of process is: _____
_____.
6. The corporation is authorized to issue only one class of shares of stock which shall be designated common stock. The total number of shares it is authorized to issue is _____ shares.
7. The names and addresses of the persons who are appointed to act as the initial directors of the corporation are:

Name                                          Address

_____

_____

_____

8. The liability of the directors of the corporation for monetary damages shall be eliminated to the fullest extent permissible under the laws effective in (name of state where corporation will do business).
9. The corporation is authorized to indemnify the directors and officers of the corporation to the fullest extent permissible under the laws effective in (name of state where corporation will do business).

The undersigned, being all the persons named above as the initial directors, have executed these Articles of Incorporation.

_____    _____
(date)              (initial director)

_____    _____
(date)              (initial director)

_____    _____
(date)              (initial director)

This document has been signed by the above initial directors as witnessed by:

_____    _____
(date)              (witness)

identified as well as the Board of Directors. Most states specify that corporations have at least one director, a fiduciary who manages the corporation and makes major policy decisions, but some do not (it must be obvious to you by now that it is *de rigueur* to check out your state's statutes and comply with what your state, in its wisdom, has set forth as incorporation requirements).

The Articles of Incorporation state the minimum amount of capital that the corporation has set aside to commence business. The Articles also designate each class of shares, the authorized number of shares of each class, and the par value (if any) of each share. In Chapter 5, on capitalizing your business, you will gain a better understanding of par value and how to fill out this section properly. Ordinarily, a simple way to allocate shares is to provide for one share for each dollar of capital initially contributed to the corporate bank account.

## Publish a Corporation Announcement in Local Newspapers

In most states, newly formed corporations are required to publish an announcement of name, intention, and the names of those responsible for carrying out the corporation's activities.

## Have Your First Board of Directors Meeting

The initial board of directors is usually selected by the original incorporator(s). After this first board of directors has been appointed, shareholders elect any subsequent directors. At their first meeting, the initial directors elect the corporate officers. The initial directors can be named in the Articles of Incorporation, but if they are not, be sure to document this selection in your corporate records (see Figure 4–2 for sample form).

**Figure 4–2**    Sample Designation of Directors

The Connecticut corporation of Smith-Jones, Inc., hereby designates the following people to serve as the initial Board of Directors of the Corporation, as acknowledged by the following signatures:

_____

Bob Smith        (date)

_____

Sue Jones        (date)

_____

Witness        (date)

## Open a Bank Account

You must open a bank account for the corporation and deposit the amount of capital, at a minimum, as declared in your application to the state. To set up this corporate account, you will need to give your banker a "corporate resolution" (also required for any other official action) authorizing this new account (see Figure 4–3 for sample resolution form). Every corporate resolution, which is simply a recording of what the company has resolved to do, is signed by the officer(s) and stamped with your corporate seal to make it official. Capitalization, or the dollars needed to fund your business, is discussed in more depth in Chapter 5.

## Assign Shares of Stock and Issue Stock Certificates

The corporation assigns shares of stock and issues stock certificates, evidence of the shareholder's ownership interest (see Figure 4–4 for sample assignment of shares form). It's not uncommon in a small start-up for one or two people, usually the president and/or secretary to initially own 100 percent of the stock and to sell off shares as the business expands and attracts investors. A stock certificate is issued to each shareholder after the corporation has actually received payment—cash, service, promise of future payment (evidenced by a promissory note; see Figure 4–5), or transfer of property (evidenced by a bill of sale; see Figure 4–6). Many small corporations prefer to keep all issued stock certificates in the official corporate record book, and that is fine.

Issuing stock to people other than the corporate officers can be tricky in that both the federal securities law and the individual state laws regulate the sale of securities—and both can be complicated. Typically, small corporations consisting solely of investors who are active participants in the daily business operations are exempt from these

**Figure 4–3**   Sample Corporate Resolution Form for Opening Corporate Account

---

The undersigned, being officers of Smith-Jones, Inc., hereby resolve the following resolutions:

1. A bank account in the name of the corporation is to be set up at First National Bank account, with the initial amount of $200,000.

2. As President of the corporation, only Sue Jones can withdraw or deposit money in the corporate account.

---

(signature, title, date of each officer)

---

**Figure 4–4**    Sample Assignment of Share Form

For value received, which is acknowledged, _____(assignor name)_____ (the "Assignor") hereby assigns all interest and benefit to ___(assignee name)___ (the "Assignee") in the ___(class)___ shares of _____(corporate name)_____ as evidenced by Share Certificate No(s) _____ (the "Shares").

The Assignor warrants the Assignee that the Shares are fully paid up and that the Assignor owns the Shares free and clear of all encumbrances.

Given under seal on ___(date)___

Signed, sealed, and delivered in the presence of:

_____
(signature of witness)

for the Assignor

_____
(signature of Assignor)

complex mandates, but some paperwork is still usually required. To find out what securities laws may apply to you, especially if you have a number of shareholders, check with the Secretary of State's Office, an attorney and the relevant state and federal statutes.

**Adopt Bylaws**

These are the general rules of the road and can be adapted to the needs of your particular business. Be sure to draw up the bylaws in a legal document (see Figure 4–7 for a sample form). A sample set of by-laws comes with your corporate kit but you should adopt, and adapt,

**Figure 4–5**    Sample Promissory Note

I, Susan Jones, promise to deposit $50,000 in the Smith-Jones, Inc., corporate account on or before June 1, 1998, to pay for 50 shares of Smith-Jones, Inc., stock which was put in my name on June 1, 1997. Failure to do so will revert my stocks to John Smith, vice president of Smith-Jones, Inc.

Signed, sealed, and delivered on June 1, 1997,

_____
Susan Jones, President

**Figure 4–6**   Sample Bill of Sales for Transfer of Property for Stock

Receipt of the below listed goods, services, or assets is acknowledged by _____(the Assignor of Stock)_____ (the "Assignor") in exchange for the sale of all interest and benefit to _____(Assignee name)_____(the "Assignee") in the ____(class)____ shares of _____(corporate name)_____ as evidenced by Share Certificate No(s) _____ (the "Shares").

The Assignee hereby sells and transfers possession of the following goods to the Assignor: ____(list of goods, services, or assets)____ .

The Assignee warrants that it owns and has the right to transfer ownership to the Assignor.

The Assignor warrants the Assignee that this sale and transfer of possessions renders the Assignor the owner of the Shares free and clear of all encumbrances.

Given under seal on __(date)__

Signed, sealed, and delivered in the presence of:

_____
(signature of witness)

for the Assignor

_____
(signature of Assignor)

_____
(signature of witness)

for the Assignee

_____
(signature of Assignee)

bylaws for your company in accordance with your state laws and business purpose. Among other things, bylaws state:

- The rights and powers of shareholders.
- The number, election, and term of office of the board of directors.
- The number, qualifications, election, and terms of office of the officers.
- Data on stock ownership and dividends.

**Figure 4–7**   Sample Corporate Bylaws Form

_____
(corporation name)
_____

By-Law No._____

The following described by-law to _____ is hereby enacted as
By-Law No. _____ of _____(corporation name)_____:

The directors and officers of the Corporation are instructed and authorized
to take such action and execute such instruments as are required or deemed
advisable to implement this by-law.

Passed by the undersigned, being all the directors of _____(corporation_____
____name)_____ on __(date)__ .


_____      _____
(signature of director)      (director's name, typed)


_____      _____
(signature of director)      (director's name, typed)
_____

- The rules of the corporation as to fiscal year, amending bylaws,
  who can sign contracts or inspect corporate books. Salaries and
  fringe benefits may also be spelled out.

**Record Minutes or Prepare Consent Forms**

Draw up a consent form for the board of directors to identify the
corporate officers and record the issuance of stock if minutes aren't
taken. If you're not keen on recording the minutes of your first—or
any—directors' meeting, this form can be used as a summary of important decisions made. Always take the time to make a record—minutes, a
corporate resolution, or a consent form—of what happens in your business. This is a legal necessity as well as a practical requirement.


# CONGRATULATIONS, YOU'RE AN INC.!

Now you've mastered the legalities of the start-up phase and you're
ready to hang out your Inc. shingle! But still, check again with the secretary of state to find out about any additional requirements. Report
what you've done to meet the incorporation requirements and verify
that you have filed all the appropriate paperwork for your state. Also,
remember, you need to apply for a tax registration number (see Chapter 10 for more on taxes).

What a satisfying experience to see the tiny company you've nurtured from a glimmer of an idea, through infancy, evolve into a full-fledged corporation! If you remember to respect its independence, keep personal agendas and funds separate, but at the same time provide guidance, you'll both flourish.

## CORPORATE STATUS

Does your corporation qualify to be in with the S corporation crowd? Is it eligible for the elite and trendy LLC status? Read on and find out about the kinds of businesses that qualify for such treatment. What is the difference between a domestic and a foreign corporation? Why would you want to form a close corporation? A professional corporation? A nonprofit corporation?

## S Corporations

Of the several types of corporations suited to the needs of small business owners, the most common kind is the S corporation, or Sub S as they are sometimes called. S corporations were created by the IRS in 1958 (and revised substantially by the Subchapter Revision Act of 1982) to allow small businesses to be taxed as partnerships, thus avoiding the double taxation levied on corporations, while still providing the advantage of corporate limited liability. A corporation can choose to have S corporation status if:

- There are not more than 35 shareholders.
- The company operates only in the United States.
- There is only one class of stock.
- All shareholders give their consent.
- The company has a tax identification number.
- Form 2553, Election by a Small Business Corporation, is filed with the IRS.

What effect does this election have? A small business corporation terminates its status as a separate *tax* entity, and all corporate income or losses are then attributable to the individual shareholders in proportion to the shares owned by each individual. The purpose is to save tax dollars by doing away with corporate "double-taxation," the tax that the corporate entity pays, and then the tax an individual shareholder pays on earnings and dividends.

## Limited Liability Corporations: The Newest Trend

The limited liability corporation (LLC), is a partnership/corporation business entity combo possessing many of the benefits of the S corporation, without the long list of requirements previously listed for S corporations, and also having some of the benefits of partnership. Like a partnership, an LLC may dissolve on the death or departure of a "member" and transfer of membership requires other members' approval. But, unlike a general partnership, the LLC allows investors to actually manage the business and not be personally liable for business debts.

Many states have been hesitant to sanction LLCs as they are a fairly recent development, authorized by states after the IRS permitted LLCs to be treated like partnerships for tax purposes in 1988. About half of the states currently have laws permitting formation of an LLC, but business experts are predicting that LLCs will become more widely accepted in the near future because of their terrific benefits to small business owners. In addition to tax savings, the filing fees are bare bones (about $60) and the paperwork is negligible.

## Closely Held Corporation

A closely held corporation is one in which the voting shares are held by a single shareholder or a "closely knit" group of shareholders. It may be "operated" in a fashion similar to a partnership and yet enjoy the protection of the corporate shield against personal liability. For those reasons, this type of organization is often chosen for businesses organized and managed by family members. The distinguishing feature is that just a few people or a single shareholder holds the corporation's voting shares, and they agree to limit the number of company stockholders as well as the transferral of stock.

Additionally, with this corporate structure, some of the formalities of running a corporation can be eliminated, such as the annual shareholders' meeting and the election of a board of directors. On the downside, if death or divorce requires the divestment of shares, some of these shares may well be complicated since outside investors may be reluctant to buy in, or family members may not want "outsiders" in.

## Professional Corporation

Every state has statutes that allow for certain groups of professionals—such as lawyers, doctors, and accountants—or firms with a sole principal and associates to establish professional corporations (PC), also called a professional association (PA) or service corporation (SC). While there used to be greater tax advantages before 1986, professional corporations still offer corporate tax advantages for what are traditionally partnership or proprietorship activities.

Organizing a PC is popular among small business owners who are in partnerships, or a businesses where individuals are closely associated with their colleagues and would otherwise run the risk of being held liable for a partner's or colleague's negligence. Small business owners also like the credibility and prestige associated with PC status and the protection and services provided by corporate state law.

## Nonprofit Corporations

Nonprofit corporations have the megaperk of tax-exempt status, which means they are free from paying taxes on the corporation's income *and* contributors can write off some of their contributions as a tax deduction, but only if the tax-exempt status is filed properly (check the timing of filing with the IRS and secretary of state). Only if your corporation is formed for religious, charitable, literary, scientific, or educational purposes can it qualify for this tax-exempt status.

## Domestic and Foreign Corporations

As soon as you legally incorporate your business, it automatically is a "domestic corporation" home based in the state of incorporation. This means it may legally operate in the "home" state in which it was incorporated. If, however, you want to extend your business dealings to other states, you must apply for "foreign corporation" status in each of the states in which you want to "do business" (it doesn't mean you've gone international).

## Maintaining the Corporate Shield of Liability Protection

Just because you have legally incorporated your company, don't breathe a sigh of liability relief quite yet. You can be held liable personally for acts of the corporation if you don't play by the rules, in spirit as well as in law.

We do not expect that anyone reading this book would purposefully attempt to set up a sham corporation to obtain corporation liability protection unjustifiably. But we don't want you to fall unwittingly into that category either. A "little knowledge can be a dangerous thing" and so we offer some advanced legal thinking to equip you with full legal armor.

The corporate shield becomes a "veil" (disguise used to hide behind) which can be "pierced" to hold principals personally liable if *the corporation is operated, either knowingly or through negligence, as though the corporation does not exist.* For example, although the legal steps have been taken to form the corporation, no corporate meetings are held, minutes are not taken, corporate resolutions are not filed, and corporate records and books are not maintained. The bottom line is, if you're going to talk the corporate talk, you have to walk the corporate walk.

Also, your corporation may not be treated as a bona fide corporation if you use the assets of the corporation as your own and add or withdraw capital from the corporation at will; or if you provide inadequate capitalization and conduct business like a sole proprietor. Remember, a corporation is an entity created by operation of law that is separate and apart from the officers, directors, and shareholders. Legally you cannot act like a sole proprietorship and still have the shield offered a bona fide corporation.

---

## KNOW YOUR KEY TERMS

- *Incorporation.* One (or more) people, the incorporators, file with the state to create a separate business entity. A corporation has four distinguishing characteristics: (1) it is a person unto itself; (2) it is created by a statute, usually by the state, and granted a charter or certificate (see following definition); (3) it—not the shareholders—is liable for its debts; and (4) it is usually granted perpetual existence so that, unlike a partnership or sole proprietorship, the death of the CEO (president) does not terminate the company's existence.

- *Articles (certificate) of incorporation (charter).* This public document, your company's birth certificate, is issued by the state to verify that the company is recognized as a singular entity with an identity separate and apart from the officers, directors and shareholders. This is how you get the official moniker, "Inc."

- *Bylaws.* These are the rules that you draft, following state guidelines, to organize and operate the corporation.

- *Incorporators.* These individuals do the original, start-up paperwork to comply with the secretary of state's official guidelines for getting the corporation underway; they often take up the reins of officers, shareholders, or directors.

- *Shareholders.* Corporations exist for the benefit of their shareholders, one (or more) of whom owns stock in the corporation. Only shareholders can elect or remove directors, amend the bylaws and charter, approve the sale of corporate assets, or approve reorganization and termination of the corporation.

- *Officers.* These personnel are responsible for the daily operations of the corporation in adherence with the bylaws. States require corporations to have certain officers; always a president, the chief operating officer, and then usually a secretary, who is responsible for the corporate records, and/or a treasurer, who is responsible for the finances. Some states allow one person to hold all offices.

- *Board of directors.* The directors are fiduciaries who manage the corporation and make policy decisions. The initial board of directors is usually appointed by the incorporator(s), and subsequent directors are elected by the shareholders.

- *Capitalization.* Simply defined, capitalization refers to the funds needed to create the corporate foundation. Since the corporation is an entity separate and apart from all the persons described previously, it must have its own capital account to be granted a charter, or certificate, from the state.

- *"Piercing the corporate veil."* What can happen if you fail to incorporate properly. Reread the preceding section!

## BASIC LEGAL RESEARCH

- *Bone up on the legalities of maintaining your corporate shield.* You might want to read two cases—*Walkovsky* v. *Carlton,* 276 N.Y.S. 2d 585 (1966), and *Teeler* v. *Clear Service Co.,* 173 N.Y.S. 2d 183 (1958)—both involving taxicab businesses in New York City, which law students read to learn the horrors of creating a sham corporation.

- *The Model Business Corporation Act.* Drafted by a committee of the American Bar Association, this act can be found in any law library.

- *State statutes for corporations.* This can be found in your local courthouse or law library.

- *Basic Corporation Law,* by Detlev. F. Vagts (The Foundation Press). This book has a cross-reference table which can be used with the Model Business Corporation Act.

- *State by state legal books about incorporation.* Nolo Press publishes a series of books—*How to Form Your Own Corporation in California [New York, Texas, Florida].*
- *How to Form Your Own Nonprofit Corporation,* by Anthony Mancuso (Nolo Press). This is a great resource book if you're interested in more information on forming a nonprofit corporation.

## KEY RESOURCES

- *The Internal Revenue Service.* For further information about filing under S Corporation status with the IRS, call the IRS and ask for the brochure, "Tax Information on S Corporations."
- *Your secretary of state or state office of corporation administration.* Refer to Appendix C for a list of state government offices that will have the forms you must complete to become an Inc., as well as staff members who can help answer any questions you have about gaining corporate status.
- *Business development councils.* City, state, and regional Business Development Councils often publish excellent publications targeted for your local area (look in the blue pages under "Government Offices, Business development").

## COURT COACH® SUGGESTS

1. *You can do it—the process of incorporating is simple!* The entire process of filling out the actual paperwork to incorporate takes about an hour or two, and it's simple enough for many small business owners to do without an attorney (an LLC is easier yet). Even if your business has only a few investors and a simple investment plan, though, it's advisable to consult an attorney to answer any questions before you start this process and review your work to red-flag any errors. It's not only expensive to backtrack and redo paperwork, it is complicated and difficult to undo mistakes at the state and federal level.

2. *Take the short, sweet, and simple course on using your phone book to help you incorporate.* Calling the secretary of state sounds like a simple proposition, but it may not be if you've never attempted to deal with your state's bureaucracy.

   The blue pages of your phone book aren't just your guide to town, city, county, state, and U.S. government departments—

but your guide to incorporating as well. When you look up secretary of state (located under state government agencies), you may be amazed to discover all the services provided to you, the taxpayer, that relate to forming and maintaining a corporation. There are specific listings of departments that can provide useful information on many topics. Use these services; *you* have already paid for the privilege with your tax dollar.

3. *Important: Read the incorporation statutes first!* These are the instructions for your corporate machine. If you're like most people, you don't want to take the time to "read the instructions" but if you do, you *will* understand the basics.

4. *You need to consult an attorney before you offer stock for sale or transfer.* State and federal laws apply, and they are both fraught with complications. This is not a choice!

5. *Purchase a corporate kit.* These bound books, available at most stationery stores for about $70, come complete with bylaw forms, fill-in-the-blank stock certificates, minute logs, and a corporate seal stamped on all of your corporate resolutions (it's fun, fancy, and looks very official!). You can also order a corporate kit from a mail-order company such as Corpex: (800) 221-8181.

6. *Be organized from the giddy-up.* You can, and should, file all your important start-up paperwork—certificate of incorporation, organization report, appointment of statutory agent for service, and application for tax registration number, in your corporate kit, and in a file in a *safe place.*

7. *Stay organized and keep adequate records.* Why is it highly important to keep track of important documents—such as the minutes of stockholders' meetings, corporate resolutions and stock transactions—throughout the life of the corporation? Because, if you are ever hauled into court, the better you and your records look, the better you'll do. And there is less chance that the court can "pierce the corporate veil." Keeping organized also makes it simple to write business plans and apply for loans or resolve disputes without having to go to court.

8. *The Leona Rule: Separate your personal finances from those of the corporation.* Open a corporate bank account and use it to pay all bills and salaries. Please don't use a personal check or credit card to pay a business expense, or vice versa, a corporate check or credit card to pay a personal expense. It complicates your bookkeeping and could make the IRS upset.

9. *Prepare legal documentation of any transactions between you and the corporation.* Treat the corporation as you would any other business associate. If the corporation borrows money from you, obtain a promissory note. If you lease property to the corporation, sign a lease agreement. Additionally, transfer any existing business contracts with your name on them into the corporation's name.

10. *Distinguish your personal signature from your signature as an officer of the corporation.* Always include your title when you sign correspondence, legal documents, checks, order forms and any other documents relating to business (Jane Doe, President, not simply Jane Doe). This clearly denotes that you're acting as an officer of the corporation, not as an individual, and that the corporation is responsible.

11. *Use the full corporate name consistently on all printed material.* Your stationery, business cards, advertising, catalogs and wherever else the corporate name appears should state the full name of your business as this is your official state-registered name. Before incorporation, you could have been Jane & Joe Doe & Company; now, you must always add your "Inc."

# 5

## GETTING MONEY: CAPITALIZATION OF A SMALL BUSINESS

### A WORKING DEFINITION OF "MONEY" FOR THE ENTREPRENEUR

It may surprise you that we have included a chapter on money in a legal guide. However, as you read through, you will discover that the dollars you raise and spend are linked in many ways to legal liabilities. For example, undercapitalizing your corporation could lead to the perception that you have created a "sham" corporation, thereby putting your corporation's liability protection at risk. Think too, about the consequences of too few cash reserves and the perils of bankruptcy when you will come face to face with legal terms and realities like Chapters 7, 12, and 13.

Financial pressure can also lead to making poor business decisions. So, a quick look at the money issue should keep you on the straight and narrow road of legal compliance.

Money for your business is dubbed capital and falls into three categories; initial, operating, and reserve. You need all three to go into business without going out of business. Many small businesses fail, not because of poor marketing, sales, service, or product, but because the business is undercapitalized; there is not enough money available, either initially or during the first few years, as the business goes through the ups and downs of its maiden voyage.

Nonetheless, one in four of *Inc.* magazine's 500 fastest growing companies in 1992 started with less than $5,000. It is important to research, research, and research so that your initial investment will materialize or turn into cash! This is particularly true for small enterprises that may be able to scrape together enough money to start up but do not have sufficient financial reserves to see the company easily through the often lean first few years.

Let's look at the three kinds of capital that you need to get your company off to a good start, and to keep it up and running while you go through the three stages of growth—losing money, breaking even, and showing a profit:

1. *Initial capital.* This covers your start-up costs, such as legal fees, licenses and permits, machinery and fixtures, deposits for utilities and your office space, and whatever else you need to be "Open for Business."
2. *Operating (or working) capital.* You use this money to buy materials for production or merchandise for sale, purchase office supplies, meet your payroll, and take care of whatever else is needed to keep the business running until accounts receivable materialize or turn into cash in hand, or until your business starts showing a profit.
3. *Reserve capital.* This is your safety net of available monies for unexpected circumstances and emergencies. You don't want to go out of business because a machine breaks and you can't afford to fix it. You may also want to earmark reserve dollars in your personal account for your personal expenses beyond the business, such as food, clothing, and shelter for a specified period, depending on how you determine the timing for paying yourself a salary from the business.

## DETERMINING HOW MUCH MONEY YOU REALLY NEED

You can plan to obtain start-up money from a number of sources: personal savings, stocks, bonds, wealthy relatives, visionary friends, lending institutions, or special funding programs. Your starting point should be transferring the "big idea" onto paper, illustrating the "big picture" with a business plan. An idea may sound great within the gentle confines of your mind, or when bounced off encouraging friends at dinner, but spelling it out in a cohesive business plan is just a "must."

This resounding note of reality will help you be honest about your expectations and will keep you focused on your goals, motivated and confident. Lenders and other investors can determine whether you can make your ideas operable in the markets you target.

While the business plan can be simple, it should include an overview of the company's goals, a physical description of the company's facilities, a detailed market analysis, initial inventory requirements and production goals, and a financial plan. For the purposes of this chapter, we are not concerned with the details of developing a business plan, only with pointing out that you often need a business plan to obtain the capital needed to realize your business. Figure 5–1 shows a sample business plan.

Two steps are crucial for determining how to capitalize your business: First, create a capital needs statement, and second, determine your net worth and personal asset availability.

## Create a Capital Needs Statement

The capital needs statement will enable you to determine how much money you will realistically need to start up your business and stay in business. This is where your three different kinds of capital, initial, pending, and reserve, come into play. You need to determine your one-time start-up expenses, monthly operating costs, and how much of a safety net you need in your savings account earmarked for capital reserve (see Figure 5–2 for sample capital needs statement). We recommend keeping at least 12 months of operating cash in reserve. You need to spend the first few months building up a clientele, marketing your business, and working out the inevitable kinks instead of worrying about making enough money to cover expenses.

Most people often underestimate the operating costs of a business. You won't if you talk to people in the know to realistically determine costs. Who can provide this advice? Local people in the same business or with a similar product are the easiest and best source of information. Besides colleagues and associations, trade associations and networking organizations and associates can be most helpful in providing you a baseline for the start-up and operating expenses pertinent to your particular business: costs for machinery, office equipment,

**Figure 5–1**   Sample Business Plan

### Background on Business

Joe's Catering is a unique venture in that there are no other catering services in Small Town, USA, and there is a marked need, as Large Employer, Inc., recently opened its corporate headquarters here with an employee base of 10,000 employees.

### Management

See the attached resumes of:

1. Joe Smith, who will own and manage Joe's Catering.
2. Cathy Jones, who will be the head chef.
3. Roger Doe, who will be the marketing director.

### Research and Development

Joe's Catering is a unique establishment worthy of financial support for the following reasons:

1. There is no other catering service in Small Town.
2. Large Employer, Inc., has expressed an interest in having company functions catered on a weekly basis.
3. Of the 5,000 individual employees at Large Employer, Inc., who responded to a survey initiated by Joe Smith, 3,000 indicated that they would hire the services of a caterer if one existed (see attached survey for more details).

### Marketing

See the attached brochure that Joe's Catering will distribute to Large Employer and other companies in Small Town (included are promotional literature, photos, and a menu).

### Operational Costs

See the attached start-up budget and operating budget for the first year of business.

### Legal

See the attached legal documents that may be of interest to you:

1. Articles of Incorporation.
2. Employment contract.
3. Pension plans.
4. Profit-sharing plans.
5. Patents and trademarks.
6. Franchise and distribution plans.

### Financial

See the attached financial documents that may be of interest to you:

1. Summary of audited financial statements for the last five years of previous business (Joe's Restaurant).
2. Cash flow and income projections for the next five years.
3. Details of outstanding loans.

Figure 5–2

| ESTIMATED MONTHLY EXPENSES | | | |
|---|---|---|---|
| Item | Your estimate of monthly expenses based on sales of $ _____ per year | Your estimate of how much cash you need to start your business (See column 3.) | What to put in column 2 (These figures are typical for one kind of business. you will have to decide how many months to allow for in your business.) |
| | Column 1 | Column 2 | Column 3 |
| Salary of owner-manager | $ | $ | 2 times column 1 |
| All other salaries and wages | | | 3 times column 1 |
| Rent | | | 3 times column 1 |
| Advertising | | | 3 times column 1 |
| Delivery expense | | | 3 times column 1 |
| Supplies | | | 3 times column 1 |
| Telephone and telegraph | | | 3 times column 1 |
| Other utilities | | | 3 times column 1 |
| Insurance | | | Payment required by insurance company |
| Taxes, including Social Security | | | 4 times column 1 |
| Interest | | | 3 times column 1 |
| Maintenance | | | 3 times column 1 |
| Legal and other professional fees | | | 3 times column 1 |
| Miscellaneous | | | 3 times column 1 |
| STARTING COSTS YOU ONLY HAVE TO PAY ONCE | | | Leave column 2 blank |
| Fixtures and equipment | | | Fill in worksheet 3 on page 12 and put the total here |
| Decorating and remodeling | | | Talk it over with a contractor |
| Installation of fixtures and equipment | | | Talk to suppliers from who you buy these |
| Starting inventory | | | Suppliers will probably help you estimate this |
| Deposits with public utilities | | | Find out from utilities companies |
| Legal and other professional fees | | | Lawyer, accountant, and so on |
| Licenses and permits | | | Find out from city offices what you have to have |
| Advertising and promotion for opening | | | Estimate what you'll use |
| Accounts receivable | | | What you need to buy more stock until credit customers pay |
| Cash | | | For unexpected expenses or losses, special purchases, etc. |
| Other | | | Make a separate list and enter total |
| TOTAL ESTIMATED CASH YOU NEED TO START WITH | $ | | Add up all the numbers in column 2 |

*Source:* "Checklist for Going into Business," *Management Aid No. 2.016* (Washington, C.D.: Small Business Administration, 1975), 6–7.

inventory, licensing and permit fees, as well as staffing requirements. Other experts who warrant a visit include:

- An insurance agent to estimate your business and personnel insurance needs.
- An accountant to determine payroll, real estate taxes, and other taxes you'll need to budget for.
- A bookkeeper to discuss efficient procedures and cost to hire.
- A clerk at city hall or the county courthouse to research license and permit fees.
- Potential suppliers who will help you estimate your operating capital needs; stationery, telephone, equipment, furnishings.
- An attorney who can provide you with an estimate of what your legal costs might be initially and down the path if you run the risk of litigation.
- The landlord (if you're renting your office space). Describe any additions/improvements you would like to make to the property and find out what the property management company will contribute.

## Determine Your Net Worth and Personal Asset Availability

The rule of thumb for capitalizing a small business is that you should try to spend as much of your own money as comfortably possible to avoid hefty monthly payments to the bank or giving up too much equity in your business to venture capitalists who normally require an equity portion before funding a new project. Before you decide how much money you need to obtain from outside sources, you'll need to find out how much money you actually have free to invest in your business by filling out a personal financial statement (see Figure 5–3).

The personal financial statement tells you your net worth, the difference between the value of your assets and the amount of liabilities or debt outstanding—assets minus liability gives you the actual amount available to invest in your business. The trick here is to determine whether an asset can be liquidated (turned into cash) or whether it can be used as collateral. The most "collateral-friendly" asset most people have is their home, and a home equity loan may be your best bet for a source of money from traditional lending sources (more on loans later in this chapter).

As far as liquidating your assets goes, try to be realistic. Just because you have a car that you could sell for $5,000 in a pinch, doesn't

**Figure 5–3**    Personal Finance Statement

| Assets | | Liabilities | |
|---|---|---|---|
| Cash (CDs) | $ 10,000 | Accounts/ | |
| Stocks, bonds | $ 10,000 | Bills payable | $ 5,000 |
| Real estate | $100,000 | Mortgage | $70,000 |
| Automobiles | $200,000 | **Total liabilities** | **$75,000** |
| | | | |
| Life insurance | | | |
| cash value | $ 10,000 | | |
| Personal assets | $ 25,000 | | |
| **Total assets** | **$355,000** | | |
| | − 75,000 (Total liabilities) | | |

**TOTAL NET WORTH** = **$280,000**

mean you could realistically rely on your feet for transportation. While savings accounts, stocks, and bonds are clearly salable assets, there are some gray areas when it comes to their liquidity, such as monies invested toward your retirement in tax-deferred accounts (e.g., 401(k) IRA). In all likelihood, the tax penalty as well as income taxes you would be required to pay to liquidate your retirement fund before the age of 55 make this a poor source of money to invest in your business. (*Note:* Most lending institutions do *not* consider retirement securities as collateral against small business loans, with the exception of funds in a 401(k) account.)

## WHERE CAN I FIND THE MONEY I NEED? (SORRY, NOT ON TREES)

This is one of life's bigger questions, and especially pertinent for entrepreneurs with big plans and shallow pockets. Finding adequate sources of start-up capital can be extremely difficult for small business entrepreneurs, since traditional lending institutions tend to be stingy with small companies that haven't yet proven their earning potential. But don't give up hope, it's not impossible.

Start by making a list of lending sources and investment sources, then weigh the pros and cons of each. Family members are the most common source of small business investment dollars and may not charge as much, or any, interest as a bank, but you don't have to live with your loan officer. Often, business partners don't make good bedfellows and vice versa.

Besides adding partners, who bring their own financial resources to the venture, which was discussed in Chapter 2, there are two additional, traditional methods of financing your company: accumulating debt by obtaining loan(s), or issuing stock and selling equity (part ownership) in your company. First, we will cover the different lending sources commonly available to small business entrepreneurs. Surprisingly, in this age of credit, many small business owners finance their enterprise with credit cards, a new development and an expensive alternative since the interest charged is generally higher than bank rates.

## Bank Loans and the Small Business Association

Usually, the traditional lending institution may give an entrepreneur a loan to start up a small business if the loan is secured by collateral. Cultivate a professional relationship with your local banker. Be prepared to put up personal assets as collateral. Your best hope of securing a loan through a bank is with the Small Business Administration (SBA).

The SBA, an agency of the federal government, will guarantee loans that banks would not otherwise make to small business owners just starting out. Not all banks want to be bothered with the paperwork involved with SBA loans, so contact your local SBA office and they will direct you to participating banks in your community. To qualify for a SBA guaranteed loan, you must meet the following qualifications:

- Must have been turned down for a conventional bank loan.
- Must be a for-profit organization.
- Must not be involved in speculation or investment in rental real estate.
- Must not be involved in the creation or distribution of ideas or opinions.
- Must meet size criteria (the maximum number depends on the type of business).
- Must have sufficient collateral to adequately secure the loan.
- All principal owners and CEOs must provide personal guarantees.
- If business assets aren't sufficient to secure the loan, liens may be placed on personal assets.
- The loan applicant must be able to demonstrate good character and management expertise.
- Generally, the applicant must provide one-third to one-half of the total assets needed to launch the business.

If you are interested in applying for an SBA loan, make an appointment to meet with a counselor at your local SBA office, who will walk you through the entire application process.

## Family Loans

Most small businesses are funded by the owner and his or her loved ones. Some entrepreneurs swear by the support their friends and family have given them in getting their business off the ground, and others curse the day they accepted money from their relatives. You must carefully consider the personal relationship you have with someone before allowing money to enter the equation. If there's already the potential for stress, borrowing money will only make things tenser. But if the loan is offered in a supportive, enthusiastic spirit, what have you got to lose?

A personal loan from a friend or relative should be treated like any other business transaction. The amount of the loan, the interest rate, and the timetable for repayment should all be documented in a note signed by all parties.

## Selling Equity/Issuing Stock

What you want to avoid is any situation where several stockholders can pool their stock to "outvote" you in any managerial decision. For example, if you brought on other investors and split up the stock ⅓-⅓-⅓ (33% each), the other two investors could vote you out of the business altogether.

Instead of incurring debt via loans, you may wish to capitalize your company by issuing stock and selling equity, or partial ownership, in your business. Selling stock to acquire capital for a small incorporated business works according to the same principles that apply to selling stock on the New York Stock Exchange for a billion-dollar corporation. The price is determined by profit potential, not asset value, and is subject to the law of supply and demand. If investors perceive that the company will give them an attractive return on their investment in a certain time frame, they may be willing to invest especially in a time when CDs, IRAs, and other conservative investments are not paying a high rate of return on investment.

When issuing stock to stockholders you want to ensure that you own at least 51 percent of the stock, to remain the majority stockholder. Certain types of investors, such as venture capitalists (discussed later in this chapter), may very well require that you give up some control of management decisions, even though you are the majority stockholder.

The primary legal concern with issuing stock is what, if any, federal or state securities laws will apply. Each state has its own statutes regulating the sale of securities. Since both federal and state securities regulations are quite complex, you must consult an attorney before issuing stock to determine which laws may apply to your company and how to comply with them.

Securities regulations are intended to protect shareholders who have invested money in the corporation but have nothing to do with its daily operations and little knowledge of management operations. They are also intended to protect honest enterprises seeking capital through public investment. The SEC has guidelines that exempt certain securities transactions from its scrutiny, the main one being the issuance of stock in a "private offering," as opposed to a "public offering."

To qualify as a "private offering," the sales of stock must be limited to no more than 25 persons and are subject to myriad restrictions. Fortunately, most small businesses issuing stock are exempt from the SEC regulations since the investment nature of small corporations is private, but you still may have to comply with some additional state statutes. Talk to you attorney.

To issue stock, you must go through several steps:

1. Incorporate the company (see Chapter 4).
2. Prepare a business plan for interested investors.
3. Depending on dollar amount needed in capital, set stock price and number of shares to be issued accordingly. Set a stock offering price low enough to attract initial investors. After you get some takers, you can raise or lower the price depending on the level of demand.
4. Develop a stock prospectus that outlines the cost of stock, minimum investment requirements, and how the money will be used to meet the goals of the corporation.

### Small Business Investment Corporations (SBICs)
These private companies are licensed by the federal government to provide financial help to small businesses in the form of equity/venture financing. SBICs purchase stock in promising small corporations and usually become involved in the business operations and management decisions. Minority Enterprise Small Business Investment Corporations provide these services exclusively to minority-owned enterprises.

### Venture Capitalists
Venture capitalists are private individuals, small investment groups, and companies that represent groups of wealthy investors looking to

buy equity in small businesses with big potential. Computer software, biotechnology, and other high-tech enterprises are typically attractive to venture capitalists. You'll need an airtight business plan and an eagerly awaiting marketplace to convince these high rollers that your idea is a winner. Often, with a few years of swelling profits to your credit, venture capitalists can be an excellent source of funding for expansion and growth into new markets.

Venture capitalists sometimes operate investment programs with state or local government to aid minorities or other special interest groups.

## KNOW YOUR KEY TERMS

- *Capital structure.* The financial framework for your company.
- *Initial capital.* The money needed to launch your business.
- *Operating capital.* The money needed to keep your business running until the profits can support it.
- *Reserve capital.* Money set aside to cover emergencies, as well as personal essentials, such as health insurance, mortgage, and food.
- *Capital needs statement.* Sets forth how much money you need to obtain to start up the business.
- *Venture capitalists.* Financiers, whether individuals, companies, or a group with substantial sums looking for attractive investment opportunities that will provide a significant return in a relatively short period of time.
- *Equity.* What you receive for partial ownership in the company, usually in the form of stock, cash, valuables, or services.
- *Shareholders.* Those who own the company as evidenced by their shares of ownership.
- *Stock prospectus.* An outline of how the stock to be issued is to be sold and how the investors' money will be used to fund the company.
- *Security.* An assurance in the form of a note, bond, stock, debenture, or evidence of indebtedness, whereby the creditor is furnished with a resource to be used in the event that the debtor fails to meet his or her obligations.
- *Debt financing.* In contrast to equity financing where stock is issued for capital contributed, capital is raised by issuing bonds or borrowing cash.

## BASIC LEGAL RESEARCH

- *How to Prepare and Present a Business Plan,* by Joseph R. Mancuso (Prentice-Hall). An extensive, step-by-step manual on developing your road map for success.
- *How to Raise Venture Capital,* by Stanley E. Pratt (Scribner's). A comprehensive guide to tapping into this source of capital for your fledgling corporation.
- *How to Plan and Finance a Growing Business,* by Donald Dible (Reston). More helpful tips to help you get the funds you need to start and sustain your business.

## KEY RESOURCES

- *Your local Small Business Administration office.* Listed in the blue pages under United States Government Offices, this is the best resource available to find out about the legal requirements of capitalization, as well as the practicalities of obtaining a small business loan.
- *Business loans from the SBA.* This publication, available from the SBA, gives you all the legal do's and don'ts for obtaining a SBA loan. Your SBA counselor can provide you with this guidebook as well as several other helpful publications.

## COURT COACH® SUGGESTS

1. *Make long-term financial planning an integral part of your business plan.* Many entrepreneurs breathe an unwarranted sigh of relief once they have secured start-up funds. The difficult truth is that once you hang out your shingle, your financial concerns have only just begun. That's why we can't stress enough the importance of long-range, realistic planning.
2. *In devising a solid business plan, don't be shy about enlisting the help of others in your profession who have achieved the success you desire for your business.* If you've got connections, use them. After all, why reinvent the wheel?
3. *Look for unconventional loans.* Many larger communities have some kind of urban development program that may offer low-interest financing, rental space in rehabilitated buildings, and

other assistance to new businesses. The SBA or your local economic development department may be able to help you find such lending sources.

4. *Approach family members for funds, armed with a business plan and a promissory note.* This goes a long way to establish a professional relationship. Your word may be your bond, but if you want to keep and maintain both relationships, put it in writing *and* adhere to the terms.

    Friends, too, need to be dealt with professionally. Before opening up your business to friends as shareholders, seriously assess their strengths and weaknesses. Someone you enjoy playing golf with may not be someone you want to deal with in a business context. The money may not be worth it.

5. *A good accountant and a good bookkeeper are "necessaries," not luxuries.* An accountant can help you formulate your business plans, estimate tax consequences, and pinpoint inaccuracies in your financial projections. Trust the truism that the money you spend consulting with an accountant will more than repay itself to your company bank account in the long run. The same holds true for a bookkeeper. Put your business structure and foundation on a safe footing. Once familiar with you personally, and with the basics of your business, a bookkeeper can advise and purchase computer programs to keep track of expenses and taxes, calculate salaries, pay bills, and determine your salary as well!

6. *Silent Partners—What are they and how do you deal with them?* An investor who takes no active part in a firm's management, but nonetheless shares in its profits and losses is called a "silent partner," or a dormant partner. This is the person whose name does not appear on the firm's letterhead and who does not take an active part in running or managing the business. Yet, because the silent partner has a financial interest in the concern and shares in the profits or losses, the law regards this person either absolutely to all intents and purposes as a partner or, at a minimum, as a partner in respect to third parties. (*Note:* Those who are active and conduct the business of the firm are known as principals.)

7. *Save, save, save, and plot and plan.* Wow! How great not to have to borrow sums from a variety of sources. There's some real satisfaction in succeeding on your own, and comfort in not taking friends and family down with you if, for any reason, your business does not thrive. After all, there are circumstances beyond your control—recessions, plant closings, snow, rain and other acts of God.

# 6

---

# INSURANCE:
# WOULD YOU BELIEVE
# YOU NEED ALL THIS?

## YOU CAN'T BUY HAPPINESS, BUT YOU CAN
## BUY PEACE OF MIND

While it's true that you can't buy happiness, you can buy peace of mind and security. It's called "insurance." The fine art of buying insurance is a delicate balance of anticipating the worst without crossing the line into the dark realm of paranoia and pessimism.

In all likelihood, you may not need all the coverage your insurance agent can—and may try vigorously to—sell you. That's because your business will probably never burn to the ground, your employees aren't likely to steal you blind, your product isn't bound to have a defect resulting in an onslaught of lawsuits, and you are a competent professional. But if even *one* of these remotely possible events does occur, you could face economic ruin. You need to protect your investment. The trick is determining which insurance you must have, which is optimal, and how much you can afford.

There are many kinds of insurance that small business owners should strongly consider. Some are mandatory, such as: workers' compensation insurance, and possibly liability or professional malpractice insurance. Property insurance, disability insurance, business life insurance, health insurance, overhead insurance, and an umbrella policy are other types of insurance to consider.

## WORKERS' COMPENSATION

You must, to the best of your ability, provide an environment free from the possibility of accidental injury to your employees. State law, comprising the laws passed by your state legislature, requires that you provide compensation for employees who suffer physical or mental injuries due to their jobs, although corporate officers can elect to be excluded from coverage under a workers' compensation policy. It's important to note that state statutes dictate that employees are eligible for workers' compensation whether the employer is guilty of negligence or not. In other words, you *must* cover your workers and buy workers' compensation insurance.

How does this work? How do you find out what your state requires for your kind of business? Your premium is based on the size of your payroll, the kinds of jobs within your organization, and the hazards your employees face on the job. Sometimes, you can lower your premium by effectuating internal safety measures that reduce the probability of accidents in your place of business substantially below the norm for your particular type of business.

Unfortunately, the premiums for workers' compensation insurance are on the upswing. Simultaneously, judges are broadening the guidelines for the types of claims that workers can file under the category of "mental duress." There have been situations of firing an employee undiplomatically, or, of asking a person to work an enormous amount of overtime, that have been the predicate for a claim in this category. (See Chapters 11–13 for more information on dealing with your staff.)

## LIABILITY INSURANCE

Liability insurance covers any claim of negligence by a third party against the company. This includes bodily injury and personal wrongs or torts done to a customer or client, causing emotional or mental duress; for example, to libel, slander, or defame.

Small Claims Courts, where the jurisdictional dollar limits range between $1,500 and $3,000 per claim, are jam-packed with lawsuits against proprietors and businesses. And jury awards in a trial court are basically unpredictable. Everyone is currently citing the case of the woman who was awarded over $1 million because her coffee was too hot at McDonald's and the server was unduly surly. Unless you work in a vacuum and have no contact with employees, customers, or suppliers, liability insurance is a must.

## Types of Liability Insurance Policies

There are four types of policies useful for small business owners that fall under the category of liability: (1) general liability, (2) product liability, (3) vehicle liability, and (4) business life. The following sections describe these policies.

### General Liability

This covers judgments up to the amount of the policy limit plus the cost of defending the lawsuit. Coverage is limited, however, to unknowing negligence, as opposed to willful and malicious behavior with the intent of injury. For example, if a customer slips on a patch of ice on your company's front steps, you could argue that you didn't realize the ice was there. But if an employee pushes a customer out the door, causing the person to fall down the front steps, chances are good that your insurer will not pay out. So, if you buy $1,000,000 worth of liability insurance and you settle a claim for $500,000, the insurance company should pay the amount and assume the legal costs of defending you.

### Product Liability

This can be quite expensive; therefore, it's important to gauge the amount of protection needed and the actual probability that your product will unwittingly cause harm to customers. The best protection is to test and think about any potential harm that might reasonably be anticipated, and then take measures to change the product and/or to explicitly extract the dangers and have clear, understandable directions for use. For example, if you are making a child's toy, you need to think about any removable part that might injure a curious child, namely, all children. Insurance can protect you so far, but it does not absolve the supplier of goods or services of all responsibility. The best protection for the business owner is not insurance, but your own competence, care, and commitment to excellence.

**Vehicle Liability**

As the Domino's Pizza deliveryman who ran over a pedestrian while trying to meet the company's promise of delivery in under 30 minutes could tell you, vehicle liability insurance is crucial for certain businesses. Not only should company-owned cars and trucks be insured, but any employee vehicle that is used in carrying out company business.

**Business Life Insurance**

This is sometimes called "key-man" insurance, but maybe in the 1990s it should be termed instead "key-person." Like regular life insurance, this insurance insures someone's life and pays out upon the person's demise. But this is premised on the concept that you, a key employee or partner, are a valuable asset and that the loss of your services to the company would create a liability endangering the company's continued viability.

Often, CEOs of major companies are insured for millions of dollars by their companies. Yet in a small business, the loss of a "key" player could be even more devastating. To calculate how much of this kind of insurance you might need, you can consider what dollar amount you company would need to stay afloat until a key player can be replaced.

## PROPERTY INSURANCE

What type of property insurance you need is partially determined by whether you rent or own the building in which you conduct your business. If you own the building, your policy will include a building and personal property coverage form that lists what property is covered.

Your building coverage should include:

- Permanent indoor fixtures.
- Outdoor fixtures.
- Property used to service the building (such as a sprinkler system).
- Any temporary structures, including additions under construction, within 100 feet of the main building.

The personal property coverage should include:

- Furniture and temporary indoor fixtures.
- Equipment and machinery.

- Inventory and supplies.
- Personal property used in the business.
- Leased personal property.
- Any personal property of others that you are responsible for.

If you are renting your business offices, your lease will include a section regarding insurance obligations. Most likely, you will need to purchase a renters' commercial insurance package policy to cover insuring the landlord against any liability suits brought against you or your product. The terms of this policy usually cover property damage due to natural disasters or personal negligence.

Many people are daunted by the legalese in these contracts. Nonetheless: read the contract; take notes on what you don't understand; and call the insurance company or your agent and be persistent until all your questions are answered to your satisfaction. Or, consult with your business attorney. Remember, there are no dumb questions!

There is not much room for negotiating a contract clause with insurance companies; and yet, you need to know what you are getting and what you are giving before you legally obligate yourself by signing on the dotted line and making your first premium payment. If you don't like what you hear, shop around!

## Types of Property Insurance Policies

Property insurance policies for small businesses come in three forms: basic form, broad form, and special form.

1. *Basic form.* Protects you from financial losses due to fire, lightning, explosion, windstorm or hail, smoke, aircraft or vehicles, riot, vandalism, sprinkler leaks, sinkholes, and volcanoes.
2. *Broad form.* Covers everything included in the basic form, plus breakage of glass, falling objects, weight of snow or ice, and water damage.
3. *Special form.* Constructed differently than the other two to cover a wider range of risks. Instead of listing what is covered, as the basic and broad forms do, the special form simply states that the business property is insured against all risks of physical loss unless specifically excluded in the policy. While this form is slightly more expensive, it's often a wise investment because it offers broader coverage (more peace of mind).

Some types of coverage are excluded from various insurance policies—even special forms. For example, earthquakes are not commonly covered. This doesn't present a problem if you live in South Dakota, but it does if you live in California. To add a specific kind of coverage to your policy, a "floater" policy can be bought for an additional fee. Here are some examples of policies you may want to consider in addition to your basic property coverage:

- *Vandalism insurance.* Protection against any criminal incidents against your property resulting in damage.
- *Water sprinkler insurance.* Covers water damage from a faulty sprinkler system.
- *Crime insurance.* Protects against theft, robbery, and forgery.
- *Fidelity bonds insurance.* Protects you against financial loss due to employee theft.
- *Boiler and machinery insurance.* Protects your business against loss due to the explosion of boilers, furnaces, engines, and similar equipment.
- *Business interruption insurance.* Protects against lost profits due to your business being interrupted by a disaster.
- *Surety bond.* Protects a business against the failure of another business to fulfill a contractual obligation.

## THE INSURANCE CONTRACT

The insurance contract, like any other legal contract, is subject to certain requirements to make it binding. Chapter 7 will cover the general requirements of drawing up and observing a legal contract.

The main legal requirement specific to an insurance policy contract is that the person obtaining the insurance (the insured) must have a legal, "insurable interest," in the subject matter of the policy, such that the insured has an economic interest in the preservation or destruction of that interest.

In other words, you can insure your house, your car, your factory, because you would be economically affected by their loss and have an interest in their preservation or replacement. But, you can't take out a policy on the Sears Tower because you heard it's going to be a particularly windy Chicago winter and you're hoping to collect if the structure blows over. You must own—"have a vested interest in"—whatever you are insuring.

In the case of life insurance, the insurable interest may be your own life, the life of a close relative, or that of a key employee whose death would affect your business. An insurance policy should "work" (pay out), if you obey the following three rules: (1) Act in good faith, (2) pay the premium, and (3) follow the terms of the policy.

On the other hand, the insurance policy contract can be deemed null and void for the following six reasons:

1. *The insurer (the company) does not act in "good faith" by honoring all valid claims and terms of the contract.* You can, as the insured, sue the insurer for the terms of your policy if the company refuses a legitimate claim, but you can also sue for the added damages caused by delay in payment. You can well imagine this is an expensive and painful process.

What's your protection? Do your homework up front. Don't buy the first product you hear about. Research the market. Ask your business colleagues what insurance company and agent they are using and whether or not they have been satisfied with the timeliness of payments, cost of insurance, and availability of service. Develop a good business relationship with an insurance agent who will be the intermediary between you and the insurance company. This costs no more dollars and can be most helpful for a time-stressed executive (one less thing for you to do).

Also, we recommend having one person in your office responsible for all the insurance reporting and follow-up. Set up a system and stay on top of the claims. If you are not satisfied, call or fax the insurance company immediately and stay on the case.

2. *Either party gives written notice of cancellation.* Usually, notice must be given a month in advance.
3. *The insured fails to pay premiums.* Most policies contain a stated grace period by which the premium must be paid or coverage is forfeited.
4. *Important contractual agreements are not abided by.* Your contract will give guidelines that you have to follow for your claim to be considered, such as immediately reporting a claim and presenting physical evidence of damage.
5. *The policy was secured under false pretenses by the insurer or the insured, such as there is no insurable interest.* The insurance company discovers that you do not, in fact, own the Sears Tower Building, for which you have purchased property insurance and filed a claim for wind damages.
6. *Certain acts are found to be illegal or otherwise violative of public policy on local and state levels.*

## KNOW YOUR KEY TERMS

- *Insurance.* Legal protection against economic ruin in case certain natural or human-made disasters occur in or to your business.
- *Insurance policy.* A legal contract between the insurance company, the insurer, and the person obtaining the insurance, the insured, that transfers and allocates certain defined economic risks if certain defined events happen.
- *Premium.* The rate that you agree to pay the insurance company for coverage, usually on a monthly or quarterly basis.
- *Deductible.* The amount that you agree to cover or pay out yourself first before your insurance policy kicks into gear and starts paying on your behalf.
- *Liability or professional malpractice insurance.* Protection for your business against lawsuits filed by any third party—customers, employees, or suppliers—claiming negligence due to faulty products or business and professional practices; will not cover purposeful misconduct or intentional wrongdoing (torts). The higher your deductible, the lower will be your premium.
- *Workers' compensation insurance.* Liability insurance mandated by the state, paid for by the employer, and paid out by the state to compensate employees who have suffered job-related physical or mental injuries.
- *Property insurance.* Covers natural and human-made disasters including fire, burglary, and shoplifting.

## BASIC LEGAL RESEARCH

- *State statutes on workers' compensation.* Found in your local law library.
- *Insurance Law in a Nutshell,* by John F. Dobbyn (West Publishing). Along with the rest of the Nutshell series, this book can be found in most law libraries and many public libraries.
- *Best's Insurance Reports, Moody's Bank and Financial Manual, and Standard & Poor's.* These three reference guides, available in your local library, rate insurance companies for financial solvency—which is important if you are expecting the company to actually pay any claims that you file.

## KEY RESOURCES

- *An insurance agent who specializes in the insurance needs of your particular business.* You may be able to purchase an insurance package that specifically addresses the needs of your business.
- *Your state insurance commissioner.* If you have any questions about your state insurance statutes, contact the Insurance Commissioner's office, which is usually listed in the blue pages under State Government Offices. If not listed, call your secretary of state office and ask for the insurance department.
- *Your professional business organizations.* Generally listed in the business section of your phone book's white pages, your professional business organization can let you know what kinds of insurance you are legally required to invest in.
- *Your state will probably have a Worker's Compensation Commission and a toll-free number to supply you with answers to all kinds of questions.*
- *Local chambers of commerce.* Listed in the City Government section of your phone book's blue pages, the chamber of commerce can give you some leads on organizations that offer discounted group rates for health, life, and other insurance.

## COURT COACH® SUGGESTS

1. *Always insure property for replacement cost, as opposed to current value.* Replacement value refers to the amount of money you would need to buy the same item in today's marketplace, while current value refers to what the item you lost is actually worth. Replacement value insurance costs a little more, but it's worth it. The actual value of most items—whether you're talking about a car, a computer, or an office building—isn't nearly what you would pay to replace them.

2. *Set insurance priorities.* Start with what you are legally required to buy: workers' compensation, motor vehicle insurance, building insurance, malpractice, for example. Next, assess what kinds of events and situations could seriously imperil your business and personal assets. Make a "wish list" of insurance and in your business plan target specific insurance options you will add, depending on your profitability.

3. *Disability insurance is a necessity, not a luxury.* What happens if you have an accident, either in or out of the workplace, and you are unable to run your business for a period of weeks, months, or even years? The results could be disastrous, as most small business owners are indispensable cogs in the mechanism that keeps their companies running smoothly—especially sole proprietors who have nobody to hand over the helm to in an emergency. In fact, if you are a sole proprietor, disability insurance may be even more important to purchase than life insurance.

4. *If you need to scrimp, increase the amount of your deductibles.* You can save a significant amount on your monthly premiums if you boost your deductibles, the expenses out-of-pocket you agree to pay out before the insurance company starts paying. Check out the math and decide for yourself on a case-by-case basis.

5. *Implement safety and security measures to make your business a better insurance risk and lower your premiums.* Simple things like installing smoke alarms, improving stairwell lighting, and adding exhaust fans can and do whittle down your insurance rates. Not to mention decreasing the chances that an employee or customer will incur an injury resulting in a lawsuit.

6. *Seek out group plans through professional associations or your town or local commercial organization.* Sometimes you can get a break on a package deal of insurance coverage—or you can, as a solo, purchase group insurance as part of an organization.

7. *Combine property and liability insurance in one policy to save money.* Many times you can buy an insurance policy that combines property and liability coverage, and costs slightly less than buying the two policies separately.

8. *Self-insure?* Consider carefully. What if you just take the money that you would have spent on insurance and stick it in a savings account? That's a great idea if you never have to file a claim with yourself. But if a disaster, even a minor one, does happen, chances are that your insurance reserve won't be large enough to cover your losses. Plus, unlike insurance premiums paid to a legitimate insurer, your self-insurance account isn't tax deductible.

However, you may want to self-insure in certain areas, like health insurance to cut costs.

# 7

# HOW TO READ AND NEGOTIATE LEASES AND CONTRACTS

## CONTRACT LAW 101: WHAT CONSTITUTES A LEGAL CONTRACT?

As a small business owner, you're likely to run across contracts often—setting up the terms of a lease, sometimes hiring a new employee, and always when supplying or receiving goods and/or services. In the good old days, as my father was fond of saying, "My word is my bond." Nowadays, your word and their word and a handshake may leave you in a sorry state.

The goal of this chapter is to acquaint you with the different types of contracts that you will encounter in starting up a small business. We will describe the essentials for setting up and negotiating these agreements to your benefit and give you tips on reading contracts like a lawyer to avoid unwanted liability.

The most basic thing you need to know is what constitutes a legal contract, or agreement that is enforceable in a court of law, as opposed to an informal agreement sealed with a handshake and a promise. A contract is legally enforceable and valid if the following elements exist:

- *Free will and adequate mental capacity of each party.* A court will deem a contract valid if the parties are found to have entered into it without duress, misrepresentation, undue influence, or inadequate mental capacity.
- *Mutual agreement on the contract terms.* Whether a contract is written or oral, the terms must be definite, as opposed to illusory, and there must be a "meeting of the minds," which means each person has thought over the terms and one person has accepted the other person's offer.
- *Consideration.* Each party gives up something of value, such as money, labor, a product, or legal rights (a tricky legal concept).
- *A specific offer with definite terms.* The offeror must submit a proposal with definite terms to be accepted or rejected by the offeree. If those terms are accepted, a contract exists. If it is signed by the offeree and delivered to the offeror, it is an express written unilateral contract; if signed by both, a bilateral express written contract. A most interesting note: If there is a counteroffer, the process begins all over. The first offer ceases to exist, and the original offeror can either accept or reject the counteroffer. And so on, and so on, and so on, until one person makes an offer the other person cannot turn down—and accepts. A done deal!

## THE FIRST STEP OF FORMING A CONTRACT: THE NEGOTIATION DANCE

As most thriving small business owners and Donald Trump will tell you, mastering the fine art of negotiation, the art of the deal, is a survival skill. The word "negotiation" is derived from the Latin word for "business," or "the absence of leisure." All business transactions—with suppliers, customers, creditors, employees and contractors—are based on this communication process used to determine mutual needs and come to an agreement for how to satisfy these needs. If an agreement that is amenable to both parties is reached, then a contract is formed and if either party withdraws without the consent of the other, that party is "in breach of the contract."

The "give and take" of negotiation requires tact, subtlety, and finesse. As stated previously, the trick is to acquire as much information as you can while imparting the least information. Therefore, it is important to be clear in your own mind about (1) what you want to gain from an agreement and (2) what you are willing to give up in exchange. Always couch your offers and acceptance as drafts or as offered "without prejudice" (meaning you can change your mind).

Contracts are usually revised a number of times before a contract with semantics and terms acceptable to both parties evolves. If hand-written changes are made to the final contract document, both parties should initial every change. In the case of extensive revisions, an addendum to the main contract should be drafted and signed and dated by both parties (see Figures 7–1 and 7–2).

Sort our your needs into three categories: (1) what you *must* have, (2) what is negotiable, and (3) what you want but could live without.

This third category is just as important to put on the table as the other two, since without some "giveaways," you put yourself in the position of dictating the terms and put the other person in the position of signing on to your script without any "give" on your part. And sometimes, with luck, the very things you are perfectly willing to give away are the very things the other party needs.

The whole point in negotiating is for both parties to feel they've won. Whenever people feel "had" or like they have been taken to the cleaners, the negotiation over the long term will probably not work smoothly, because the disgruntled party may not fulfill that part of the agreement and the other party consequently will not reap the "benefit of the bargain."

**Figure 7–1**   Sample Addendum to a Contract

This document serves as an Addendum to the contract between _____(name of first party)_____ (hereby referred to as the first party) and ____(name of second party)____ (hereby referred to as the second party) on ____(date)____.

The first and second party agree to the following changes:

In all other respects, the terms of the original contract are still valid.

The undersigned agree to the terms of this addendum,

_____        _____
(signature of first party)                        (Name of first party, typed)


_____        _____
(signature of second party)                      (Name of second party, typed)

**Figure 7–2**    Sample Contract for Services

This contract confirms that _____(name of service provider)_____ will render the following services to _____(name of client)_____ under the following circumstances:

1. We will provide the following services: (describe)
2. We will charge for the services as follows:
3. Our invoices will be mailed on the last day of each month that services are provided.
4. Invoices are payable upon receipt and bear interest on the unpaid amount at the rate of _____% per annum compounded daily.
5. If the client is, or becomes, incorporated, the individual accepting the terms of our engagement on behalf of the client also personally guarantees payment for our services.
6. This contract is valid for services rendered during the following time period:



The undersigned agree to the terms of this contract,

(signature of service provider)

(Name of service provider, typed)

(signature of client)

(Name of client, typed)

This brings us to the "Statute of Frauds." Sounds interesting, but what is it? The celebrated English Statute of Frauds, passed in 1677, has been modified and adopted in nearly all states. Its distinguishing characteristic is the provision that certain classes of contracts must be in writing and signed if a suit or action is to be maintained.

Simply stated, for many contracts, if you don't have it in writing, you can't go to court and sue on the contract. Under the Uniform Commercial Code (UCC § 2-201), a contract for the sale of goods for $500 or more must be in writing and signed by the party to be charged if it is to be enforceable by an action or defense. It is most intriguing that what began way back in the 17th century continues in our modern society as we are still concerned about closing the door on any fraud or perjury.

This is not to say that an oral contract isn't binding—in theory, that is. While an oral contract can be binding, the problem is that in a dispute the situation of "he said, she said" makes proof of the terms difficult, if not nearly impossible. Hence, it is always advisable to put it in writing. A written document not only serves as a reminder of promises made but makes responsibility for a breach of contract much easier to determine.

## CLAUSES AND ATTACHMENTS: YOUR CONTRACT'S BODY PARTS

A written document needn't be lengthy to be legal, as long as the basic services to be provided and promises made are spelled out. It's optimal to have it signed by all parties (see Figure 7–2 for a basic service contract). Two caveats: First, the more details you include in the contract, the less chance there will be for broad interpretation of the terms, which can lead in turn to misunderstandings and breach. Second, a contract will be construed in a court of law against the maker. Therefore, if you have prepared the contract and the other party interprets it differently than you do, the court can view your interpretation as less credible because the terms may be self-serving.

During negotiations, never say, "This clause is a deal breaker." Whenever pushed up against a wall and given an ultimatum, most people's reaction is to think or say, "I don't think so." This is a power tactic that can boomerang and torpedo a good deal. All the time, effort, and expenses expended on this point can be wasted when egos and knee-jerk reactions are engaged.

What if there's a clause that you and the other party are both reluctant to budge on? Is it a deal breaker? Maybe yes, maybe no. In deciding what to do, take the perspective of a good accountant and consider that whatever has been invested is "sunk money"—it's been spent, so to speak. What you need to do is focus on where you are going from here; how much it will cost in financial and human terms; how important it is to your priorities; and whether you are willing to compromise.

Deal breakers require the most creative problem solving, not black and white thinking. Offer resolutions and compromises. If you cannot reach a compromise, agree on all the other points, and seek a neutral third party—a judge, or arbitrator, or an objective independent person—to come up with a solution.

## CONTRACTS THAT THE SMALL BUSINESS OWNER MAY ENCOUNTER

As a small business owner, you will likely encounter a wide range of contracts that fall into three categories: business-to-business, leases, and employment contracts. While the fundamental elements of contracts within these groups are similar, each contract has its own intricacies. This is said by way of warning you *not* to use form contracts—the ones provided in this or any other book—*without* tailoring them to meet the needs of your specific situation.

## Business-to-Business: Defining the Terms of Your Relationship

Whenever you enter a relationship with another businessperson, whether it's an individual freelancer who occasionally writes advertising copy for you or the multimillion-dollar manufacturer who distributes your product worldwide, both parties need to be clear on the terms of the relationship.

Clauses commonly found in business-to-business contracts include:

- The names, business titles, and addresses of the offeror and offeree.
- The date that the contract is signed and the length of term.
- A listing of the considerations, or things of value, being exchanged. This would include the work specifications and the amount of money to be paid.
- The time lines for rendering of services, completion of work, and payment of money, including payment schedule.
- Specific guarantees of quality of labor and materials, and remedies if services or products are defective.
- Conditions allowing either party to terminate the agreement.
- Consequences, remedies, and relief for breaches of the contract.
- A statement as to which state's laws apply to the interpretation of the contract.

## The Lease: The Landlord/Tenant Contract

When setting up your business, one of the first contracts you will likely encounter is a lease. Commercial leases are usually long and complicated, with much boilerplate language (definition: the small print repeated in every similar contract, often in small print), and as written, usually protect the interests of the landlord more than the tenant. (Here's a perfect example of how in a dispute, your interpretation and understanding can be given more weight since the contract will be construed against the maker.)

Read and understand every paragraph before signing. Since a lease is enforceable and operative from the moment of execution and obligates you to pay for the entire time stated in the contract, regardless of whether or not your business has staying power, you need a solid business plan in place *before* you legally obligate yourself to this major expense.

Leases are theoretically negotiable, just as all contracts are. But the willingness of your potential landlord to take part in the negotiations dance depends on (1) the desirability of the property (remember the three most important elements of a successful business are *location, location, location;* (2) the personality of the landlord; and (3) market conditions. Assess all three by research and information gathering. You might learn that the landlord has had this space on the market for a long time, or the former tenant packed up in the middle of the night and left the landlord stranded. Information is power.

On the other hand, you may very well be able to decrease the monthly payments up front for increased payment at the back end as most landlords view the lease on a total dollar return over the full term. Hence, if the landlord expects to earn $24,000 on this space over two years, you may pay less than $1,000 for the first six months or first year for an increased payment in the second year. This graduated rental increase over the term eases your cash flow initially, and the landlord receives the total rent over a term of years.

Above all else, focus on your needs. If possible, compare the dollar per square foot being requested of you with the dollar per square foot being requested of other tenants in the building. If you find a landlord willing to do some give and take, here are some of the basic lease elements to consider:

- *Rent charges.* Commercial rent is charged on a cost per square foot basis; this base charge is the guaranteed amount to be paid to the landlord monthly. There may also be additional charges for maintenance, tenants' association fees, real estate tax, and heating and air-conditioning charges on top of that, but most commercial leases are net, net, net.

- *Duration.* Leases can be written to cover any period of time. Generally, the longer you are willing to lease, the lower the rent should be. A short-term lease is very desirable, though, until your business has its sea legs. Either way, you should request a clause giving you a first option to renew the lease at a stated rent fee to protect against (1) unseemly rent hikes at the discretion of the landlord, or (2) having your space rented out from under you at the end of your term.

- *Option to sublease.* Just in case your business experiences initial cash-flow shortage or folds due to a downturn in the market, you want to include a clause that allows you to find another suitable tenant to share or rent. If you are successful and up and running, you will probably want to stay in your location.

- *Insurance.* The lease outlines what insurance the landlord has, as well as what insurance the tenant is required to carry. Ask for a copy of your landlord's insurance policy to review with your agent to make sure there aren't any duplications such as covering the landlord's liability for personal injuries and damages to the building as well as your own liability.

- *Maintenance responsibilities.* Make sure that the landlord's responsibilities are spelled out as clearly as those of the tenants. If there are improvements to be made, now's the time to clarify who will do them and when and who will pay and how they are to be paid for.

- *The right to expand.* If expansion is likely to be in your future, it wouldn't hurt to include a clause guaranteeing you the right to be notified about adjacent space or larger quarters opening up in the building before the landlord makes these spaces known to the general public. If you are a good tenant, this is a plus for both landlord and tenant.

- *Security deposit.* Tenants typically plunk down two months' additional rent as a security deposit, to be returned upon amiable termination of the lease. You should ask the landlord to hold the deposit in an interest-bearing bank account for your benefit, meaning you receive it back, plus the statutory interest, or to place it in escrow with a third party if you're unsure about the landlord's solvency.

- *Term lease/percentage lease clause.* A term lease is the standard and states that a given amount of rent is paid for a specific amount of time. Another option is a percentage lease, in which the landlord is entitled to a percentage of the renter's income instead of a fixed amount of rent.

## Employment Contracts

As your business grows and you find yourself in a position to hire employees—either on a contract, full-time, or part-time basis, you may want to use some form of employment agreement. This can be quite short and simple (see Figure 7–3 for sample employment contract).

**Figure 7–3**    Sample Employment Contract

---

This employment agreement is made between _____(name of employer)_____
(the "Employer") and _____(name of employee)_____ (the "Employee") on
__(date)__.

The terms of employment are as follows:

1. The Employer agrees to employ the Employee and the Employee agrees
   to work for the Employer in the position of _____
   _____.

2. Employment commences on _(date)_ and terminates only upon written
   notification of two weeks' time by the Employer or Employee.

3. The Employee shall perform the following duties and have the following
   responsibilities, although it is understood that this is not an exhaustive
   list and may be changed as the Employer sees fit:

4. The following statutory holidays are paid vacation days for the Employee:

5. In addition to statutory holidays, the Employee is entitled to _____ additional days of paid vacation in the first year of employment, subject to
   change thereafter.

6. The Employee is entitled to _____ days of paid sick leave in the first year
   of employment, subject to change thereafter.

7. The Employee may not take any paid days off during the first
   _____ months of employment.

8. Subject to statutory deductions, The Employer shall pay the Employee a
   gross cash salary, inclusive of any statutory vacation pay, and other pay
   outlined in this contract, equivalent to _____ dollars ($_____) per
   annum in biweekly installments not in advance.

9. The Employer shall make the following fringe benefits available to the
   Employee:

10. The Employer may terminate the employment of the Employee without
    cause on _____ weeks' notice to the Employee. However, the Employer
    reserves the right to terminate the Employee's employment without no-
    tice for cause, including but not limited to death, incapacitating illness,
    incompetence, or failure to follow reasonable employment requests, at
    any time.

*(Continued)*

**Figure 7–3**    *(Continued)*

11. The Employee promises to keep the Employer's business secrets confidential during and after the term of employment and the Employee also promises that, on the termination of the employment with the Employer for any reason, the Employee will not operate a similar business or in any way aid and assist any other person to operate such a business in the state of _____ for a period of _____.

12. If any provision or part of any provision in this agreement is void for any reason, it shall be severed without affecting the validity of the balance of the agreement.

13. The terms of this agreement remain in effect until amended in writing by both parties.

14. The Employer will review the salary and benefits outlined in this contract on a yearly basis, as well as give the Employee a written and verbal performance review.

15. There are no representations, warranties, conditions, terms, or collateral contracts affecting the employment contemplated in this agreement except as set out in this agreement.

16. The Employee acknowledges ample opportunity and advice to take independent legal advice in connection with the execution of this employment agreement.

17. This agreement is governed by the laws of the State of _____.

The undersigned agree to the terms of this contract on <u>(date)</u>,

(signature of Employer)
(name of Employer, typed)

(signature of Employee)
(name of Employee, typed)

There are a few basics that you should consider when designing an employment contract, including:

- Service to be performed.
- Time constraints, if any.
- Compensation.
- Where the work is to be performed.
- Term of employment, if the position is only valid for a given period of time.
- Actions that will result in termination of the contract.

For more information about hiring and firing employees, see Chapter 11. If you chose this option, please consult an attorney.

## KNOW YOUR KEY TERMS

- *Contract.* An agreement between two or more parties in which there is an offer and acceptance and in which the rights and obligations of each party are spelled out.
- *Express contract.* A written or oral agreement in which the terms are explicitly spelled out and each party agrees to abide by the terms.
- *Implied contract.* An agreement in which no discussion of terms takes place, but the actions of each party make it clear that an agreement has been made.
- *Bilateral and unilateral contracts.* Two basic types of agreement. A bilateral contract implies an exchange of promises, like the marriage vows, while a unilateral contract implies a promise by one party in exchange for an act by the other.
- *Lease.* The legal agreement between the renter and owner of property allowing use for a period of time.
- *Sublease.* An interest in leased premises granted to someone by the tenant.
- *Sublet.* A lease by lessee of premises during unexpired balance of the term.

## BASIC LEGAL RESEARCH

- *The Uniform Commercial Code Rules.* Can be found at any law library and many public libraries in the same section of references as your state statutes. Commercial law can be a sticky wicket, but the Uniform Commercial Code (UCC) rules help uncomplicate the process of contracting for the sale of goods. These rules, which were enacted in 1940, cover all the branches of commercial law and have been adopted in all states except Louisiana (which has adopted key portions of it). The UCC covers sales, warranties, commercial papers, bank deposits and collections, letters of credit, bulk transfers, warehouse receipts, bills of lading and other documents of title, investment securities, and secured transactions.

- *Contracts in a Nutshell,* by Gordon D. Schaber and Claude D. Rohwer (West Publishing). An overview of contract law.
- *The Complete Legal Guide for Your Small Business,* by Paul Adams (John Wiley & Sons). A good reference book written for laypersons.
- *Business Contract Forms,* by Robert J. English (John Wiley & Sons). Ideas for creating your own standard contracts for vendors, clients, and so on.
- *Getting to Yes,* by Roger Fisher (Penguin); *Swim with the Sharks,* by Harvey Mackay (Ballantine); *Power Plays: How to Negotiate, Persuade, and Finesse Your Way to Success in Any Situation,* by Robert Mayer (Random House). Books with some great tips about the fine art of negotiating.

## KEY RESOURCES

- *An insurance agent.* It wouldn't hurt to get some advice about the division of insurance between you and your landlord.
- *A real estate broker.* Have your broker explain the terms of your lease. Remember: There are no dumb questions.
- *A banker.* The loan officers at your local bank can be very helpful in advising you about small business loans to meet your lease obligations.

## COURT COACH® SUGGESTS

1. *If your company has corporation status, always sign contracts as a corporate officer to avoid personal liability for meeting contractual obligations.* Sometimes, as with a small commercial bank loan, you may be required to sign with a personal guarantee as well. And, you always have the choice to leave the money behind if you don't want to provide an additional personal guarantee.
2. *Make sure the other party is authorized to sign the contract.* If the other party is a corporation and is not being represented by the CEO or president, you may want to request seeing a board of directors' resolution or corporate bylaws authorizing the party to sign contracts on behalf of the corporation.
3. *If you have any doubts as to the ability of the corporation you are contracting to fulfill a contract, request a personal guarantee clause.* This commonly used clause acts as a personal guarantee that

the individual signing the contract will undertake all contractual obligations if the corporation is unable to do so. In other words, you are assigning personal liability to the person signing the contract that is not normally applicable when dealing with a corporate entity.

4. *When doing the negotiation dance, let the other person lead sometimes—but make sure the negotiator doesn't step on your toes.* Compromise is the key to success, which can mean a delicate balance between getting your own needs met and being sensitive to the other party's similar desire. Remember to keep in mind what it is you want to gain from an agreement, and what you are willing to give up.

5. *Separate your own demands into requirements, and prioritize them.* Remember, there are three categories of demands: (1) can't live without, (2) negotiable, and (3) giveaways (the fudge factor).

6. *If a contract has gone through a number of revisions, both parties should initial and date each page so that everyone has a valid copy of the final draft.* When a contract travels back and forth between parties a number of times, it's easy to forget who agreed to what when. Having both parties initial each page, or even each specific revision, is a good safeguard against memory loss in the final analysis of a contract.

7. *Don't rely on form contracts for major transactions.* Any business transaction you are undertaking—from buying large quantities of production materials, to renovating your work space, to hiring employees—probably has some unique aspect that reflects your company's specific needs. While form contracts are a good starting point for devising business agreements, never use them verbatim.

8. *Have an attorney review any contract you devise before you implement it in your business practices.* When it comes to signing legally binding contracts, better safe than sorry.

9. *Even though oral contracts are legally binding, they are difficult to prove in a court of law.* The days of basing business deals on a person's word and a handshake are long gone (if they ever did, in fact, exist). Even if you are doing business with a friend whom you trust implicitly, there's always the chance of misinterpreting the spoken word. The moral of this story: Always put it in writing!

10. *As Harvey Mackay advises in his book,* Swim with the Sharks, *"Say no 'til your tongue bleeds."* When you finally start hearing something from the other side that sounds like an offer to which you could say "yes," start giving it serious consideration and say so.

# 8

# FRANCHISES, LICENSES, AND PERMITS

## FRANCHISING: LICENSING AN ALREADY ESTABLISHED BUSINESS

The concept behind franchising, which really took off in the 1950s, is that you hitch your wagon to an already proven shining star, reduce your risks, and profit from someone else's name recognition, as well as that company's trial-and-error mistakes and experience. Of the estimated half-million franchised businesses in the United States, 9 out of 10 are retail enterprises.

One of the attractive advantages of a franchise is that for an initial investment ranging from several thousand to several hundred thousand dollars you can have a business. If you have always yearned to be an entrepreneur in a certain field but lack an original moneymaking idea or capital to finance a business, this may be the avenue to pursue. But, and this is a gigantic BUT, if your franchise is to succeed, you must *research the company.*

### The Franchise Contract

The franchise contract is an agreement between you (the franchisee) and the franchising company (the franchisor). The basic terms of this contract set forth the following common terms for the franchisee:

The franchisee:

- Has permission to operate under the parent corporation's trade name (usually well-known).
- Is bound to operate the business in accordance with the parent company's policies and marketing procedures.
- Must pay a franchise fee and other start-up fees.
- Has access to professional assistance from the parent company in many phases of setting up and running the business, such as site selection, construction of the facility, equipment to use, inventory control and bookkeeping methods, advertising and promotional strategies, employee training.
- Does not have the option to close shop without the permission of the franchisor within the contractual period of time (usually one year).
- Must pay a fee to the franchisor for the first six months of operations.
- May be required to purchase equipment, goods, and supplies from the franchisor, often at a marked-up price.

As to the franchisor, he or she:

- May elect not to renew the contract if sales don't meet the expectations spelled out in the agreement.
- May include a "buy-back" clause, which allows the franchisor to repurchase the franchise at will. (This is obviously not an attractive option for the franchisee who intends to financially excel.)
- Receives a percentage of the income that the franchise earns.
- May charge the franchisee employee training fees.

## The Offering Circular

As a start, you should review the mother company's "offering circular," a document required by the Federal Trade Commission, which regulates franchises nationwide. The offering circular provides prospective franchisees with details about the franchise's financial, legal, and operational policies. Most franchises use a "Uniform Franchise Offering Circular," tailored to their particular franchise. This document may include:

- A description of the franchisor's business and the franchises being offered.
- Identity and business experience of persons affiliated with the franchisor.
- The litigation history of the franchisor and of the people connected with it.
- Bankruptcy history, if any, of the franchisor.
- Initial fees required from the franchisee to the franchisor.
- Any other fees to be paid to the franchisor and the conditions for refunds.
- An estimate of the franchisee's initial investment, including expenses for real estate, equipment rental, construction and remodeling, inventory, and any other payments necessary to start operations.
- Obligations of franchisee to purchase or lease from designated sources.
- Obligations of franchisee to purchase or lease goods, services, and equipment from specific suppliers.
- Financing arrangements.
- Obligations of the franchisor to support the franchise.
- Exclusive area or territory to minimize competition.
- Trademarks, service marks, trade names, logotypes, and commercial symbols.
- Patents and copyrights.
- Obligation of the franchisee to participate personally in the actual operation of the franchise business.
- Restrictions on goods and services offered by the franchisee.
- Renewal, termination, repurchase, modification, and assignment of the franchise agreement and related information.
- Arrangements with public figures to promote franchise operations.
- Representations regarding earnings capability.
- Information regarding existing franchisees.
- Financial statements.
- Contracts the franchisee will sign upon purchase of the franchise.
- Acknowledgment of receipt by prospective franchisee.
- A copy of the franchise agreement.

## Check It Out, Two, Three, and Four Times Over

Before signing a franchising agreement, do all your homework. Perform a background check on the company with the related trade organizations, the local chamber of commerce, the Better Business Bureau, or Dun & Bradstreet. Check with other managers of local outlets to see what they have to say about the parent company. Do this at a scheduled business appointment, off-site, and not on the fly in a casual manner. You want the real scoop and need to develop some kind of trust with the other franchisees if you expect to hear the true financial story.

You should also have your attorney, accountant, and banker review the agreement and circular. They can pinpoint potential pitfalls and coach you to negotiate the most favorable terms.

You should include in your discussions all those who will be working with you in the business and all adult family members who will be financially affected by this decision. You want their input, positive and negative, up front because their support is crucial to your success. If they have concerns, listen to them carefully; they may be throwing a more objective eye on the picture than you are, particularly if you are gung-ho to get started.

It's important to remember that not all franchisors are created equal. This potentially lucrative business attracts fly-by-night companies out to make a quick buck at your expense, as well as honest profitable smaller franchises and highly reputable and established chains that offer an opportunity to get on-the-job management training as well.

Simply put, the primary reason franchisees fail is that they have not done enough in-depth research. Besides having professionals review the franchisor's proposal and speaking with other franchisees about the pros and cons of their experience, it is essential that you:

- Visit other local franchises as a customer.
- Read in-depth about the industry and trends in general.
- Check with business organizations to get a read on your local economy and market.
- Confer with a financial advisor about your financial health and cash-flow prospects, and get a realistic picture of the financial struggle, if any, up front.

Then, and only then, are you ready to even entertain the idea of plunking your money down.

## LICENSES AND PERMITS

We've already touched on the licenses and permits you'll need to operate as a sole proprietor, partnership, or corporation (see Chapters 3 and 4). You also need to consider government licensing regulations you must comply with as a member of your chosen profession, a member of the local business community, an employer, and a manufacturer of products.

The federal government generally is not involved with regulating small businesses; the handful of exceptions include businesses involved in drug production, firearms, tobacco or alcohol products, preparation of meat products, and investment advisory services. But each state and each local government has its own licensing and permit requirements.

Don't worry. This is not as complicated a process as it sounds because most states have a department of economic development, or department of commerce, equipped to act as a one-stop shopping center for licenses and permits. Many states even offer a handbook to guide you through the maze of licenses and permits applicable to small business owners and/or your specific profession. Likewise, your local chamber of commerce or a local attorney specializing in commercial matters can supply you with a list, or outline, and other information about local legal requirements for your business.

Understanding all the licenses and permits your business will need before hanging out your shingle will enable you to factor into your budget any filing fees, as well as any remodeling or equipment purchases that may be legally required.

To give you some idea what might be required in your state, the following regulations are often applicable to small business start-ups:

- *Tax registration.* The federal government requires every new business to apply for an employer identification number (see Chapter 3), and S corporations need to file an additional form (see Chapter 4). Call the local IRS office to receive this application form. Your state department of revenue, or treasury department, can also tell you what local tax laws apply to your business (see Chapter 10).

- *Professional licensing.* Even if you're not a doctor, lawyer, accountant, or other professional traditionally required to have a license, your state may require a license or proof of adequate training in your occupation of choice. Acquiring your professional license may be as simple as supplying your certificate of training, or it may entail passing a written exam and/or undergoing a background check.

- *Labor Department registration.* Any business employing workers must obtain a state unemployment tax number, and register with the state office administering the laws on unemployment compensation and workers' compensation. Your business may also need to meet certain state safety codes to protect your employees on the job. Check with your state Department of Labor.

- *Licenses for products manufactured or sold.* Check with your state Department of Economics or local Chamber of Commerce to see if the products you are planning on manufacturing and selling require a license (for example: food, liquor, firearms).

- *Environmental regulations.* As a small business owner, you probably won't have to deal with any environmental agencies at the federal level, but you will at the state, regional, and local levels. Of particular concern is the disposal of waste, hazardous and nonhazardous, and recycling of paper, bottles, and cans. Check with your town government about recycling plans and pickup.

- *Local health department regulations.* You may have to pass a periodic inspection by the local health department if your company's sanitary conditions are an issue as, for example, in food preparation. The health department is also sometimes involved with environmental concerns such as radon testing and asbestos removal.

- *Building codes and permits.* Your local building inspector will probably need to make sure your place of business passes muster and meets your city's safety regulations. If you do need to make renovations—either by choice or the inspector's request—you'll need to get a permit from the local building and safety department.

## KNOW YOUR KEY TERMS

- *License or permit.* Authorization by the federal, state, regional, or city government for a person to undertake a certain activity or provide a certain service that would be illegal without such authorization (e.g., the work-related activities of an electrician or operator of a restaurant).

- *Franchise.* Authorization by a company (e.g., Baskin-Robbins, McDonald's) to use its name and/or sell its product, under the stipulations laid out in a franchise agreement.

- *Uniform franchise offering circular.* A document, prepared by a company offering a franchise, that explains the company's financial, legal, and operational details.
- *Licensing agreement.* The contract evidencing the sale of a license permitting the use of patents, trademarks, or other technology to another firm.
- *Letter of intent.* Customarily, a letter that reduces to writing a preliminary understanding of the parties entering into a contract.
- *Nondisclosure agreement.* A written document you prepare for the signature of the person to whom you plan to reveal confidential commercial information.
- *Creative license.* Authorization to use a trademark or to reproduce a good, or permission to provide a service under a licensing agreement or in the broadest sense, permission by a competent authority to perform.

## BASIC LEGAL RESEARCH

- *Franchising,* by William L. Siegel (John Wiley & Sons).
- *Uniform Building Code.* Most cities base their legal requirements for commercial spaces on these guidelines for building or remodeling. You can find this document at a law library, or possibly your city government offices or the local safety department.
- *Directory of Franchising Organization,* by Small, Samuel, and Pilot Books Staff (Pilot Books).
- *Evaluating Franchise Opportunities* (Small Business Administration).

## KEY RESOURCES

- *The U.S. Department of Commerce.* This federal office can provide you with information about franchising opportunities, including the *Franchise Opportunities Handbook.*
- *The Federal Trade Commission (FTC).* This organization regulates franchises nationwide. If you suspect fraud, this is the place to contact.

- *The International Franchise Association (IFA).* You can get valuable information on IFA members by purchasing their membership directory (1350 New York Avenue, NW, Suite 900, Washington, DC 20005).
- *Your local Small Business Association, chamber of commerce, and state department of economic development.* All these offices can help you decipher what licenses and permits your business is required to obtain.
- *Your local library reference section.* Here's where you'll find loads of information about your industry of choice in general, as well as how different industries are faring in your neck of the woods.
- *Trade publications.* Subscribe to magazines in your field at least one year prior to making any final decisions about investing in a franchise.
- *Business magazines.* Keep up to date on trends in and out of your field.
- *Newspapers.* The *Wall Street Journal* is de rigueur for many businesspeople. *Barron's* and the *Financial Times* also are widely read. Our personal favorite is the *New York Times* (Saturday edition Money Page).

## COURT COACH® SUGGESTS

1. *Make a checklist of licenses and permits you need to acquire, and regulations you need to comply with, before signing a lease for office space.* This will help you determine if the space meets the government's needs as well as yours, and will help you create a realistic start-up budget.

2. *When considering a franchise, accept the rosy picture the sales representative paints for you at face value.* This person works on commission, and your signature on the dotted line means money in his or her pocket.

3. *Buy with extreme caution an already established and vacated franchise unit, even if it's recommended by the sales representative.* Chances are, there's a good reason the last owner closed down shop—and it's not because the person was making money hand over fist.

4. *Research extensively before investing your money in a franchise.* And when you're tired of researching, research some more (we know we've said it before, but it bears repeating).

5. *You are your best test market.* If a franchise appeals to you, it's probably going to appeal to others like you and may be worth investigating further. Trust your instinct.

6. *Don't mortgage your house or jeopardize your children's college education to buy a franchise.* Remember, the success rate of the less expensive franchises does not compare to that of the Blockbuster Videos and McDonald's of the world.

7. *If you have a profitable business, consider licensing or franchising it.* It has worked for others, why shouldn't it for you?

8. *If you see a need, develop your own business with an eye to franchising or spinning off other locations.* Here's one in the "Woe's me" category that has a lesson to be learned: In the early 1960s, one of the authors was six months pregnant and in dire need of an ice-cream fix. It was pre-Baskin-Robbins and the proliferation of ice cream franchises that followed, and the author walked 10 city blocks in Manhattan to find an ice cream cone!

9. *When selling a license or franchise to someone else, don't be too eager to qualify that person in your desire to expand.* It is imperative to handpick your first few licenses or franchises as success breeds success. The opposite, unfortunately, is just as true.

10. *Visit another location of the franchise you are planning to purchase—and sample the wares on-site.* The quality and service you encounter will be a good indicator of the support that the franchise owner receives from the home office.

11. *If you come across an extraordinarily well-run franchise but can't afford to buy an outlet, investigate it as a potential stock purchase for your portfolio.* After all, one of the authors recalls being impressed by a McDonald's burger in 1966 and still regrets passing up the chance to buy stock at $15 per share!

# 9

## PROTECTING YOUR INVESTMENT: INTELLECTUAL PROPERTY LAW VISITED

### WHAT'S IN A NAME?

Giving your business, product, and/or service an identifying name makes you the official owner for all the world to know. This is an important step in the process of transforming your visions into concrete reality. It also protects you from those who would pirate your property, an asset, and profit handily without your consent. This can be a creative and rewarding process, but—as with most aspects of setting up a business—there are some important legal steps to follow.

After all, little can dampen the spirit of embarking on a new venture more than printing up your stationery, business cards, and sign; planning a media campaign; and unveiling a name for your business, only to find out that another business owns the intellectual property rights. (For additional information on the legal requirements of naming a sole proprietorship, partnership, or corporation, see Chapters 3 and 4.) Still worse is the discovery that someone else has pirated your concept before it has a chance to hit the marketplace. Hence, the trademark or service mark was invented.

## PROTECTING THE NAME OF YOUR BUSINESS, PRODUCT, OR SERVICE

Legally, whoever protects a name first is the rightful owner; the first in time is the first in right. When contemplating a name for a business, product, or service, your first step, then, should be to contact your secretary of state to determine if any other entity has "reserved" your name of choice. This is called conducting a name search, and can be done at a state and federal level (if you want to reserve the name vis-à-vis all other owners nationwide).

If the coast is clear, go ahead and reserve your name. Thereafter, you trademark or service mark it if a service is provided by your business to impede anyone else statewide from co-opting your name or mark.

### Trademarks (™) and Service Marks (℠)

If you're planning to open a branch of your company in a number of states, or market your product nationally, you'll need to conduct a national name search and reserve your mark with the federal Patent and Trademark Office (PTO). One way to do this is to catch a flight to Washington, DC, and spend a great deal of time at the PTO's main search library, where the PTO maintains a record of all active trademark registrations and pending applications. A simpler option is to hire a company that specializes in national name searches (see Key Resources at the end of this chapter). Your local library may have catalogs of reserved trademarks, but your best bet here is an attorney specializing in intellectual property because this can be tricky stuff.

It's important to note that you are not legally required to register your trademark anywhere. Previous use of a trademark determines legal ownership. However, registration nationally and in the states where you plan on conducting business gives you firm protection by serving notice to other entrepreneurs—on a state or national level—that you have staked a claim to a name. Nobody else can register a trademark that's already on the books.

Once your trademark (or service mark) is registered officially, you obtain a certificate, which is proof-positive that you are the sole owner of the name you have chosen for your business, product, or service.

From then onward, you are free to put an ® next to the company, product, or service name, signifying that you have registered your trademark or service mark.

## PROPER CARE AND FEEDING OF A TRADEMARK OR SERVICE MARK

Once your business, product, or service name has legally become a trademark or service mark, you need to use it consistently and properly to protect your claim to exclusivity. Aside from registration federally and by state, here are some other actions you can take to make sure your trademark is doing its job:

- *Always use the proper symbol to denote a name as a trademark or service mark.* You should make others aware of your trademark or service mark by using ™ or ℠ following the name. When you register federally with the PTO use the ® symbol (e.g., Court Coach®). If a trademark or service mark isn't federally registered but is registered by a state.

- *Take immediate action on learning that another business is using your trademark or service mark illegally.* It is illegal for anyone else to use the same trademark or service mark, signify a ®, or register a similar or identical trademark. To maintain the exclusiveness of your potentially valuable trademark or service mark, always nip infringements in the bud by sending a letter requesting that the illegal usage cease to the user or to the agency that may regulate the user if such agency exists (e.g., American Bar Association for lawyers). You can file an action in court to seek an injunction, that is, a court order barring the use of your trademark. A dispute about who is first in time may be difficult to prove if you have not registered your trademark, but have simply denoted your mark with ℠ or ™.

- *Always use your trademark or service mark in conjunction with your product name or service.* The trademark or service mark should really function as an adjective, describing the product. For example: IBM computer, Kleenex tissue, Jell-O gelatin. Once the general public starts thinking of all gelatin as Jell-O, or all computers as IBMs, the trademark's value weakens.

- *When planning your business start-up, you need to factor in the time required to register a trademark—about 12 months from start to finish if you use the services of an attorney.* When printing up business materials, you need to use a trademark or service mark

($^{TM}$ or $^{SM}$), until your mark is registered. Therefore, it is important when printing to know how much printed material you will need and use during the waiting period. You don't want boxes and boxes of fine letterhead with the wrong marks.

## PROTECTING YOUR IDEAS FROM INFRINGEMENT

In the eyes of the law there are two types of mental subject matter: intellectual products, which qualify as property, and ideas that haven't yet been developed into products or services, which do not qualify as property. You can't protect an idea legally.

So, the conundrum is how to protect your ideas that aren't classified as property while developing a product or service. "Loose lips sink ships," yet you need to explain what it is that you're developing to associates, banks, and investors. Your best bet for safeguarding your idea is to require those people to whom you wish to reveal your proposed product or service to sign a nondisclosure statement (see Figure 9–1 for sample). This document states:

- You are the originator.
- The other party didn't have anything to do with the development of the idea.
- The other party will not use the idea without your permission.
- The other party will not reveal your idea to anyone else without your permission.

If you are seeking a patent from an invention and want to make a disclosure statement legally binding, you must send a description of the idea to the Commissioner of Patents, along with a letter requesting inclusion in the Disclosure Document Program. The Patent Office will assign your idea a Disclosure Document number, which protects your idea for two years.

If you are not dealing with a patent, but with a trade or service mark, make sure that you keep well-organized, dated notes while your idea is in the development state. In your file, include documentation on research you have conducted, funds expended, and important conversations and transactions with other parties and most particularly, examples of use and their dates. These notes could be crucial in establishing you as the originator of an idea in court, should you suffer an infringement of your rights.

**Figure 9–1**  Sample Nondisclosure Statement

The undersigned employee of _____(company name)_____ (the "Company") hereby promises to keep the Company's business secrets, including but not limited to customer, supplier, logistical, financial, research, and development information, confidential and not to disclose the Company's business secrets to any third party during and after the term of employment.

If any part of this promise is void for any reason, the undersigned accepts that employment may be severed without affecting the validity or enforceability of any other parts of the employment contract.

The undersigned agree to the terms of this contract on __(date)__ ,

(signature of Employer)

(name of Employer, typed)

(signature of Employee)

(name of Employee, typed)

## PATENTS

To protect a unique product you have spent days, weeks, months, and years perfecting and inventing from being copied without your permission, a patent is in order. After your initial expenditure of personal capital and before you can attract investors, or begin manufacturing your invention, you will need to obtain a patent.

Once your invention is registered with the PTO, you gain exclusive rights to make, use, and sell the product throughout the United States. The first step is to fulfill the requirement of "first inventorship" (a classification ascertaining that you have not merely reinvented an already existing product).

The PTO maintains a classification by subject matter of patents in the United States. These files are available for public inspection in the PTO's search room in Arlington, Virginia. While you can conduct a patent search yourself, it may be advisable to use the skills of an attorney who specializes in patent law for this important first step. Only after your product is patented can you affix "patented" after the name of your product, with your patent number.

## COPYRIGHTS

Literature, music, art, and computer programs can all be copyrighted, and you should be aware that copyright law applies to unpublished as well as published works.

As an author of an original work, you are protected by the Copyright Act of 1976, which states five exclusive rights given to copyright owners for 50 years past the length of their life: the rights of reproduction, adaptation, distribution, performance, and display.

To officially hinder the use of your intellectual subject matter without your permission, you need to register your product with the Federal Register of Copyrights. The process entails filing an application form along with a small fee and two copies of the work to be copyrighted.

Any product that is under copyright status should have a copyright notice attachment (see Figure 9–2) with the following information:

- The copyright symbol: *The Entrepreneur Small Business Legal Guide* ©.
- The word "Copyright," or the abbreviation "©."
- The year of first publication.

Many people are unaware that there is a simple way to copyright your material without registering it with the Federal Register of Copyrights. You can skip the paperwork and fee that goes along with filing your copyright with the federal government. All you need do is attach the copyright icon (©) to the title of your work, and a court of law will deem that you have put the world on notice of the original nature of the work. Of course, registering it with the federal government makes your case stronger.

The exclusive right to use original materials that a copyright provides is subject to several exceptions. The "fair use" exception covers

---

**Figure 9–2**    Sample Notice of Copyright

---

Copyright 1996 by Smith-Jones, Inc.

All rights reserved.

Purchasers are authorized to reproduce portions of the contents without prior permission, providing reproduction is for personal use only. Inquiries about reproducing that entire document should be addressed to: Smith-Jones, Inc., 1900 Main Street, Darian, CT.

---

most of the bases. This states that an original work can be reproduced for classrooms and other noncommercial purposes. For example, libraries and archives can usually reproduce single copies of written works for noncommercial purposes.

Four criteria are considered in determining fair use (after the fact, of course):

1. *The purpose and nature of use.* The work must be used in a nonprofit or educational context that is not commercial in nature.
2. *The proportion and importance of the portion of the work used in comparison to the entire work.* Let's say, for example, that one paragraph out of 400-page textbook was copied by a graduate student for his 100-page thesis. It could be argued that the portion of the original work copied was so small that it had little bearing on the outcome of the 100-page "original" work of the student.
3. *The nature of the work.* This relates to how the court defines the term "original." Let's say you're writing an "original" script for a TV commercial about your restaurant, Joe's Taco House. Using the Taco Bell commercial's jingle and filling in your restaurant's name is clearly more blasphemous than copying a section of a math textbook to describe how your tacos are shaped exactly like an isosceles triangle.
4. *The use's effect on the value of the work, including its potential market.* If Mrs. Jones' first-grade class makes t-shirts depicting Barney Dinosaur to wear in a school play, it's a very different scenario than if Joe's T-Shirt Shop makes the same shirts and sells them to Mrs. Jones's first-grade class (and anybody else who wants them).

## KNOW YOUR KEY TERMS

- *Intellectual Property.* Basically, a tangible product produced by your unique intellect.
- *Trademark.* Any word, symbol, design, or slogan that identifies and distinguishes the products of a company.
- *Service mark.* A mark, word, symbol, design, or slogan that identifies and distinguishes the services of a company.
- *Trade name or business name.* Describes a business as separate from the product or service it offers, and applies more to the goodwill of a business.

- *Nondisclosure statement.* A document that should be signed by potential investors, associates, and anyone else with whom you share your product development plans. It swears them to secrecy and protects you from their infringement of your ideas.
- *Copyright.* The exclusive right of an author or proprietor to print or otherwise reproduce an intellectual product.
- *Patent.* The exclusive right to make, use, and sell an invention throughout the United States.
- *Registered/Patented.* The filing (or registering) of a trademark, copyright, or patent with the appropriate federal office in Washington, DC, and/or your state office for the secretary of state.

## BASIC LEGAL RESEARCH

- *Trademark: How to Name Your Business and Product,* by Kate McGrath and Stephen Elias (Nolo Press).
- *How to Protect Your Business, Professional, and Brand Names,* by David A. Weinsten (John Wiley & Sons).

## KEY RESOURCES

- *The Commissioner of Patents, Washington, DC 20231,* can give you more information about filing for a patent.
- *The Federal Register of Copyrights, Library of Congress, Washington, DC 20559,* can give you more information about registering materials for copyright.
- *The Federal Patent and Trade Office* has a register of attorneys who specialize in representing applicants in the preparation of patent applications. For more information, call (703) 557-4636.
- *National name search services.* Two well-known services are Prentice-Hall Legal and Financial Services: (800) 543-4502; and Trademark Research Corporation: (800) TRC-MARK.

## COURT COACH® SUGGESTS

1. *If you have a computer and a modem, you can save money by using on-line name search services.* For about $10, well below what the name search consultants charge, you can conduct your name

search using a subscriber database (Compu-Mark, IntelliGate, or Dialog).

2. *Lawyers specializing in trademarking, copyrighting, and patenting your product or services are listed in your yellow pages under this category: "Attorneys, Intellectual Property."* Or, you can contact your state or local bar association to get a list of attorneys in your area. Be sure to shop around for an attorney who may have experience with the particular product you are copyrighting.

3. *Always use your mark icon to protect your exclusive rights.*

# Part II

# THE LEGALITIES
# OF RUNNING
# A SMALL BUSINESS

# 10

## DEMYSTIFYING THE TAX BASICS

The tax laws' complicated nature makes them a common source of difficulty for small business owners. Although as a solo, you need only to make quarterly estimated tax payments that include self-employment tax, once you start hiring employees, payroll taxes get thrown into the mix. This chapter is by no means a guide for doing your taxes on your own; by all means, do use an accountant. But we hope to provide you with a basic foundation for understanding your tax responsibility so that you don't learn this lesson the hard way by making costly mistakes and/or having to deal with an IRS audit.

### THE VALUE OF A GOOD ACCOUNTANT

Why, you may be asking yourself, is it highly advisable to hire an accountant? First, you'll have more time to concentrate on other important tasks—like marketing and courting new clients. Second, you'll save money and have peace of mind that the company's financial matters are well organized and up to date from the outset. Third, you will avoid raising "red flags" inadvertently with the IRS. If your budget does not allow for a full-time accountant, at least use an accountant as a consultant to set up your books and review your tax returns each year. You may even find that hiring a part-time bookkeeper to handle payroll, accounts payable and receivable, taxes, and other financial records pays for itself.

## Justification for Hiring an Accountant

You'll really understand why hiring an accountant is a wise investment if you ever actually have to deal with the IRS. Let's take, for example, a worst-case tax scenario: You've fallen behind on your taxes and have been summoned by the IRS to have a little chat with an IRS agent. As you can well imagine, this is a high-stress situation where a slip of the tongue or flare of the temper may result in having your business flattened by the IRS.

Enter the accountant, who has the advantage of knowing the art of talking to the IRS agent, familiarity with tax law and the intricacies of your business's finances. The accountant can logically and respectfully explain to the IRS agent that money can't be obtained from a stone, and the agent may very well accept a negotiated payment schedule or agree to an alternative regarding overdue or unpaid taxes. The end result: Your accountant has more than earned her keep by keeping you on the straight-and-narrow with the IRS in what could have been a fatal situation for your business.

## Further Justification for Hiring an Accountant

Let's further explore how to dig yourself out of the financial hole created if you fall behind on your taxes, as this has proven to be the beginning of the end for many small businesses. The trouble starts when you make the pivotal mistake of ignoring your taxes for the first year, in the hopes of using that money as operating capital and making up for lost taxes the next year. Bad move! Inevitably, tax time will roll around again and you will be tempted to use the same strategy (if you were lucky enough to avoid detection by the IRS the first time, that is).

While the IRS may take a few years to catch up with you, chances are good that it will do so. In fact, the IRS gets its tax dollars in about 90 percent of all delinquent tax cases—one way or another.

Here's what happens when the IRS does catch up with you. (Warning: It's not a pretty picture.) Until a business's back taxes are paid in full, the IRS can and will charge interest—considerably higher than market rate and compounded daily on the unpaid balance—as well as penalties. In addition, interest will be assessed on the unpaid balance of penalties and interest. If your small business is unable to pay off its tax liability, the IRS can shut you down (a very nasty scenario) and will take enforced collection action to collect its money. This may very well result in your declaring the business bankrupt (also a very nasty scenario).

Another worst-case tax scenario—and justification for hiring an accountant—is payroll taxes (further discussed later in this chapter). Some business owners short on cash decide to bypass payroll taxes for a period of time, until they build up their bank account. This is definitely an unwise idea, not to mention unlawful!

It can take the IRS as long as two years to contact you about delinquent payroll taxes. Meanwhile, the business is using payroll tax funds to cover operating costs, so there's a double financial whammy when the IRS catches up with you. A far better alternative is paying your taxes on time and applying for a loan from a bank or a wealthy relative. Other alternatives are using corporate credit cards as a backup or taking an equity line of credit on your home.

It should be mentioned that there is a 100 percent penalty for responsible parties who fail to pay the withholding or payroll taxes for employees. So, as you can see, your tax headaches—and justification for hiring an accountant—increase as your small business blossoms.

## INCOME TAXES LEVIED ON YOUR BUSINESS

Chapters 2 and 3 touched briefly on how your business's status, whether sole proprietorship, partnership, C corporation, or S corporation, affects your financial commitment to the IRS. As you will see in this section, your choice of business organization is a choice between significant differences in federal income treatment.

### Income Taxes Levied on Sole Proprietorship and Partnership

The income tax reporting procedure for sole proprietors, really no more than the alter egos of individuals, is relatively simple, since all of the business's profits or losses can be reported as personal income. All that's needed is a Schedule C, reporting the profit or loss of the business, attached to your personal Form 1040. The profit or loss is then listed on the 1040 as other income from business activity, and the taxes are calculated accordingly.

Remember, a sole proprietor is also responsible for the self-employment tax on *net* Schedule C in addition to income tax. The major tax advantage of a sole proprietorship is that business deductions, such as depreciation, can be taken personally as well. This can result in considerable tax savings.

Income earned in a partnership is reported to the IRS in the same way as income earned in a proprietorship. The partners each report their share of business income on a separate line on the 1040 personal income tax form. Instead of a Schedule C, a U.S. Partnership Return of Income, Form 1065, is filed indicating how much each partner earned. All depreciation allowances and investment tax credits for the partnership are deducted against the partners' share of net income or losses for the year. Remember that the partners may also be responsible for self-employment tax (for more information on sole proprietorship and partnership, see Chapters 2 and 3).

## Income Taxes Levied on Corporations

A corporation, like any business, is formed by associates to conduct a business venture and divide profits among investors. Associations, unincorporated syndicates, groups, pools, or joint ventures may be treated as corporations. While this is a plus for liability, it's a definite minus when it comes to paying taxes because of double taxation. What's that, you say?

Here's where taxes become a bit more complicated. As you'll recall from Chapter 4, a corporation is viewed in the eyes of the law as an entity, an "it" with a legal identity separate from the officers and any others who have a vested interest in the company.

Thus, a corporation pays income taxes separately from shareholders on profits before dividends. Double taxation refers to the fact that the corporation pays income tax on its earnings and then when these earnings are distributed, the individual pays tax again on these earnings. In small businesses, where most shareholders are also employees earning a salary, the individual shareholders must pay income tax on that salary. Working owners could wind up paying taxes on their salaries *and* on dividends distributed from corporate profits.

Luckily, there is a way around this double taxation. Most small or closely held corporations employing all the stockholders distribute all the company's earnings as salaries and bonuses, tax-deductible by the corporation as a business expense. Thus, the corporation is left with no taxable income, and all earnings are reported through the owners. The IRS, however, looks at compensation to ensure that it is reasonable.

The other option is for a small corporation to declare itself an "S" corporation and terminate its status as a separate *tax* entity. All corporate income or losses are then attributable to the individual shareholders in proportion to the shares owned by each individual. See Chapter 4 for more information about regular corporations and S corporations.

## Limited Liability Corporations

The limited liability corporation (LLC), a fairly new concept in business organization that is not yet accepted in every state, gives you the best of both worlds: the tax structure of a partnership and the limited liability of a corporation. An added note: Organizations of professionals, doctors, and lawyers are generally treated as corporations for tax purposes.

## TAXES LEVIED ON YOU AS AN EMPLOYER

As mentioned earlier, once you hire employees, the taxes you pay (as well as your paperwork) increase. Remember, hiring even one employee qualifies you for employer status with the IRS. This is one reason that small businesses often utilize temporary-help agencies, freelance workers, and independent contractors for short-term needs.

## Payroll Taxes

Before we get into the specific payroll taxes you'll be responsible for as an employer, here are the basics of what you need to do to stay square with the IRS:

1. The first step is to obtain a federal Employer Identification Number (EIN). The IRS requires all businesses except most sole proprietors to obtain an EIN number by filing IRS Form SS-4. *Note:* If a sole proprietor pays payroll taxes, an EIN is required.
2. The second order of business is opening a bank account solely for Social Security (FICA) and federal income taxes (FWT) withheld from employees' paychecks.
3. FICA and FTW withholdings are deposited in your bank account for taxes along with a federal tax deposit (FTD) coupon on a regular basis. Typically, this deposit is made on a monthly basis, depending on the size of the tax deposit.
4. You'll also need to file the information regarding the FICA and FWT taxes on a quarterly basis with the IRS on Form 941, the Employer's Quarterly Federal Tax Return.

Now that you have the payroll tax basics under control, here's a rundown of your payroll tax responsibilities once you decide to take the big plunge and become an employer.

### Federal Income Tax Withholding

You'll need to obtain a supply of Employee's Withholding Allowance Certificates, Form W-4, from the IRS for employees to record their yearly withholding allowances (number of dependents). This, along with the size of the employees' salaries, determines the amount of money that should be withheld from their paychecks to cover the federal wage tax (FWT) and Social Security tax (FICA). The completed W-4 is maintained by the employer.

### Social Security and Medicare Taxes

According to the Federal Insurance Contributions Act (FICA), your employees are entitled to old age, survivors, disability, and hospital insurance, which are financed by Social Security and Medicare taxes levied on both the employee and employer. For more information about these taxes, see the IRS publication, Circular E, Employer's Tax Guide.

### State and Federal Unemployment Taxes (FUTA)

Unlike FICA, FUTA is not deducted from the employee's wages, but is paid solely by the business. The FUTA rate for 1995 is 6.2 percent of the first $7,000 of the employee's wages for the year. That rate is reduced to 5.4 percent for employers who pay all state unemployment taxes. For more information on federal regulations, contact the IRS. State regulations vary.

### State or Local Income Tax

In addition to the federal income tax, most states and cities levy a local tax on employee wages. This tax must also be withheld from the employee's paycheck. For more information, contact your state and city department of revenue office.

### Disability Tax

This tax is regulated on a state level. In some states, the disability tax is handled by the department of employment security, in others by different departments.

## Self-Employment Tax

Sole proprietors and partners are subject to paying a federal self-employment tax. This is a Social Security tax for people who work for themselves and don't automatically have Social Security tax withheld from their paychecks. This tax is computed and reported on

Schedule SE, Self-Employment Tax, which is attached to the 1040 personal income tax form.

## Excise Tax

Excise taxes are levied on the sale of certain articles, on certain types of transactions and occupations, and on the use of certain products. This tax is not included in the selling price but is charged separately by the manufacturer or the retailer. Businesses subject to excise taxes must file Form 720, Quarterly Federal Excise Tax Return. If in doubt, call your local IRS office to find out if your business is subject to excise taxes.

## TAX DEDUCTIONS FOR SMALL BUSINESSES

Although the IRS has been reviewing business deductions more stringently in recent years, there are still plenty of ways for small business owners to whittle away income taxes. Any expense incurred by your business, that is ordinary and common to your type of business, is deductible, including (among other things) depreciation of company-owned property, advertising, promotional materials, insurance, employee benefit programs, legal services, office expenses, car mileage, and business-related meals and entertainment. For a complete examination of what business expenses can be deducted, see IRS Publication 535, *Business Expenses*.

## Depreciation

The major category of deductions for most small businesses is depreciation, which has been the yearly deduction of a portion of the *cost* of an item that has been used solely for business purposes. Any piece of company property—equipment, machinery, vehicles, furniture, fixtures, and so on—with a useful life of more than one year is subject to depreciation. Intangible property, such as copyrights, can also be depreciated.

To be depreciable, business property must meet three basic requirements. It must be:

1. Used solely for the purpose of conducting business (or else only part of the item is deductible).

**2.** Have a useful life of more than one year.

**3.** Be something that wears out, or loses value from use.

There are two methods of depreciation: straight-line depreciation and accelerated depreciation. The straight-line method involves deducting an equal amount each year over the projected lifetime of the property, not including the first year in which only a half-year's worth of depreciation is allowed. Accelerated depreciation involves writing off larger amounts of the price of an item in the years immediately following its purchase. This allows for greater tax savings during those crucial, and often lean, start-up years.

Another option is to write off up to $17,500 of depreciable assets in the year of purchase, but this can get a little tricky. If you purchase more than $200,000 in depreciable assets in one year, the $17,500 is reduced by the same amount you exceed $200,000. Also, the amount you write off can't exceed the total taxable income that your business received in that year.

## Employee-Related Tax Deductions

In many cases, employee benefits qualify as tax deductions although there are exceptions; it's wise to consult an accountant as to which deductions your business qualifies for before investing in a benefits program. Here are some of the employee benefits that may qualify as tax deductions:

- Profit sharing.
- Pension plans.
- Life insurance.
- Health insurance.
- Relocation expenses.
- Educational assistance programs.

Employee wages can also be deducted if your business meets the following qualifications:

- The wages are ordinary and necessary expenses for the operation of your business.
- Services are rendered for the wages paid.
- The wages are reasonable for the services rendered.
- Payment was made during the tax year.

# A FINAL NOTE ON TAX DEDUCTIONS: STAY IN YOUR FOXHOLE

It's important to remember not to get overzealous in your deductions; keeping a low profile is rule number one in avoiding an audit. And, make certain you can document, with receipts, any expenses that you claim. Burgeoning travel and entertainment expenses are particularly suspect. It's wise to write down the reason for each expense on the back of the receipt and in your checkbook in case your memory fails you when you're sitting across the table from an IRS agent during an audit. Most credit card receipts have a fill-in-the-blank form for you to jot down the name of your business invitee, date, and purpose.

## KNOW YOUR KEY TERMS

- *Gross income.* "All income from whatever source derived" (Internal Revenue Code § 61).
- *Imputed income.* The earnings of a taxpayer who works solo or uses his or her own property.
- *Deduction.* The amount subtracted from gross income or adjusted gross income when computing taxable income.
- *Business and investment deductions.* All "ordinary and necessary expenses paid or incurred during the taxable year in carrying on any trade or business" (Internal Revenue Code § 162).
- *Credit.* The amount a taxpayer is permitted to use against taxes payable for sums withheld from wages and prepaid amounts (Internal Revenue Code §§ 31, 32).
- *Capital asset.* For purposes of capital gains and losses, "All property held by the taxpayer is a capital asset" arising in sales of (certain kinds of) property (Internal Revenue Code § 1221).
- *Annual accounting period.* For the determination of income and deductions on an annual basis, the allocation of items to a particular year, either fiscal (you pick the end-of-the-year date to close the books) or calendar year (Internal Revenue Code § 442).

## BASIC LEGAL RESEARCH

- *Federal Taxes 2d Ed.* (Prentice-Hall) and *CCH Federal Tax Guide* (Commerce Clearing House). These tax guides can be found in law libraries or the reference department of your public library.

- *Julian Block's Guide to Year Round Tax Savings,* by Julian Block (Dow Jones-Irwin). You can find this easy-to-use guide in most bookstores.
- *U.S. Master Tax Guide (1995)* (Commerce Clearing House). Published on a yearly basis, this book is not intimidating because it is beautifully organized. You will easily find the answers to all tax questions in here, so it is well worth the cost of purchase.
- *Stand Up to the IRS,* by Frederick W. Daily (Nolo Press). A guide to dealing with IRS collectors and defending yourself in an audit.

## KEY RESOURCES

- *Your local IRS office.* IRS publication 334, *Tax Guide for Small Business,* and 583, *Taxpayers Starting a Business,* are available through your local IRS office, or by calling the IRS office: (800) 829-3676.
- *A Certified Public Accountant who specializes in small business tax returns.* There are accountants who have developed a niche in small business tax issues, who may be able to save you a substantial amount by ferreting out tax deductions not visible to the untrained eye.
- *Small Business Administration.* Several pamphlets addressing taxes, including *Steps in Meeting Your Tax Obligations* and *Getting the Facts for Income Tax Reporting,* are available.

## COURT COACH® SUGGESTS

1. *Remember: Ignoring the tax man is not a good strategy for financing the operational costs of your business.* We know, we've said it before. But it bears repeating, so tattoo this tip on your brain!
2. *Hire a reasonably priced, per hour, accountant/bookkeeper if possible.* Look around for an at-home professional who may advertise in your local newspaper, or advertise yourself.
3. *Invest in computerized programs to process your internal accounting.* Keep an in-depth analysis of hours worked per employee, accounts receivable, and detailed, sophisticated monthly billing statements. Send billings out on time and follow up on your collection rules (for more on collecting your money, see Chapter 16).

# 11

## HIRING AND FIRING YOUR STAFF

### MAKING THE TRANSITION FROM SOLO TO "THE BOSS" (THE BUCK STOPS HERE)

Hiring (and firing) employees can be a complex, and sticky, web of state and federal statutes and common-law concepts for the unsuspecting first-time employer. In fact, a single employee termination could trigger accusations of the violation of dozens of statutes that sometime overlap and contradict each other. To make matters more complex, employment litigation has become somewhat of a national pastime, much of which centers around unlawful hiring and firing practices, and unsafe or hostile conditions of employment.

One small-company president, quoted in the April 1994 issue of *Inc.* magazine, summed up the views of many business owners, attorneys, and judges. After spending $50,000 on legal fees fighting a wrongful-termination charge, he said: "We've been in business and owned by the same family for 80 years. We had a nice reputation in the community. The fact that this employee was able to drag us through the courts on an utterly worthless claim and cost us all this money and aggravation made it clear to me that the system is out of control."

Nevertheless, we hope there will come a time when your fledgling business gathers enough steam to warrant hiring one, or several, employees to help keep the ship afloat and divide the labor load. No doubt, you may have looked forward to this day of passing on various aspects of your workload and sharing the stress involved with running your thriving company. But, like many changes, there are pluses and minuses.

One of the biggest challenges you'll go through is learning to be the boss. This involves taking responsibility for all mistakes (not just your own), managing people with different personality styles (many times you'll think it would be easier to do it all yourself), and becoming astute at choosing staff, knowing that if an employee does not pan out, you must swing the hatchet without incurring disgruntled employee wrath at a costly litigation.

## The Best Defense Is a Good Offense

What's a well-meaning entrepreneur on the verge of becoming a first-time employer to do for protection? Think like a lawyer! Conceptually protect yourself from liability by understanding and using the legal doctrine of the sword and shield. The sword symbolizes attack, or offense, and the shield symbolizes defense. The $64,000 question, whether you're interviewing potential employees or discussing the possibility of termination is, "How can I protect myself?" In other words, know the applicable legal rules of the road for hiring and firing so that you don't make a mistake that is legally indefensible.

## THE ETIQUETTE OF HIRING

In hiring any employee, it's important to choose someone who shares your vision and company goals, and who fits into your corporate structure, no matter how large or how small. For most small business owners, this is an extremely personal decision, since you are taking into your company "family," someone you will probably be spending more time with than your spouse and children.

You go a long way toward choosing the right employee by obtaining the right information to make sure the employee has "the right stuff." You need to ask artful questions when interviewing and verifying his or her history of employment because you are severely limited by the law as to the questions you can ask a potential employee; and the former employer is under legal constraints as well not to defame or prevent employment.

Intuition is also a great source of information, not only your own, but also that of your staff. A new employee should pass "the office smell test" before being considered in the running for position among the ranks. You might want to include associates in the interviewing process of a potential candidate for a position. And, by all means, take into consideration the opinions of all other personnel who are clued in to observe and engage the applicant in consideration.

All adverse reactions (anything from a condescending tone toward receptionist to a dirty raincoat) as well as positive reactions (enthusiasm, positive energy, good sense of humor) should be duly noted and carefully weighed before making your final decision. In this fashion, you will gradually build a wonderful team of dedicated, smart professionals (who are also diverse in personality and style).

Hence, your final step in hiring should be to factor in all the information you have gathered. If you think someone's lied to you, the person probably did and should be eliminated from your choices. By the same token, if you truly believe someone's basically trustworthy and honest in expressing the intent to be a vital member of your team, hire that prospect!

One last thought about the hiring process: Take your time making any decisions about bringing someone on board and ask for and check references. Offering someone a job is easy, but the repercussions of hiring the wrong person—namely, getting rid of the person—is legally and emotionally difficult, if not traumatizing, unless you are a trained hatchet person. Learn to interview by reading some of the books suggested at the end of this chapter.

## The Job Interview

The best defense is a good offense and thus, walk gently and carry a small stick. The "do unto others" golden rule of diplomacy you learned in nursery school can be most helpful in appeasing bruised egos. For example, virtually anyone who's been on the job interview circuit knows that the phrase, "We'll keep your resume on file" is code for, "You didn't cut the mustard for the position." Which one would you rather hear?

Starting from the time you interview a potential employee, your management style may be one of your best preventive measures for avoiding any employment litigation. Would-be employees who are miffed because they didn't make it past the interview process are ripe for charging you with a discrimination suit.

A letter to applicants who didn't make the grade is a business, but not legal necessity (see Figure 11–1). It's nice to let people know as

**Figure 11–1**    Sample Employment Rejection Letter

My Company
1 Main Street
Rowayton, CT 10000

Dear _____(applicant's name)_____ :

Thank you for your interest in the position of _____ at ___(Company name)___ . We regret to inform you that we are unable to offer you a position with our company at this time. However, we will keep your resume on file for future reference. If a position becomes open that matches your skills, we will certainly keep you in mind.

We wish you the very best in your job search.

Sincerely,

_____(signature of President, Owner, or Personnel Manager)_____

soon as possible if they didn't get the job, as hanging in the inertia of ignorance is not a very comfortable place to be, and everything you do is good (or bad) P.R.

Anyone's list of the most uncomfortable situations in life would surely include job interviews. This anxiety-provoking experience would have to be somewhere near the top of the list for interviewers and interviewees alike (maybe right after public speaking). The trick for the employer is to get a feel for the person sitting across the desk, without asking any impulsive or inappropriate questions.

Thinking like a lawyer, you need to strike a balance between the job applicant's right to privacy and your right to make an informed choice and to know specifically exactly what you can expect from this individual as to performance and restrictions on the person's ability to perform.

Watch out for these sensitive areas when compiling a list of interview questions or an employment application form:

- *Avoid asking questions that don't pertain to a legitimate business concern.* Legally, the applicant's personal life is none of your business. Supposedly, job performance has nothing to do with marital or economic status, sexual orientation, weight, religious status, political affiliation, desire to have children, or hobbies. But if the applicant's resume lists hobbies or interests or membership in organizations, that line of questions can be pursued gingerly. Let the interviewee "volunteer" information.

- *Information about race, sex, color, and national origin can be obtained only for business purposes.* Employers can legally request this information for certain federal record-keeping rules.
- *In some states, you can't inquire about whether or not the applicant made previous claims for workers' compensation.*
- *Never ask about criminal arrests.* You may inquire about actual convictions, (which differ from arrests in that the person is "innocent until proven guilty" under our system of justice); however, it must be clear that the q & a will be considered only in relation to specific job requirements.
- *Don't discuss the applicant's feelings about labor unions or ask whether the person belongs to a union.* Again, if the person lists union membership on a resume, or has been referred to you by a union, you can carefully broach the subject.
- *Avoid questions about the employee's physical and mental condition.* Taboo questions include, Have you been tested for AIDS? Have you undergone any psychological counseling? Is any surgery on the horizon? How many sick days did you take at your last job? and questions of this ilk.
- *Don't inquire about personal habits, including smoking and drinking alcohol.* While you are legally allowed to designate your office as a nonsmoking environment, you can't refrain from hiring someone because the person is a smoker—that's called discrimination in at least 15 states. Check your local statutes. (Please note that making an unvoiced observation yourself—that the person's clothes reek of cigarette smoke, or that the interviewee's eyes are bloodshot and speech is slurred—is allowed, and you'd be remiss not to notice these traits.)

The Equal Employment Opportunity Commission (EEOC), the government office that oversees employee rights, further complicated the process of interviewing job applicants in May 1994. New government guidelines on how to conduct job interviews without running afoul of federal disability-discrimination laws were issued with the –intent of further protecting mentally or physically disabled employees from discrimination. The problem is that the guidelines make distinctions that many bosses and personnel departments find difficult to understand.

One of the most contentious aspects of the new guidelines is that they sharply restrict employers' rights to ask questions about the specific accommodations that an applicant might need. Employers can only ask applicants whether they can do tasks "with or without reasonable accommodation." They can't ask about the type of accommodation that would be needed until after a job offer is made. Labor lawyers say that restriction may put companies in the uncomfortable position of "unhiring" disabled people who accept conditional job offers if the necessary accommodations can't be made.

To find out more about the fine points of these very specific guidelines, contact the national office of the EEOC at (800) 669-3362 and ask for the *Enforcement Guidance on Pre-Employment Disability-Related Inquiries* publication. (More information regarding the EEOC's role and guidelines can be found in Chapter 12.)

## After the Interview and Before the Job Offer

Once the potential employee passes the interview process, there are other hiring aspects to consider:

- *Drug testing.* Consult with an attorney who specializes in labor law before even suggesting a drug test. Depending on the job, the jurisdiction, and the type of drug testing involved, legal restrictions may apply.
- *Medical testing.* While your insurance company may require that all new employees undergo a physical examination to qualify, you are not at liberty to enforce this rule before the offering and acceptance of a job has transpired.
- *References.* In addition to asking applicants to sign a form permitting you to contact former employers and personal references, request written references when possible.
- *Personnel records.* Permission to speak with an applicant's former employers is not the same thing as the go-ahead to peruse their personnel records. Again, written permission is advisable, but quite honestly, no former employer will reveal this information to you in all probability. The former employer owes you nothing, may even be a competitor, and could risk liability.
- *School and college transcripts.* Most schools won't release transcripts to anyone but the student in question. The applicant will need to obtain these for your review. Hence, if time is of the essence, make this qualification known to potential applicants in your advertisement of the position, since this could easily delay the process.
- *Criminal records check.* Depending on the nature of the work, you may want to consider hiring a private service to conduct a criminal records check, although it's advisable to inform the applicant before embarking on this process.

- *Lie detectors.* Currently, lie detectors are permitted by federal law as long as applicants are judged on the basis of whether or not they lied on the test, and not on information derived from it (such as whether they were ever arrested or have a chronic illness).
- *Evaluating skills.* There's no legal reason you shouldn't administer a skills evaluation test to make sure your potential employees live up to their resumes.
- *Compliance with the Immigration Reform and Control Act.* The Immigration and Naturalization Service requires you to obtain written verification from applicants that they are legal residents of the United States.

## Reference Check: Name, Address, and Serial Number

My mother taught me long ago, "If you can't say something nice, say nothing." This should be the response you expect to hear when you "check." That's because the former employer risks liability for a "bad" reference. Again, listen for what is *not* said.

Remember the "don'ts" of interviewing. Don't inquire into any of the potentially lethal problem areas:

- Marital status.
- Weight.
- Age.
- Race.
- Pregnancy status or number of children.
- Religious affiliation.

If any of these considerations are important to you, you must use your own powers of observation or inquire indirectly by focusing on statistics on the applicant's resume.

Don't interview anyone, even a temporary worker, without reviewing a written resume, even if it's written on the back of a napkin. And, hire no one without first checking the person's references.

## The Job Offer

The important thing to remember here is, don't write the offer, say it, or even imply it unless you mean it! Make certain you spell out clearly all the elements of the offer: title; responsibilities; salary and bonus, if any; when you expect the person to start and finish, if time-limited; as well as all conditions of employment or company rules.

Once you have offered an applicant the job, you can't legally offer the job to someone else (although this very thing happened to both of the authors in the dog-eat-dog city of New York). Consequently, you need to set a deadline for the applicant to accept or reject your offer. If you offer a job with certain terms and conditions and the applicant comes back with changes in the terms (a "counteroffer"), as we pointed out in Chapter 7, the entire negotiation process starts over again. You can now either accept or reject the applicant's new offer, since the terms have been changed. This can be a rather lengthy game of give-and-take until both parties agree on all terms of employment.

Revisiting our discussion of contract law (Chapter 7), you now know that on your written or oral acceptance of the written or oral offer, the contract has been made. Since this is a done deal, you are legally bound to have the desk or work space ready and waiting, and your employee is bound to show up on time for work on the appointed date. If either person doesn't follow through on the terms of employment, the contract has been breached (see Chapter 12 on employee rights and Chapter 14 on your rights as an employer).

Even if there is no written employment contract (and there usually is not), oral contracts are also often binding in a court of law. An oral contract is a verbal (face-to-face or over the telephone) offer and acceptance, a "meeting of the minds" not memorialized in writing. The problem with an oral contract is the ease with which one person can dispute the other person's understanding. If it can be demonsrated that there is no "meeting of the minds," there is no contract.

Sometimes even an offhand comment can be construed as an "implied" contract, as for instance, a spoken promise of upward mobility ("There's much room for advancement") or job security ("No one ever gets fired"). Your employee handbook and personnel policy statements can give rise to an implied contract. When you scrutinize your written materials, cast an eye on whether or not an employee could "infer" from the wording some guaranteed right or "perks" (perquisites) not intended by you. Don't wait for 20-20 hindsight; 20-20 foresight is much better.

Written, signed contracts are the easiest to prove in a court of law since both parties are bound by their written word as evidence of the required "meeting of the minds." For an oral or implied contract to be upheld in court, there usually has to be something written and signed by the party being sued (who is usually the employer) as evidence of intent. This could be a letter, a memo, or the employee handbook (discussed more in Chapter 12).

## Firm Brochures and Employment Policy Manuals

What you put in writing could be construed by an employee or court of law as creating some employee right. Make sure you shield yourself with careful writing, careful editing, and review by all principals in your business. Even a firm brochure has been used to infer an implied right to certain work conditions or to abolish the doctrine of "at will" employment, so that a court might find an employee has acquired "a right" to a job, or you have relinquished "the right" to let the employee go.

This is tricky and risky business. The bottom line is, before you officially commit anything to writing—an employee handbook, a statement of firm policy and procedure, or even a company brochure—shield yourself from problems by having a lawyer review the materials.

Keep organized files documenting your company's compliance with all policy procedures to the letter of the law.

## Statute of Frauds

Even if you say absolutely nothing to an employee about the terms of the job, four basic employment terms can be assumed and will be assumed by a court of law, and must be present in every employment situation:

- The wages are reasonable.
- The location of the job is where the employee is.
- The work to be performed is something the employee is capable of doing.
- The employer or employee can terminate the employment situation at any time by either party's choice (subject to the "employment at will" exemption covered in the next section).

To protect profits and your business, there are other terms of employment you should consider putting in writing, either in an employment contract or the employee handbook.

### Protection of Your Trade Secrets

If you anticipate that an employee will be in a position where access to a trade secret is possible—such as a baker who has access to the family recipe that launched your cookie conglomerate, or a software tester who's helping you work the glitches out of games you're developing to market on the Internet—be sure the person signs a nondisclosure form (see Figure 9–1, in Chapter 9).

## Ownership of Copyright

Original works of authorship are subject to copyright law. Who owns a copyright can be problematic. If an employee writes or draws something original and if the work, whether literary, musical, dramatic, pictorial, or audiovisual is done is "within the scope" of employment, then the employer is considered to be the author and owns the copyright. However, if the creator is deemed to be an independent contractor, then the employer does not maintain the copyright. Have the independent contractor sign a statement waiving this privilege if you, as the employer, intend to own any copyright generated by persons other than yourself during the course of their employment (see Figure 11–2).

## Ownership of Patents

To promote industrial progress and economic growth, the United States Constitution secures to inventors the exclusive right to their discoveries for a limited time (Art. I, Sec. 8, Cl. 8). Technically, an employee who invents a product on the job may own the invention

---

**Figure 11–2**    Sample Waiver of Copyright Privileges

---

The undersigned (the "employee"), as an employee of Vanity Press, Inc., hereby waives the privilege of copyright ownership for the following:

1. Any materials written by the employee and published of by Vanity Press during the entire time period of employment by said company.
2. Any materials written by the employee during working hours (8:00 AM–5:00 PM, Monday–Friday), regardless of whether or not they are published by Vanity Press, will legally belong to Vanity Press.

Any violation of this agreement may result in termination at the discretion of Vanity Press.

---

(date and signature of employee)

---

unless there is a written contract clause reserving ownership to the employer.

### Noncompete Clause

This contract clause states that the employee will not go after your clients, or market share, for a certain period of time after leaving the company. However, your noncompetitor clause should not run afoul of antitrust laws (remember, Ma Bell); hence the need to tread lightly and consult an attorney.

### Benefits, Fringe and Mandated

This subject will be covered at length in Chapter 12.

## THE ETIQUETTE OF FIRING

You need to handle firing employees at least as carefully as hiring employees, maybe more so since most of the rapidly multiplying employee litigation cases center around wrongful termination and accusations of discrimination. Trends indicate that at a jury trial, a sympathetic verdict for the plaintiff employee may be the outcome. Out of 120 suits surveyed by the Rand Corporation in 1988, 66 percent were won by employees. A 1991 California study found that plaintiffs were victorious 75 to 80 percent of the time. So be very sure that both you and the employee are clear on exactly why he or she is being let go.

## The Best Defense Is a Good Offense, or How to Avoid Wrongful-Termination Litigation

Here are some Court Coach® tips that could keep you safe from being on the wrong end of a wrongful-termination suit.

### Establish Written Termination Guidelines

All your company's procedures, for hiring and promoting as well as firing, should be outlined in your employee handbook (see Chapter 12). Unlawful, illegal behavior should subject the employee to immediate dismissal.

### Know How to Deal with Illegal Acts

Even though you may be a very small company, you need to behave like a big company when dealing with employees illegal acts such as selling or using drugs on the job. Do not ignore any illegal activity occurring at your workplace; document it immediately; start investigation of the employee's work space and questioning of the alleged wrongdoer and, possibly, previous employer. Confront the situation head-on. Be pleasant and with sound evidence, fire on the spot. Escort the defused employee to his or her desk; watch while the employee packs up and make sure that there is no reason to return; remember to collect keys, pass cards, and other security papers or access materials; and provide a personal escort to the door.

### Keep Thorough Records

On a day-to-day basis, keep records of even "small" employee failures, like repeatedly arriving to work 5 minutes late, or failing to write down phone messages, failing to file documents in a timely fashion, and the like. What might be considered insignificant as an isolated instance could be cause for termination if occurring on a repeated basis. Nonetheless, there are employers who have the temerity to fire at once with no second chances. One friend of mine, working on a temporary basis as a fill-in office worker, was asked not to return when she missed the morning train and arrived at work an hour late because her briefcase had been lost. It goes without saying that glaring omissions or dereliction from responsibilities should also be recorded.

### Provide a Written Warning

If an employee does something that may be significant enough for termination, or cumulatively has jeopardized the job position, give written notice and a limited amount of time to correct the behavior (see Figure 11–3). This "second chance," showing your good faith, will serve you well in establishing your position in a court of law or with the union arbitration process or a grievance board.

### Devise an Evaluation Form

Periodically (quarterly or biannually), have a face-to-face formal evaluation session with each employee. This way, all employees know where they stand and you have written documentation as to the progress, or lack thereof, in an employee's performance.

### Encourage Employees to Report Other Employees' Misdeeds

This really cuts against the American grain where "telling" is seen as unacceptable "ratting." However, the miscreant employee is hurting the company as a whole, taking money out of your pocket (even if it is dollars translated into wasted nonproductive work time) playing rather than working, and upsetting the morale of other employees. Have an open-door, strictly confidential policy that promotes the flow of information to you about employee problems.

**Figure 11–3** Sample Termination Warning

**Internal Memorandum**

DATE:

TO:      (Employee's name)

FR:      (Supervisor's name)

RE:      Warning of Termination

---

Please note that the following behavior was observed, and recorded in your
employee file, on _(date)_ :
(A brief yet thorough description of the behavior)

Consider this due warning that if the above-described behavior is observed
again, this will be grounds for your immediate dismissal. If you have any
questions, or would like to discuss this issue further, please feel free to call
me and arrange an appointment.

---

## Obtain Adequate Documentation

Make sure you have sufficient documentation for the charges
leading to termination. Don't accuse an employee of incompetence unless you can back it up with documentation. If you need time to gather
your evidence, consider a suspension first.

## Handle All Termination Actions Consistently

This will deter charges of favoritism.

## If Possible, Have a Witness

The presence of another manager or partner when you fire an employee may come in handy if there are any questions later on, and will
aid in keeping emotions of all concerned under control.

## If Possible, Part Amicably

Try to let an employee down slowly and keep on good terms with
the terminated worker. Several weeks' severance pay and benefits will

help to ease the sting of termination, and may keep you on speaking terms with a former employee from whom you may need information in the future. Also, disgruntled employees naturally are more likely to bad-mouth you in the community. Not to scare, but newspapers are replete with stories of former employees who come back to the workplace, gun in hand.

## Chip, Chip, Chipping Away at Employment at Will

During the early 1980s, a revolution in the process of firing employees began taking place. Previously, a common-law doctrine known as "employment at will" was recognized in most courts of law. This doctrine allows an employer to fire whomever they like, for whatever reasons they choose—so long as a discrimination isn't involved or there's been no violation of a written, oral, or implied contract. It also allows the employee to quit at will.

As employees started gaining more rights through state and federal legislation, decisions in various courts have chipped away at the doctrine of "at will" employment. By 1989, 45 states had accepted a number of legal theories eroding the "at will" doctrine. And, in 1992, a landmark report from the Rand Corporation indicated that only five states still maintained this once universally accepted policy: Louisiana, Mississippi, Georgia, Florida, and Delaware. The following three major court-sanctioned principles have chipped away at the core doctrine:

1. *The implied contract exception.* Courts have held that employee rights may be inferred or implied, even though no written contract exists. (Sometimes these rights may be implied from the language in the employee handbook, which we will cover in Chapter 12.)
2. *The good faith and fair dealing exception.* This evolving concept is based on the assumption that any employer/employee relationship is predicated on the mandate of acting in good faith and dealing fairly with all employees. Under this thinking, there must always be a valid, and provable, reason for dismissing an employee. By way of analogy, when we return a perfectly good item of merchandise and the clerk asks, "Reason for return?" There is never a box for (1) "I don't like it anymore," or (2) "Changed my mind." The store assumes that if a product has been purchased and is in perfect condition,

you will keep it. Rightly or wrongly the employee of the 1990s makes a similar assumption, and courts may support it, too.

3. *The "public-policy" exception.* We have public-policy goals to promote a fair, well-functioning society. When a person initiates an activity or tries to ensure that public-policy goals are implemented, for example, by exposing an illegal activity (whistle-blowing), a retaliatory firing will not be tolerated by many courts. This is because we want to chill intimidation by wrongdoers and encourage individuals to expose and weed out corruption.

## EMPLOYEES OR INDEPENDENT CONTRACTORS?

A recent survey by the General Accounting Office, which reports to the Internal Revenue Service (known to all of us as the IRS), estimates that the government loses $20 billion per year due to the misclassification of employees as independent contractors. As might be expected, this loss does not make the government happy. Consequently, the IRS has been looking more closely at how businesses are classifying their employees—and you could face a stiff fine if you've made a mistake.

### How to Avoid a Misclassification Disaster: Defining the Independent Contractor

If you are unsure whether a person working for you falls into the category of employee, look for these key characteristics determined by the IRS, which distinguish an employee from an independent contractor:

- Must follow your instructions about when, how, and where the work is to be done.
- Attends training sessions provided by the company.
- Does not subcontract work to other individuals.
- Works full time, primarily on the company premises.
- Prepares oral or written reports at the employer's request.
- Is paid on a preset periodic basis, as opposed to straight commission or a one-time fee.
- Uses tools and materials provided by the employer for the work done.
- Is directly affected by the overall financial stability of the company.

- Can be discharged at will by the employer, and has a right to quit at will.

## The Pros and Cons of Hiring Employees versus Independent Contractors

Both independent contractors and full-time employees have their advantages. Small business owners can save on a number of costs by hiring independent contractors, including Social Security tax (FICA), unemployment tax (FUTA), workers' compensation insurance, health insurance, and other benefits that are legal requirements for full-time employees on your payroll. Not to mention the time investment to file the necessary IRS paperwork and keep proper records (see Chapter 10 on taxes).

On the other hand, if you can afford to hire full-time employees, including an office manager or bookkeeper to handle the paperwork, there are significant advantages. The biggest, and most obvious, advantage of employees is that they work only for you. Therefore, there are no worries about competing with other companies for the time and attention of a contractor who is in demand (competent, skilled, has a good reputation).

The other major advantage of employees over contractors is control. Employees are legally bound to do what you want, and they can learn to do it your way, a boon for consistency, smooth transitions, and a cooperative environment. Employees are usually better team players than independent contractors, who may be working for a number of businesses simultaneously, and have the legal right to get the work done in any manner they please.

---

### KNOW YOUR KEY TERMS

- *Employer.* You, if you have any people working for you and you are paying them wages or salaries.
- *Wages.* Compensation given to a hired person for services rendered, based on time worked or output of production.
- *Salary.* Instead of an hourly rate, the money one receives from an employer at a stated rate, usually by year or month.
- *Employees (according to the IRS).* Workers who perform services exclusively for you. They are responsible for doing the work

themselves, exactly to your specifications and under the supervision of your company. You can fire them, or they can quit, at will, according to the doctrine of at will employment.

- *Independent contractors (according to the IRS).* Workers who may offer their services to a variety of companies at any one time, work under a contract, hire assistants, and use their own facilities or equipment to get the job done. You can't fire them unless they don't meet the specifications of the contract.

- *Employment at will.* A common-law doctrine or concept that works two ways: The employee can quit at any time for any reason; and conversely, the employer has the right to terminate a worker's employment for any reason not wrongful (e.g., as long as discrimination isn't involved)—and there's the catch.

- *Employment contract.* An agreement between employer and employee providing the terms and conditions of employment. An employment contract can be written, oral, or implied. There are even provisions for an employment contract by default if none of the preceding are in place.

- *Wrongful-termination litigation.* A small business owner's worst nightmare, a lawsuit initiated by an employee alleging infringement of a right or breach of contract resulting in damages.

## BASIC LEGAL RESEARCH

- *Your Rights at Work,* by Darien A. McWhirter (John Wiley & Sons). Gives a good overview of your employees' rights from their standpoint.

- *Your Rights in the Workplace,* by Barbara Kate Repa (Nolo Press). Another book to give you a good overview from the employee's side of the fence.

- *The IRS Audit Manual.* Provides a detailed list of 20 factors to help you determine whether or not an individual qualifies as an employee.

- *The Bureau of National Affairs weekly Bulletin to Management and biweekly newsletter "Fair Employment Practices."* These two publications will keep you up to date on the state and federal employment laws and related issues that could affect your company. A subscription to both costs $200 annually. Call (800) 372-1033.

---

**KEY RESOURCES**

---

- *Equal Employment Opportunity Commission in Washington, DC.* The EEOC can provide you with more information about employment discrimination. Call their information and publication center: (800) 669-3362.

---

**COURT COACH® SUGGESTS**

---

1. *Consider contracting with an outside service to act as your personnel department.* Hiring and overseeing employee personnel needs can be a time-consuming process. If you plan on hiring more than several employees, but not an office manager, consider contracting with a service that specializes in personnel leasing. In effect, these contractors act as the personnel department for a number of small companies at the same time. There are two big advantages: You save management time and they do all the paperwork.

2. *Time-share staff jobs.* By accruing employees to share a position, you can often attract superior workers with excellent skills, education, and experience who have other commitments, particularly to family.

3. *Allow partners and associates to work a 30-hour or 3-day week, instead of the standard 40-hours in 5-days, and pay at the same rate as formerly, but a decreased percentage.* These workers focus on the tasks that need to be done, not just on punching the clock, and will often work on their own time at home. You offer them job security and an opportunity to keep their hand in until they can return full time, and you won't have to rehire and retrain for that position.

4. *Get more/give less. Always "get" as much information as you can in any given situation, and "give" as little as possible.* This is the kind of legal tactic that good, smart lawyers and negotiators use constantly—much to the chagrin of their opposing party. If you learn this one tactic, you will have benefitted yourself ten times over the purchase price of this book. (But it takes practice—try it on your kids or spouse!)

5. *You already know that the best defense is a good offense.* Your best defense against discrimination in hiring and wrongful-termination charges is being aware of the legal rules of the

road, your rights and liabilities, and the employee or job applicant's rights.

6. *Use the following broad definition of trade secrets, and protect all of yours.* A trade secret is *anything* tangible you have that the other guy doesn't have—a formula, pattern, device, plan or process, tool, or mechanism—which gives you an opportunity to obtain advantage over competitors who do not know or use it. It's your secret formula known only to you and to those employees in whom it is necessary to confide. Treat it with care and concern—it's your baby!

7. *Consider having an employment lawyer give your interview questions for potential employees the once-over as well as critiquing your exit interviews.* Considering the EEOC's stringent new guidelines for protecting the rights of the mentally and physically disabled, this would be an extremely wise and proactive move to keep yourself trouble free.

# 12

# YOUR LEGAL RESPONSIBILITIES TO YOUR EMPLOYEES

## LEGALIZING YOUR COMPANY POLICIES

The goal of this chapter is *not* to provide step-by-step directions on how to write an employee policy handbook. Rather, we want to acquaint you with sensitive areas of federal employment law that you need to address in thinking through and devising your company's policies. Each state also has its own employment laws (see Basic Legal Research and Key Resources at the end of this chapter for help in researching these laws). So, be sure and also contact your state's labor department to make sure you've covered your bases in complying with state law.

## THE EMPLOYEE POLICY HANDBOOK: CLARITY AS A LITIGATION ROADBLOCK

More and more employers are learning the hard way that a sexual harassment or age discrimination suit can sink a business of any size by destroying its reputation and bank account. Discrimination claims have risen sharply in recent years. In 1993, some 270,000 allegations were filed with the U.S. Equal Employment Opportunity Commission

(EEOC), by 150,000 complainants. The number of complainants, up from 125,000 in 1992 and 110,000 in 1990, is expected to continue rising.

Employee relations are becoming increasingly complex, and even the smallest businesses with only one employee should consider outlining exactly what corporate culture that employee can expect to encounter. The handbook should cover policies regarding:

- Job descriptions.
- Promotions and salary reviews.
- Benefits.
- Holidays, sick leave, vacation time.
- Grounds for dismissal.
- Hearing policies and reporting procedures.

An employee policy handbook, by spelling out the company rules for employees, can be a roadblock to litigation. In many states, it can be used legally as evidence of an implied contract guaranteeing certain benefits and creating certain responsibilities by the employer and rights for the workers. The lesson here is: Be careful not to make any promises about the working conditions or terms of employment unless you're 100 percent sure you can keep them, because just by accepting your offer of employment, an employee may be entitled to these conditions and benefits.

## LEGAL REQUIREMENTS: THE BASICS

Before you begin to formulate company policies regarding what you expect from employees during business hours and what they can expect to receive in return, you need to become familiar with what the government expects from you as an employer. First, you need to understand how federal and state laws applicable to employment issues work in relationship to each other, and as they apply to you.

Then you can decide how you want to meet these basic requirements and still attract first-rate employees who are satisfied with benefits, while maintaining your profit margins.

### Wages and Hours: The Fair Labor Standards Act

Your employee policy handbook should clearly outline the following:

- The hours your business operates and that employees will be expected to be on the premises.

- Wages and bonuses.
- Employee incentive programs.
- Any policy regarding overtime pay.

The Fair Labor Standards Act (FLSA) states the federal government's guidelines for what constitutes fair payment for a day's work—and, for that matter, what constitutes a day's work. The FLSA covers all employers whose annual sales total $500,000 or more, or who are engaged in interstate commerce. The exception to the preceding is an unincorporated family business that comprises only family members.

The FLSA, passed in 1938 to squelch the horrendous labor practices born during the depression, has been continuously amended and revised. As a result, this is one of the most complicated employment laws that you'll need to contend with. The major areas covered include:

- The right to overtime pay, one-and-a-half times the regular rate, for any hours exceeding a 40-hour workweek (for exemptions, see following section).
- Federal minimum wage standards (each state also has a minimum wage requirement, which may be higher than the federal standard).
- Equal pay for equal work for men and women.
- Restrictions on child labor (under 18 years of age).

## Employees Who Are Exempt from the FLSA

Employees in a number of categories qualify for immunity from the FLSA requirements, such as overtime pay. The most common exemption claimed is the "white-collar" exemption, defined as follows: "Anyone employed in a bona fide professional, executive, or administrative capacity who earns a minimum of $250 per week on a salaried basis." Sounds simple enough, but wait, there's more.

While many businesses include any salaried employee in the white-collar exemption category, you need to examine the employee's duties as well because the Labor Department does. In fact, a number of states are aggressively cracking down on businesses that mistakenly include employees in the white-collar exemption category when their duties may disqualify them.

To qualify as an exempt executive, the employee must:

- Be primarily responsible for managing others, and direct the work of two or more people.
- Have the authority to hire and fire other employees, or to order such hiring and firing.

- Devote no more than 20 percent of work time to other nonmanagerial tasks. Certain retail and service companies are allowed 40 percent of nonmanagerial time.

Administrative and professional employees have similar requirements, but the definitions change slightly with salary level. If the weekly salary exceeds a certain level, fewer requirements are mandated. As you can see, you need to check this out initially, and as you expand.

## Health and Safety (OSHA Requirements)

The federal Occupational Safety and Health Act (OSHA) obligates employers to "furnish a place of employment free from recognized hazards causing or likely to cause death or serious physical harm." In other words, if you know a potentially hazardous condition exists, fix it or face the possibility of a fine if an OSHA inspector from the federal or state department of labor stops by for a spot check.

How does the state enter the picture? In reality, small businesses rarely are graced with a visit from an OSHA inspector because there aren't enough of them to regulate every place of business. And workplaces with 10 or fewer employees are exempt from safety inspections unless they fall in a high-risk safety category. OSHA publishes minimum standards for each industry, as well as a self-inspection checklist.

It's wise to keep your place of business's health and safety conditions up to snuff to lessen the chances of a lawsuit brought on by an employer or customer. If your business deals with producing or handling food, the employee policy handbook should cover sanitation guidelines that comply with both the federal OSHA statute, as well as state OSHA laws if your state has them.

## Federal Nondiscrimination Laws: Title VII

As we discussed in Chapter 11, it's illegal to refuse to hire or terminate employment on the basis of race, skin color, gender, religious beliefs, national origin, physical handicap, age, sexual preference, or marital status. Most of these biases are covered under Title VII of the federal Civil Rights Act of 1964, which created the Equal Employment Opportunity Commission (EEOC) to oversee the workplace standards set in the act (for a list of unlawful practices covered by Title VII, see Appendix G).

And while Title VII made employment discrimination on the basis of sex illegal in 1964, only recently has sexual harassment in the workplace been recognized as a form of sexual discrimination. We're sure you've noticed that it has become an increasingly common employee accusation and the root of many headline-grabbing lawsuits nationwide.

Your employee policy handbook should clearly express your strong disapproval of any form of sexual harassment, as well as procedures for reporting grievances and sanctions that will be issued within the company for any well-founded complaints. It wouldn't hurt to include the EEOC's official regulations and guidelines on the subject of sexual harassment. You can acquire these guidelines by calling the national office of the EEOC: (800) 669-3362, or contact your local EEOC chapter.

## Other Federal Nondiscrimination Laws

Sexual harassment isn't the only form of discrimination suit that is gaining speed these days—from the well-founded to the bizarre. Consider the lawsuit that a former Chemical Bank employee filed on being fired for poor hygiene habits. Not only was her appearance habitually unkempt, maintained Chemical Bank, but she emitted an odor that offended both coworkers and customers.

After several warnings to lather up more regularly or risk termination of her position, the latter occurred. The former employee maintained that she had a skin condition that forbade her from bathing more than once a week and sued Chemical Bank for somewhere in the range of $1 million for emotional damages due to discrimination. The charges were dismissed, but nonetheless, this type of case brought against a small business owner could result in weeks tied up in court and thousands of dollars worth of attorney fees.

Then there's the case of the former cafeteria manager at the Smithsonian Institution's National Museum of American History who filed a human rights lawsuit because his boss had addressed him as an "old fart." The boss in question maintained that the plaintiff brought the offending nickname on himself by referring to himself as an "old-timer" who belonged to the "old school." But the jury thought otherwise, and awarded the plaintiff $400,000. This is a prime illustration of three Court Coach® adages to remember about office "jokes":

1. One person's joke is another person's offensive comment.
2. It's OK for me to joke about my weight (skin color, sexuality, age, etc.), but if *you* make a similar joke it may be the basis for a lawsuit.
3. When in doubt, don't.

Since the passage of Title VII in 1964, a number of additional federal laws have been passed to address discrimination; you would be wise to take note of the following:

- *The Pregnancy Discrimination Act of 1978* prohibits discrimination on the basis of pregnancy, childbirth, or related medical conditions.
- *The Age Discrimination in Employment Act*, enacted in 1967, prohibits discrimination against people 40 to 70 years of age.
- *The Americans with Disabilities Act*, enacted in 1990, prohibits employers with 15 or more employees to deny employment to job applicants with disabilities. As the result of a July 1994 amendment, you must also accommodate any disabilities of employees.
- *The Labor Relations Act*, with its various amendments, makes it illegal to discriminate against workers for belonging or refusing to belong to a labor union.

## EMPLOYEE BENEFITS: THE LEGAL REQUIREMENTS AND BEYOND

While employee benefits such as health insurance, private pension plans, and a family leave policy aren't legally required for small businesses unless your business meets certain criteria, most job seekers worth their salt consider them mandatory criteria for accepting a long-term career position at a small company. As a small business owner, every employee you hire is an essential worker and thus a key element in the success or failure of your business. For this reason, you need to be able to offer your workers an attractive benefits package up to par when compared with other businesses in your industry.

When thinking about providing more than you need to, you might be motivated by the knowledge that the pool of trained, able workers is shrinking due to significantly lower birth rates; and there's stiff competition to recruit and retain the cream of the crop at all levels of the workforce. Remember, too, loyalty is a fossil. The skilled workers of the 1990s have an acute sense of their value and won't hesitate to move around if they perceive that their employer is not meeting their personal, as well as professional, needs.

### Health Insurance

It is a very common misconception that health insurance is a legally required benefit for all full-time employees, paid for by the employer. In reality, federal law does not mandate company-sponsored health insurance, and only a few states have passed laws to that effect (e.g., Hawaii requires employers to provide coverage to employees earning more than a certain amount). In fact, more than eight million employed workers have no health insurance, and millions more are underinsured.

Providing health insurance is expensive—typically exceeding $3,500 per year for each employee—and many small business have been pruning their benefits as a cost-cutting measure. But the cost of not providing at least some form of health insurance plan may be quite high in itself. You may not be able to attract, or keep, a top-notch staff if your health insurance policy is inadequate, and in addition, a good employee without coverage who becomes ill or is in an accident may be forced to return to work unrecovered, or to quit and find a job with coverage. Depending on your budget, here are some options for shouldering some, or all, of your employees' health insurance premiums:

- Pay for a portion of the cost of health insurance premiums.
- Offer a "cafeteria style" of benefits, including health insurance, in which employees receive a lump sum of money to spend on benefits in any manner they please.
- Investigate group insurance plans and offer to pay for specific insurance that you can afford.
- Cover employees, but not their family members.

If you decide to offer health insurance, federal law requires you to offer (but not pay for necessarily) continued insurance coverage to former employees for up to 18 months following termination. This law, called by its acronym COBRA (Consolidated Omnibus Budget Reconciliation Act) covers all former employees who were enrolled in a company insurance plan, including spouses, except those that were fired due to gross misconduct.

## Workers' Compensation

In Chapter 6, we covered how to insure your company, including workers' compensation insurance, which protects your company against liability incurred by employee injuries on the job.

## Unemployment Insurance and Social Security Disability Insurance

These federal insurance programs for workers are paid for either partially or fully by taxes levied on employers (see Chapter 10 for more information on payroll taxes).

## Pension Plans/Welfare Plans

Private employers are not required by law to provide their workers with retirement plans. Additionally, those employers offering pension plans are not required to pay any minimum amount of money into the plan. However, employers who do offer a private pension plan must comply with the provisions of several federal laws, as stated by the Employee Retirement Income Security Act of 1974 (ERISA). Under ERISA, a pension plan does not have to include all workers, but it must spell out exactly who is eligible and be structured not to discriminate against certain classes of workers (older workers, women, minorities, or clerical workers as opposed to managers).

When offering a plan, employers must give employees several explanatory documents:

- A summary plan description, explaining the basics of how the plan operates.
- A summary annual report, outlining the plan's financial status and operations.
- Survivor coverage data, explaining how much the plan would pay to a surviving spouse in the case of the employee's death.

If you decide to do away with an existing pension plan, you must notify employees in writing at least 60 days before the plan ends. Welfare plans under ERISA, and almost all other types of employee benefit plans, are not considered pension plans. ERISA requirements are not as stingent for these, for example, health insurance and accidental death insurance plans.

## FAMILY-FRIENDLY POLICIES

Most small business entrepreneurs aren't required to comply with the federal Family and Medical Leave Act (FMLA) because it applies only to businesses employing more than 50 employees (some state FMLAs include businesses with more than 20 employees). Nonetheless, you should consider implementing family-friendly policies addressing child care and elder care to attract and keep valuable employees. Recent studies by the Families and Work Institute in New York, among others, consistently show that employees at family-friendly companies have more loyalty for their employer and are more productive on the job because of reduced stress.

At the very least, you should consider granting employees—men and women—the same 12 weeks of unpaid leave afforded under the FMLA for circumstances including the birth or adoption of a child, family health needs, or an employee's own health needs. Other inexpensive family-friendly benefits for small business owners include:

- *Flex-time work hours.* An alternative to a strict 9–5 regimen that allows parents to schedule appointments for their children before or after work, and take them to school or day care with less stress.
- *Taking vacation an hour at a time.* A number of companies are implementing this innovative policy that lets parents leave a few hours early to attend an occasional soccer game or otherwise spend some quality time with their family.
- *Part-time telecommuting.* With the aid of a fax machine, computer, and modem, many jobs can be structured so that the employee can spend one or more days a week working from home.
- *Information services.* This could range from a small library of videos, books, and pamphlets on parenting issues to a toll-free resource-and-referral counseling service if your budget allows.

## DEFINING YOUR EMPLOYEES' RIGHT TO PRIVACY

The issue of privacy involves a balancing of two rights—the employer's "right to know" versus the employee's right to privacy. Recently, the media has been focusing on this issue of privacy in the workplace regarding drug and alcohol use, AIDS testing, information regarding off-duty activities, and the extent and manner of record keeping. In Chapter 11, we briefly covered employees' rights to privacy in the context of hiring and termination, but this subject bears closer examination.

The basic rule of thumb is, whatever employees do on their own time that doesn't affect their job performance is "none of the employer's business"! The problem, however, is that there is not a bright-line test distinguishing a legitimate business concern about employees' off-duty behavior that might affect business performance and inquiries that constitute an invasion of employees' privacy. As a consequence, court decisions, and your own company decisions, must be made on a case-by-case basis, delicately balancing one interest against the other to reach a fair determination.

If you as employer suspect that an employees' off-duty behavior, which may cause you concern, manifests signs of addiction to drugs or excessive use of alcohol on a regular basis, you need to collect evidence to back up your suspicions before confronting the employee in question.

Addicts, as you may know, are quite adept at sidestepping the issue and often allege, "It's not a problem." Your evidence makes the problem a concrete reality, and your dialogue should inform the employee why it is a problem for you. Then issue a written warning, stating that if the behavior doesn't change, specific disciplinary actions will be taken (which should be outlined in the employee handbook).

As we stated in Chapter 11, mandatory AIDS testing is prohibited by law. Drug testing is allowed in certain circumstances, subject to the Drug-Free Workplace Act. If job safety is a consideration, or the employee will be dealing with confidential data (such as a secretary at the Pentagon), drug testing may be allowed.

---

## KNOW YOUR KEY TERMS

- *Employee policy handbook.* A manual defining the corporate culture of your company, as well as the obligations of the company and its employees.
- *Equal Employment Opportunity Commission (EEOC).* A federal government agency overseeing employee rights regarding discrimination in the workplace.
- *The Fair Labor Standards Act (FLSA).* Guidelines enacted by Congress establishing fair wages and hours.
- *The Occupational Safety and Health Act (OSHA).* Another federal law establishing safety and sanitation standards in the workplace.
- *Employee Retirement Income Security Act (ERISA).* Laws that outline the requirements for employer-sponsored pension plans.
- *Family and Medical Leave Acts.* State and federal laws with provisions that regulate time off for family and medical problems; they require companies with more than 50 employees (in some states, more than 20 employees) to allow employees 12 weeks of unpaid time off.

---

## BASIC LEGAL RESEARCH

- *Law in the Workplace* (American Bar Association). An overview of state and federal employment laws. Send $3 to ABA Public Education Division, 750 Lake Shore Drive, Chicago, IL 60611.
- *How to Comply with Federal Employee Laws,* by Sheldon I. London (London Publishing).

- *Fair Employment Practices Cases,* (Bureau of National Affairs). A compilation of legal cases pertaining to employment law that can be found in most any law library. It is a great reference for seeing how the courts have ruled on various employment issues in the past.

## KEY RESOURCES

- *U.S. Department of Labor.* Can provide you with a list of federal employment regulations. Call (202) 219-6666
- *Your state labor department.* Here's where you can find out what employment laws affect your business (check the government listings in the blue pages of your local telephone book).
- *Your state commission on human relations* (or human rights and opportunities) deals with discrimination complaints.
- *International Foundation of Employee Benefit Plans.* For pamphlets covering a variety of employee benefit issues, call (414) 786-6700.
- *Pension and Welfare Benefits Administration.* For more information about ERISA rules and pension plans, call (202) 254-7013.
- *The Pension Rights Center.* This organization can also provide additional information about pensions. Call (202) 296-3778.

## COURT COACH® SUGGESTS

1. *Include a disclaimer in your employee policy handbook, stating that the handbook is not a contract.* While the handbook outlines the general policies of the company, each employee should also have an individual employment contract that details that person's particular terms of employment.
2. *Put a date in the title of the employee policy handbook* (The 1995 John Doe Company Handbook), *and note the right to make changes in the future.* Any changes should be dated as well.
3. *Include a procedure in your employee policy handbook that covers grievances and disputes pertaining to material in the handbook.* Naturally, this procedure would not mention going to court. Mediation, arbitration, and negotiation are all options that are discussed in Chapter 13.
4. *Always have an attorney who specializes in employment law review your employee policy handbook, and consult with the attorney before making any changes in the handbook.* Employment law can be tricky business, as you've probably gathered from this chapter.

If you haven't yet grasped that truth, you will by the end of the next chapter!

5. *Considering the extent of drug and alcohol addiction in our time, it would be surprising if you did not occasionally encounter this problem with some employee.* Keep in mind that the addicted person needs help. You might want to have another compassionate person, a friend perhaps, speak with the employee. You could also consider an extended leave of absence. Point the addicted person in the direction of a 12-Step program, such as Alcoholics Anonymous or Narcotics Anonymous.

6. *Loyalty to your workers creates a faithful workforce that may see you through lean times.* And so it goes, what goes around comes around. If you are not happy with your employees' attitudes, discover the source of the problem. Chances are, that somewhere someone is disrupting the flow of the workplace. It's your job to weed that person out and deal with the problem effectively for the good of the entire workplace (even if the difficulty is having you as a boss!).

7. *You create the corporate culture most by your own mental attitude, as well as your actions.* Do not be in the position of the pot calling the kettle black on the premises at any time—not just during regular working hours. This means no drinking, gambling, or placing of bets (the Super Bowl pool may qualify as an exemption, however).

8. *It does not astonish women who have worked outside the home that 50 percent of them have experienced some form of sexual harassment.* Statistics like this and the larger-than-life television images of Clarence Thomas and Anita Hill have brought this illegal behavior in the workplace to the forefront. But what exactly constitutes sexual harassment, many people are wondering aloud these days?

   Legally, we have adopted two separate definitions of sexual harassment: (1) behavior that is sexually offensive and unwelcome, and (2) a hostile environment. Quite simply, it is offensive and unwelcome conduct characterized by unwanted sexual advances made in the context of an unequal power relationship.

   Treat all complaints seriously and *never* look the other way.

9. *Some more tricky EEOC guidelines.* Keep in mind that, according to the EEOC, an employer is responsible for its acts and those of its agents and supervisory employees. An employer may be responsible also for acts of nonemployees on the company premises (vendors, clients). Hence, the importance of your employee policy handbook.

# 13

## WHAT TO DO WHEN EMPLOYEE GRIEVANCES COME TO A HEAD

### EMPLOYMENT LITIGATION: LEGALIZED BLACKMAIL?

The American workforce of the 1990s has evolved into a global and cultural melting pot, as well as a hotbed for employment litigation. Employment litigation has risen by more than 2,200 percent over the past two decades and now accounts for an estimated one-fifth of all civil suits filed in U.S. courts. Employers and the legislature alike are struggling to defuse the wide range of red-alert buttons that can undermine a company's productivity and profits. This is crucial for small business owners, as legal defense costs in employment lawsuits can easily catapult into the $200,000 range.

The best remedy for employment litigation is avoidance, a pound of prevention and knowledge being worth at least two pounds of cure (see Chapters 11 and 12). But if you do wind up on the wrong end of an employment lawsuit—which can happen even to the most sensitive employer, due to lack of information or a bad apple employee—there are some strategies you can use to minimize the damages to your reputation and bank account.

Given our philosophy that information is power and knowledge is your best defense, this chapter will explain the most common types of employment litigation charges, how to avoid going to court, and what to expect if you do wind up in court. Although unions aren't as common as they used to be, we'll also cover how to deal with employee grievances brought before a union.

## TORTS VERSUS CRIMINAL ACTS

From the Latin *torquere,* "to twist," a tort is a private injury. A crime is a public wrong against society, tried before a grand jury or other criminal court with a judge and jury, for which the perpetrator must compensate society as a whole—usually by going to jail. The plaintiff in a criminal suit is the state on the behalf of the alleged victim, who is usually a witness. Most suits involving employees are "torts," as opposed to "criminal acts," although some employment litigation suits can fall into both categories.

A simple definition of a tort is that it is any wrong committed against a person by another person or organization. Because we as a society don't want employees going around injuring someone's reputation, job opportunities, or feelings, has established a remedy and a punishment, namely money damages, to make injured persons whole again, to put them back in the position they were in before the injury occurred. But, to recover a dollar amount, the victim must demonstrate that the "tortfeasor" (the bad guy) had a legal duty (alleged) to the plaintiff; that in some way, the defendant breached that duty; and that the victim was injured. The worse the injury, the higher the award can be.

Two main legal criteria separate criminal acts from torts: burden of proof and evidence. For a successful civil suit, a civil plaintiff needs only to prove to a judge or jury by a "preponderance of evidence," that he or she is entitled to the relief being asked for (such as back pay and job reinstated). That is, the judge or jury must find that the evidence favors the plaintiff over the defendant by this standard of proof. (*Note:* In some cases, the standard of proof can be "clear and convincing," a much higher standard of proof.)

While crimes are defined by statutory laws, passed by the legislature, torts are defined by common-law precedent. We will consider three torts that were defined in the twentieth century, primarily as a result of employment grievances: wrongful discharge from employment, infliction (intentional or negligent) of emotional distress, and invasion of privacy, as well as the torts of assault, battery, and defamation.

For a criminal prosecution, the defendant must be proven guilty by proof "beyond a reasonable doubt."

## Common Employee Grievances That (Might!) Qualify as Torts

Most employee grievances that escalate into litigation suits arise from intentional acts against a person, or "interference with the person." Here are some common examples of behaviors in the workplace that qualify as torts and are tried in civil court.

### Wrongful Discharge
This refers to any discharge that violates a public policy such as an employee's civil right against discrimination based on sex, race, or age. Under the doctrine of employment at will (I work for you as long as I want and you work for me as long as I want), you can fire an employee; you just can't fire anyone wrongfully (for the wrong reason).

### Assault
These are physical actions, such as raising fists or wielding a weapon, that creates apprehension or fear of a battery. An employee must have the impression of immediate harm to his or her body. Do not lose your cool and menace or threaten a worker with physical injury, ever.

### Battery
Any unlawful intentional touching—actual contact with the employee—constitutes battery. You cannot pat your secretary's body, even as a "joke."

### Defamation
You may not spread untrue rumors or otherwise communicate falsehoods about an employee that harm his or her reputation. You might be accused of defamation by giving a terrible reference to a potential new employee.

### Intentional Infliction of Mental Distress
This is intolerable and offensive behavior done "on purpose" that results in the disturbance of the employee's emotional well-being. The employee is upset, but you didn't really mean it and you should have known better.

### Invasion of Privacy
To infringe on an employee's right to keep a private life private in the workplace, it must be shown that there has been (1) the public dis-

closure of a private fact, (2) the publication of information placing a person in a false light, or (3) an intentional intrusion on a person's private life; and there must be harm to the employee as a "person" of ordinary sensibilities: mental suffering, shame, or humiliation (see Chapter 12).

## FEP: The States Have a "Say" about Fair Practice and the Common Law of Torts

On a state-by-state basis, fair employment practices (FEP) statutes or laws have been passed. Some are strong and may be an extremely effective tool for an employee challenging any number of employment practices, including sexual harassment. Note, however, a few states have no FEP laws. Most importantly, some states allow money damages; some do not.

If your state has no allowance for an award of money damages, an employee can still proceed under the Federal Civil Rights Act, except, of course, if you have a company with fewer than fifteen people. When that Act does not apply, your aggrieved employee can still sue under a variety of common-law tort theories in state court.

As an employer, your best defense to avoid a high-figure tort judgment is (1) hire a lawyer and (2) argue that the states' Workers' Compensation law should apply. This law allows recovery only for physical injuries, not emotional injuries.

## The Double Whammy: When Employee Grievances Qualify as a Tort and Criminal Offense

Some employee grievances qualify as both a tort and a criminal act if Congress or your state legislature has deemed that the offense is great enough to pass a law forbidding it. Usually state governments take their cue from Congress, and after the passage of a federal law, individual state legislatures follow suit.

Federal antidiscrimination laws are covered extensively in Chapter 11, but it's worth noting again the four federal laws that have generated most of the glut of employment litigation in the courts today:

1. *Title VII of the Civil Rights Act of 1964.* Prohibits discrimination on the basis of race, religion, sex, or national origin.
2. *The Age Discrimination in Employment Act of 1967.* Protects workers who are at least 40 years old from discrimination.
3. *The Americans with Disabilities Act.* Outlaws discrimination against people who are disabled, including the obese.

4. *The Civil Rights Law amendments, enacted November 1991.* Provides that employees claiming discrimination based on Title VII (including religion, sex, and sexual harassment) or the Americans with Disabilities Act can receive punitive damages between $50,000 and $300,000, depending on the employer's size. Although this law was passed with the best of intentions, it has resulted in what some legal experts call a litigation gold rush by disgruntled employees who feel they have nothing to lose.

## EMPLOYEE GRIEVANCES AND LABOR UNIONS

The federal National Labor Relations Act (NLRA), passed in 1935, established labor unions as employee champions against the often unfair whims and unjust demands of management. During the next 25-plus years, roughly a third of the workforce belonged to powerful labor unions and relied on the union steward to present any grievances to management. But union membership began to wane in the late 1950s as political corruption within the ranks and unfair union practices came to light. The passage of the Equal Pay Act in 1963 marked the beginning of a crusade by Congress to expand employee rights under federal law. In effect, the courts have taken over much of what used to be covered by union grievance procedures.

As a small business owner, you probably won't be dealing with any labor unions, but the NLRA is nonetheless a law you may need to contend with. Employees can sue employers, as well as unions, for violations of the NLRA. The basic components of the NLRA that may affect small business owners are:

- An employer may not interfere with or restrain employees who are exercising their rights to organize a labor union, bargain collectively, and engage in other concerted activities for their own protection.
- An employer may not encourage or discourage membership in a labor union by hiring and termination policies, or employment conditions that discriminate.
- An employer may not discriminate against employees who have filed charges or testified under the NLRA.
- An employer must negotiate fairly with the union that represents its employees.

If you must resolve an employee grievance with a labor union, the local chapter of the National Labor Relations Board (NLRB) will need to get involved. Your local NLRB can help resolve any union-related problems that require an investigation and hearing.

## AFTER CHARGES HAVE BEEN FILED: DAMAGE CONTROL

As we learned in Chapter 11, the best way to avoid a standoff in court with an employee is to outline your company policies and procedures in an employee policy handbook that is required reading for all new staff. But what can you do after the damage has already been done, or is perceived to have been done, and an employee files a lawsuit? Fear not, an expensive litigation trial is not necessarily the only way to proceed. Three viable alternatives for employee disputes are negotiating a settlement out of court, mediation, and arbitration.

## NEGOTIATING A SETTLEMENT

If you act on your own, an excellent tactic is to find out from the local courthouse clerk how long it is taking your court to put this kind of lawsuit on the docket. It could be years! And even though you may have done nothing wrong, when you factor in the time value of money and ongoing worry, you may decide to make a money settlement to make a lawsuit go away. On the other hand, you may have a high tolerance for this stress or great confidence in your position, and feel more comfortable just hanging out and waiting for time to dissipate animosity and work in your favor.

Negotiating a settlement out of court is always cheaper, and usually less adversarial, than relying on a judge or arbitrator to make a decision for you. Keep in mind, though, that the nature of discrimination and other employment litigation charges is extremely volatile. Chances are good that an employee who has reached the point of filing charges against you is not going to be willing to sit down and have a chat about the abuse the person perceives as having occurred. Perhaps, though, your attorney and the plaintiff's attorney could negotiate a settlement and avoid the publicity, added expense, and time delay that comes with a day in court.

Never "finalize" a settlement without attorney advice since you may not know how to finalize a settlement so that it is really put to rest once and for all.

Let's say, for example, that Sally Secretary accuses you of firing her because she is a woman. In fact, you fired her because she couldn't type. A typing test, with an unbiased witness presiding, reveals that

Sally types only 23 words per minute. This is slightly off from the 85 words per minute cited on Sally's resume, so the two of you agree that she has been let go for due cause. End of case, you can return to running your business—right?

Wrong. You must draft a document (or several documents) for the grievant's signature to truly finalize this case and make sure it doesn't come back to haunt you (see Figure 13–1 for sample document). This document should include:

- A release clause, stating that you are free from any legal obligation to pay damages for the job termination.
- A disclaimer of wrongdoing on your part as an employer.
- A nondisclosure and noncompete agreement.

Now, you can get back to running your business, fully confident that Sally and her discrimination suit are out of your life forever.

You also need attorney advice to finalize a settlement. You need to draft and execute a general release for the grievant's signature, and possibly a disclaimer of wrongdoing and nondisclosure agreement to put this to rest for once and for all. And there are other concessions that can be negotiated.

## Mediation

Mediation is the process in which a neutral third party, usually an attorney or professional employee relations mediator, is hired to help the disputants negotiate. This can be a useful method of separating the emotions in a situation from the facts. Many workplace disputes have more than one side, and the mediator sits everyone down and makes sure that all sides are heard. For example, one man's "innocent" dirty joke may sound like sexual harassment to his female coworker, even if the intent wasn't there. The mediator puts all versions of the problem on the table and, in a perfect situation, helps find a solution that's acceptable to both parties—without going to court.

The real beauty of mediation is that you are not bound to accept the mediator's recommendations. In other words: It couldn't hurt to try it. Even if no solution can be reached without the help of a judge, mediation can still be a good idea as a precursor to court. Everyone goes to court with a clearer idea of what the other person believes happened—or what story they'll tell in court—as well as what outcomes the other parties hope for.

Your local small business association or bar association may be able to provide you with a mediator; or you can look in the yellow

**Figure 13–1** Sample Negotiation Contract for Dismissal of
Discrimination Charges

This contract for dismissal of discrimination charges against __(name of company, or individual being sued)__ , is made between __(name of ex-employer)__ ("The Company") and __(name of ex-employee)__ ("The Plaintiff") on __(date)__ .

The terms of this contract are as follows:

1. The Plaintiff hereby drops all charges of discrimination against the Company, and any employees of the Company.

2. The Plaintiff hereby agrees to all terms of unemployment compensation outlined in the termination of employment contract, and will not seek further compensation from the Company.

3. The Plaintiff hereby agrees that the Company, or any employees of the Company, are not guilty of any acts of discrimination against the Plaintiff during his/her time of employment with the Company.

4. The Plaintiff, as an ex-employee of __(company name)__ hereby promises to keep the Company's business secrets, including but not limited to customer, supplier, logistical, financial, research, and development information, confidential and not to disclose the Company's business secrets to any third party after the term of employment.

5. The Plaintiff hereby promises not to gain employment with any competing company, or compete for __(company name)__'s clients for a period of one year after termination of employment.

6. The Plaintiff acknowledges ample opportunity and advice to take independent legal advice in connection with the execution of this agreement.

7. This agreement is governed by the laws of the State of _____ .

The undersigned agree to the terms of this contract on __(date)__ ,

(signature of Employer)
(name of Employer, typed)

(signature of Plaintiff)
(name of Plaintiff, typed)

pages under "mediators" (this is becoming a big business). You can also call several national mediation services (see Appendix E).

## Arbitration

Arbitration is similar to mediation in that a third party is brought in to hear each disputant's view of the circumstances surrounding a case, but the resemblance ends there. Arbitration does not have the "meeting of minds" aspect that mediation has. When two feuding factions decide to take their case before an arbitrator (usually a retired judge or attorney), they also agree to accept the arbitrator's judgment as a legal decree—whether both parties like it or not. Arbitration is usually much less expensive and time consuming than litigation. There's also the added attraction that, unlike a trial, arbitration proceedings are private and not open to public scrutiny.

The American Arbitration Association is a good place to start looking for an arbitrator (see Key Resources at end of chapter).

## WHAT TO DO WHEN LITIGATION IS IMMINENT

If the worst-case scenario comes to pass and find yourself facing a court date, it's time to read Chapter 17, which covers representing yourself in court and working with an attorney in various capacities.

---

### KNOW YOUR KEY TERMS

- *Crime.* This is a public wrong prosecuted by the government, for which the law provides punishment or recompense to society.
- *Misdemeanor.* Like a crime, it is an offense against the state or federal government. In common parlance, it refers to something of a less serious nature carrying a lighter punishment.
- *Tort.* This is a private, or civil, injustice committed by one person or organization against another person or individual's property, for which the individual may be compensated in money damages.
- *Negligence.* This legal deficiency results when a person fails to exercise such care as a reasonably prudent person would exercise in similar circumstances. It could be characterized as inadvertent or thoughtless.

- *Burden of proof.* Whoever has the "burden" must establish by evidence a requisite degree of belief. The degree of belief required in a criminal suit must be "beyond a reasonable doubt," and in a civil suit one must convince the trier of facts by "a preponderance of evidence."
- *Evidence.* If you can see it, smell it, hear it, taste it, touch it, it's evidence. Or, it can be proof in the form of witness testimony, documents, or objects used in court to induce belief in the mind of the court or jury.
- *Common versus statutory law.* As distinguished from the statutory law established by an elected legislative body, Congress, or your state's equivalent, common law is the law flowing from court decisions of general or universal application.
- *Eggshell skull theory.* This is one of our favorite legal theories, which you can apply to life as well as to legal matters. So, what is this tort idea? It means you must take your victim as you find the victim, with a thick skull or an eggshell-thin skull.

## BASIC LEGAL RESEARCH

- *Index to Periodicals of Law.* Found in any law library, this index lists all the laws currently on the books. This is a good source if you want to include the actual discrimination laws in your employee policy handbook.
- *Sexual Harassment,* by Joel Friedman, Marcia M. Baumil, and Barbara E. Taylor (Health Communications, Deerfield Beach, Florida). This book will give you a very good background on what the law views as sexual harassment.
- *Getting Past No: Negotiating With Difficult People,* by William Ury (Bantam Books). This is a good guide to the basics of negotiating.

## KEY RESOURCES

- *The American Federation of Labor and Congress of Industrial Organizations (AFL-CIO).* For prounion information, call (202) 637-5000.
- *The National Right to Work Committee.* For antiunion information, call (703) 321-9820.
- *The American Arbitration Association.* The main office is in New York City; call (212) 484-4000. There are regional offices in more than 30 cities nationwide (see Appendix F).

---

**COURT COACH® SUGGESTS**

---

1. *Nip all potential lawsuits in the bud.* Whether you are right, wrong, or indifferent, you do not want to set a precedent for other employees to follow, whether you settle before trial or go the distance.

2. *When an employee comes to you with a complaint about harassment or other forms of discrimination, utilize your most effective tools for avoiding litigation:*

   Listen to the employee grievance.

   Treat the employee with respect.

   Ask the employee what relief he or she is seeking.

   Give the employee's request careful and thoughtful consideration; refer employee to proper procedures.

   If necessary, consult with others for more objective perspectives.

   Respond promptly (as in immediately) before the employee spreads personal discontent throughout the work environment, gathers support, and works up a full head of steam that no amount of reason will defuse.

3. *Know how to recognize sexual harassment when you see it, and make sure you're not a participant.* See Chapter 12 for more on this timely issue being discussed at office water coolers, movie theaters, parties, and in courtrooms across the United States (see Appendix G for a list of unlawful employment practices that the EEOC enforces, including sexual harassment).

# 14

# THE OTHER SIDE
# OF THE FENCE:
# YOUR RIGHTS AS
# AN EMPLOYER

## RELAX, YOU HAVE SOME RIGHTS TOO!

After reading Chapters 10 through 13, which focus on how the law protects employees, you, as an SBO may now feel overwhelmed by the tough line the law expects you to hew as a responsible business owner. You may also feel a tinge of vexation accompanied by the gut reaction: "Hey, what about me? I'm doing all the worrying and risking my money, don't I have any rights?" Reassuringly, the answer to that question is "Yes, you do."

While we touch on your rights as a vendor and customer in Chapters 1 and 16, you'll be pleased to discover that you also have rights as an employer.

Your basic right as an employer is contractual—performance by your employees for payment by you. Flowing from that right is the right you also have to hire and to fire, based on standards of performance. You also have a right to set the standards of performance for your workplace and to monitor employees to make sure they are living up to these standards. Finally, you have the right to determine pay scales and whether or not to offer additional benefits. Read on as we examine these rights, and what you can do when they are violated.

## CONVEY YOUR EXPECTATIONS (OR TERMS OF EMPLOYMENT) CLEARLY TO EMPLOYEES

In the employer-employee relationship, it is the employer who has the right to establish guidelines called "terms of employment." These can be carefully outlined in an employee policy handbook (see Chapter 11). As long as you spell out the rules and consequences in advance by giving adequate notice, failure to comply with these terms can, and should, be grounds for termination.

### The Employment Policy Handbook Revisited: Doing It Your Way

You should consider incorporating the following terms of employment into your company's policy.

**Honesty**
It would seem unnecessary to state in written form that you expect honesty in all dealings, a statement that seems like a no-brainer, but you do. A statement that honesty must be maintained in all relationships among employees, between employer and employees as well as in all business-related activities, suffices.

The computerized office has certainly increased the opportunities for dishonesty. If it comes to light that an employee has knowingly tampered with information in your company's computerized files, for example, take the following steps:

1. Check all available forms of information (files, telephone logs, computer hard drives, and disks) that may document the irregularity.
2. Interview any and all related personnel who might have knowledge or responsibility. It is difficult to vigilantly monitor your employees.
3. Give the employee an opportunity to be heard in a manner that meets due process requirements.

In sum, you are not only within your rights, you must protect yourself and your business and your other employees by investigating all avenues of wrongdoing immediately and with the thoroughness of a police detective.

## Due Process Procedures

And, oh by the way, what is due process? Later in this chapter, we will explain what to do when your rights as an employer are violated. In the meantime, include the ways in which employee/employer grievances are to be dealt with; who to contact, how, when and where, with time parameters delineated.

## Well-Defined Performance Standards

Small business owners frequently assume that employees know exactly what their duties are when, in fact, work boundaries and expectations are unclear. You need to spell out in no uncertain terms, in writing, what your expectations are for each job and that failure to comply with these objectives is grounds for discipline or even termination. If clear performance expectations have never been established, verbally and in writing, disciplining or firing an employee for subpar performance becomes almost indefensible in a court of law because there are no benchmarks against which to judge performance.

Case in point: In the recent case of *Burrill* v. *GTE Government Systems Corp.*, reported in the May–June 1994 issue of *Business Horizons*, plaintiff Burrill was hired as the manager of GTE's Colorado facility to solve a series of problems. The crux of the problem was that Burrill was not given an explicit job description laying out his duties. When he was subsequently terminated because of alleged poor performance, he filed a wrongful discharge suit against the company. Although GTE moved that case should be dismissed, the judge ordered it to go to trial based on the fact that Burrill never received a written description of his duties.

Now, we know you aren't GTE, but even in a tiny company taking a few minutes to draft a job description that lists the parameters of responsibility is a matter of self-preservation. This need not be an elaborate document, just simple and straightforward. In actuality, you should take this step before you even advertise for a position opening up at your company—and certainly before the interview process begins. Writing a job description will force you to clarify your own thinking about what skills the job requires, and what you need personally from the worker because every business has its own unique needs.

## Adherence to the Rules

All company policies outlined in the employee policy handbook must be followed. While there are plausible reasons to create exceptions to almost any rule, the rules outlined in the employee policy handbook should be adhered to strictly. One problem in not following through is that the inactivity on your part about requiring compliance can be seen as a waiver of your rights. Even if you have only one employee, you must act immediately on any employee failure. If, to achieve your profit margin, each employee must bill six hours a day to clients, an employee who hands in a time sheet with only four hours of billable time per day needs to be told!

## Alcohol and Drug Use and Abuse

While schoolchildren are taught that alcohol is a drug, as a society, we still accept alcohol abuse more regularly than drug abuse. Many an employer has a bottle of hard liquor in the desk drawer to offer a client, or just to have a "pop" at the end of the day. And it's perfectly acceptable for many employees, especially in the trades, to have a beer on-site at lunchtime with their sandwiches. It's our opinion that no alcohol should be consumed in a work environment, either during or after working hours. And, what's good for the employees is also good for the boss (end of sermon).

Legally, there is no law that we know of forbidding a small business owner or employee from consuming alcohol in the workplace. But alcohol dulls the senses and could create a liability, an accident, or an assault or fight between employees, or a verbally abusive exchange between an employee and customer.

Impairment from drug or alcohol use could be a stated term for termination. But you don't want to have to exercise your right to terminate unnecessarily and lose a good worker. Consequently, you might also consider establishing standards or procedures for identifying and reporting an addiction or abuse problem and treatment options. Strict confidentiality standards are a must so that you don't step on your employee's privacy rights.

On a state level, workers' compensation claims are being denied for employees hurt on the job because they were drinking or taking drugs, and substance abusers may also lose their unemployment benefits. A number of industries have adopted self-policing drug abuse regulations, and in 1988, Congress passed the Drug-Free Workplace Act, requiring any company that does $25,000 in business with the government to show that it has a policy for keeping drugs off the premises. This law is now being replicated at the state level.

## Smoking

Whether you are a smoker or a nonsmoker, you need to accept the reality that you may have employees from both camps. Keep in mind that while it's perfectly legal to have an office policy saying that smoking isn't allowed inside the premises, it's also totally illegal not to hire prospective employees because they smoke. Therefore, perhaps a designated smoking area outside the building (or inside the building if your local and state government allow it at your kind of business establishment) is the answer.

### Search and Surveillance

Some businesses also reserve the right to search and use surveillance if employees are suspected of carrying drugs. Be sure and clarify your stance on these tactics in your policy handbook so that everyone knows what to expect. And remember the Constitution and the prohibition about unreasonableness.

## What to Expect from Employees beyond Your Legal Rights

The employee policy handbook would be a novel to rival the length of *War and Peace*, not to mention an insult to most people's intelligence and upbringing, if you included *every* mode of behavior acceptable and unacceptable in the workplace. Yet (and this is harder for some of us to believe than for others), there are many people who simply haven't grasped the nuances of proper office etiquette, not to mention social grace or grace under pressure. And there are others who simply never learned the nuances of treating others with common dignity and respect (this is no excuse!). In either case, you may have to tutor an employee in the fine art of office etiquette.

An employee's lack of experience, or family training, is not theoretically your problem. But in reality, when you hire an employee, you get the whole enchilada. This can be tough to handle delicately. More than one lawsuit has involved employer/employee conflict over body odor, loud obnoxious behavior, or inability to get along with others in the workplace—characteristics that may make an employee "unfit" personally despite being well qualified professionally.

Even if the following traits aren't spelled out in the employee policy manual, it is not off the norm to expect your employees to:

- *Dress appropriately.* This can mean something very different if you work at a factory that manufactures widgets rather than an advertising firm catering to Fortune 500 clients. Observant new employees will deduce the dress code from fellow employees, and especially from you as the boss. Friday dress-down day is a freebie bonus we support.
- *Speak with respect toward everybody—whether addressing the janitor, the letter carrier, or clients.* This is one of those common decency rules that everybody should have learned as a six-year-old.
- *Adhere to commonsense office social procedures.* Basically, from 8 to 5 (or whatever your office hours are) employees are being paid to do their job, not to engage in long social exchanges at the water cooler, make lengthy personal phone calls repeatedly,

or use the office computer and other equipment for personal business.

- *Maintain an acceptable level of personal hygiene.* You'll recall we mentioned in Chapter 15 that the court upheld Chemical Bank's decision to fire an employee whose lack of personal hygiene offended colleagues and customers. Although this is an extreme case, it illustrates that employers have a legal right to expect those working for them to demonstrate certain socially acceptable behavior or risk being let go.

## HOW TO PROCEED WHEN YOUR LEGAL RIGHTS AS AN EMPLOYER ARE VIOLATED

A bird's eye view of termination protocol was outlined in Chapter 11, but a quick review may be of benefit here. You are on steady ground if you can answer "yes" to the following four questions before you decide to end an employment relationship:

1. *Has the employee disregarded a company policy presented in the employee policy handbook or outlined in the employee contract . . . or verbally stated as office procedure?* We've covered this point extensively, but it bears repeating one more time: Write down all company policies in the employee policy handbook so that you are not left with the third alternative: "I told him so!"

2. *Is the record of the events leading up to termination documented and complete?* One of the most critical aspects of terminating an employee is documenting evidence of unsatisfactory job performance, the paper trail we defined at the outset. Every employee should have a file that includes job evaluation forms and any warnings about conduct, memos about projects that weren't carried out per your instructions, as well as any citations for jobs well done so that you can accurately weigh the value of the employee.

3. *Have you followed due process and company procedures for terminating employment?* Just as you expect employees to follow company rules for conduct on the job, so should you follow the procedural guidelines for terminating employment. These guidelines should be written down clearly in the employee policy handbook.

4. *Has the employee been made aware that the end is near?* This last point is, perhaps, the most important because the spark that ignites many wrongful-termination lawsuits is the sense of

injustice an employee feels when abruptly let go. You might think that the employee should know of your dissatisfaction, but denial is a rampant disfunction. In fact, the employee might assume that if you've never said anything (just made faces!), everything is fine. Remember: we don't want any surprises.

To avoid that element of surprise, consider issuing a clear notice of warning, designating rules of probation and a limited amount of time to correct an undesirable behavior before letting an employee go. Note on the warning that termination can occur at any time during the probation period and performance must remain satisfactory even after probation ends.

If the behavior continues, a notice of termination (the pink slip) may be in order. This written document serves two purposes:

1. It informs the employee of the exact reason for termination and clearly documents the course of events that led to your decision. It also states when the termination is effective and what benefits the ex-employee will or will not be eligible for (unemployment, health insurance for a given time, monetary compensation).

2. It serves as an important piece of evidence should a wrongful-termination suit be filed. The Court will be impressed that you took the time to spell out, and document to the employee, the reason for dismissal. This document will also serve to jog your memories about the events, as the case may not go to court for a number of months or, more likely, years.

A notice of termination, complete with clear documentation of the events that led up to your decision, may even deter a wrongful-termination suit. Although the ex-employee probably won't be any less angry about your decision, he or she may think twice about going up against you in court if you show your proof beforehand.

At this point, you may want to review Chapter 13, in case the employee contests the termination. If a day in court is looming in your future despite all your best efforts, turn to Chapters 17 and 18.

## YOUR RIGHT TO CREATE YOUR OWN UNIQUE WORK ENVIRONMENT

As the business owner and boss, you have the right to shape your work environment from employee dress code to fixtures and furnishings as you please, as long as what pleases you is not illegal or immoral.

Creating your space, your logo, your unique modus operandi is probably one of the most satisfying aspects of running a small business—so relax, have fun, and be creative!

## Let Your Fixtures and Furnishings Reflect Your Personality

If you are taking unfinished or "raw" space and starting from scratch, you need to check out and comply with a whole host of regulatory codes including environmental, health, safety, and building codes. Check these out with your town zoning, lawyer, commercial broker, leasing agent, and/or landlord. For example, in the Court Coach® offices, the building lease stipulated that the carpet had to be a commercial grade and fire retardant. (Luckily, a color available was a most exquisite shade of dark aqua.) It was also permissible to have a carpenter install wood molding instead of the commercial plastic molding, and the aesthetic result was legal as well as pleasing to the eye.

Once you get a handle on the regulatory guidelines of your interior design, let your imagination go—but not too wild! Remember, you want to have an office environment that's attractive to everyone who enters, and not all potential clients will share a passion for fuscia walls and day-glo orange carpeting.

## Safety Counts

Keep an eye out for safety too; anyone coming to your premises is a "business invitee" to whom you owe a limited duty to carry on activities with reasonable care for the person's safety. This is a negligence standard, a commonsense general duty to use reasonable care. Dangerous items for sale should be in locked cases. Ladders and other items that can fall on customers (which often seem to be the cause of injury) and thus the subject of lawsuits should be carefully monitored. Accidents can and do happen, but legal fault is only cognizable in the law where you acted negligently. Ask yourself, "Would a reasonable person place a fixture that is easily toppled in an area of heavy customer traffic?"

To limit your liability, give your business invitees notice by posting signs of potential sources of danger, such as the following:

- Very hot water. Use Caution.
- Not for use by children under the age of [supply age].
- Shopping carts tip easily. Use seatbelts for small children.

And when in an impromptu, ad hoc situation, like wet floors or ice on the sidewalk that might pose a danger, post a sign (even a hand-written note on a bathroom paper towel if necessary) to alert business invitees and your employees of danger.

And think carefully about whether you might be creating an *inherently* unsafe situation in your office or business. For example, are the tiles for the floor in your restaurant too slippery? Test them out before you invest big dollars only to find you have created a beautiful environment but unsafe condition. Always "person-proof" your environment, with an eye to safety beyond just compliance with building code standards.

## Uniforms: Don't Make Your Employees Wear Anything You Wouldn't

A vision that comes to mind is a coffee shop I frequented in college where the waitresses wore white uniforms that had been, obviously, shortened (poorly in most instances) to the point of skimpy. The young women's discomfort was so conspicuous that I asked one of them about it. The owner, she said, insisted that they shorten the uniforms at least a certain number of inches above the knee, and if they didn't like it, they didn't have to work there.

Today, with sexual harassment in the consciousness of most people, an employer might not be so bold, not to mention crude. Contrast that situation, however, with the Playboy bunnies with their fluffy cottontails and high heels or the Las Vegas showgirls? Would these "uniforms" pass the legality test as a known condition of employment? Ordinarily, the legal question here comes under public decency statutes and municipal and local ordinances. We could get into the whole topic of topless bars, but we are working under the assumption that not too many readers will be engaging in that business. Nonetheless, you would do well to think about all the laws and regulations affecting such an establishment and analyze your business and its liability in your particular line of business.

## Flexibility

Being a small business owner affords you the luxury of offering workers the benefits of flexibility—extras such as time off to pick up a sick child from school, attend traffic court for a speeding ticket, or avoid rush-hour traffic on a holiday weekend by leaving early. There's a real joy in having the right and the ability to make your workplace a more humane, nurturing environment. And there's a further reward in seeing your flexibility spill over into happy experiences in the office and more relaxed congenial workers.

On the other hand, there is the temptation to expect that you can make extra demands of your workers that aren't necessarily part of their job description. This could lead to legal claims against you as your employer rights do not extend to requiring workers to provide services for which they are not hired. Sometimes, too, the family atmosphere of a small business inadvertently blurs the boundaries between each person's job responsibilities in a manner not found in larger, less flexible businesses.

The CEO of IBM, for example, would not dare to ask the office manager to empty the trash or bring coffee to a client. But, neither will same CEO answer the phone when working late and expecting a call or run a package to Federal Express at 7:00 P.M. to make the next-day deadline. Guess who will also be working late and dashing? The secretary.

The Court Coach® philosophy on flexibility is that in a small office with few workers, the focus needs to be on *work product* while avoiding an unacceptable blurring of boundaries that may leave someone without a job description. In other words, it's a balance of rights. Everyone needs to be willing to bend a little to get the job done, but how much is "a little" and how much is "a lot"? Although the small business owner should be able to expect a little give on the part of his or her employees in return for a flexible office atmosphere, err on the side of caution in your expectations.

One obsessive nitpicker can poison this flexibility with a "it's not my job" attitude. And so, once again, we point out the importance of picking your office family with extreme care, an ounce of preventive thought being worth any number of pounds of cure. Everybody in a small business has a stake in the business's profitability, so employees that come in with a rigid mind-set about responsibility may not work out for you, the business owner.

Seek out flexible employees who are self-starters and task-oriented, whether it involves staying late or working weekends to prepare for an important presentation, or turning down the heat, or taking responsibility for something mundane like throwing the soda cans in the recycling bin.

Please, no prima donnas, female or male. Prima donnas have a strange domino effect on other employees and soon create an office atmosphere dominated by contentious finger-pointers whining, "Why me." The Court Coach® office policy, imparted at the initial job interview to all prospective employees, is "Leave your ego and your tiara at the door."

## A FINAL NOTE ON THE ONGOING DEBATE OVER YOUR RIGHT TO TERMINATE EMPLOYMENT

Many people think civil rights laws are meant to stop discrimination in hiring, and they are. But their practical effect is also to prevent discrimination in firing. Only about 5 percent of the approximately 1,000 calls per year fielded by the National Employment Lawyers Association relate to questions about hiring.

Many believe this trend by disgruntled ex-employees to file discrimination suits, sometimes without justifiable cause, is stacking the legal deck against employers and forcing them to hang onto unproductive or otherwise undesirable employees purely to avoid a legal battle. This is not the result intended by these laws.

Some people, such as celebrated legal theorist Richard Epstein of the University of Chicago, even call for the abolition of all civil rights laws as they apply to the private sector because these laws are evolving into something very much like a right of job tenure for those they seek to protect (see Chapter 11 for more on wrongful-termination litigation). Epstein argues that the pressures of competition and the need for talented employees would in itself make discrimination in the workplace disappear. After all, why would an employer fire a productive worker?

All that said, civil rights laws are symbols of the United States' traditional commitment to fairness and are not likely to be abolished. This means that employers need to be vigilant in protecting their own rights, a process that begins with knowing what those rights are, and how to protect them. As a start, you may want to read this chapter again and take good notes (for more information on terminating employees, see Chapter 11).

## MORE RIGHTS VIA THE FREEDOM OF INFORMATION ACT (FOIA) AND OTHER FEDERAL PUBLIC ACCESS/STATUTES

Even heads of large corporations can be reduced to Jell-O at the thought of wading through the red tape that's often required to obtain information from government agencies. Since a small business owner must deal with scads of government agencies for everything from zoning regulations to health and safety compliances, a working knowledge of how to use these powerful statutory tools may be helpful. When FOIA came along in 1966, the process was made easier. We hope to familiarize you with FOIA and other public access statutes, but this is by no means even a complete overview of the public access laws. It is simply a sampling to whet your appetite for knowledge (see Basic Legal Research and Key Resources in this chapter for further information).

The Freedom of Information Act (FOIA) 5 USC § 552 is one of three federal laws that were designed to give the public access to government information. In this chapter, we will focus most on FOIA and the federal Privacy Act (FOIA/PA) 5 USCA § 552a. The other federal public access laws passed subsequently are the Government in the Sunshine Act (1976), the so-called "open meeting law," and the Federal Advisory Committee Act (1972) which gives the public the right to attend Federal Advisory Committee Meetings.

Before FOIA was passed, the public was denied access to information and decisions, sometimes made behind closed doors by government agencies. But, John Q. Public still had to adhere to and comply with the results of those decisions. The Freedom of Information Act and the public access laws that followed it have changed this picture and brought government agencies out into the sunshine.

Public access laws give the public access to public records and individuals the right to examine their own personal records. FOIA (and FOIA/PA) applies only to the executive branch of the federal government and specifies that government agencies must publish the following information in the *Federal Register,* a huge compendium found in most major libraries and all law libraries:

- How the agency is organized.
- How the public can get information from the agency.
- Descriptions of agency functions.
- Formal and informal procedures that determine agency functions.
- Rules of agency procedures.
- Descriptions of agency forms, and where to get the forms.
- Agency instructions concerning the scope and contents of its papers, reports, or examinations.
- Agency rules for implementing federal laws.
- General agency policies that affect the public.

Most states and many municipalities have privacy and open records statutes of their own on the books. These may be quite different from the federal statutes, so check with your state's office of attorney general or secretary of state, or your city's corporation counsel.

The old adage "You catch a lot more flies with honey than with vinegar" is as true as it is trite—especially when dealing with the oft-harangued public servants working at government agencies. And not all agencies and officials are alike. Some are cooperative, and some find imaginative ways to avoid release of information. Keep asking.

---

## Know Your Key Terms

- *Employer.* The person who has control over what workers shall do and how.
- *Employee.* The person who performs the services at the direction of and under the control of the employer.
- *Independent contractor.* A person who works for another but is not under the direct supervision or control of the other in the physical performance of the work.
- *Title VII and other civil rights laws.* The laws that codify our civil rights and protect against discrimination based on sex, race, religion, age, or sexual preference (see Chapters 11 and 12 for more information on their impact on employer/employee relations).
- *Freedom of Information Act (FOIA, pronounced foy-yah), 5 USC § 552.* Legislation, passed in 1966, and significantly amended in 1974, that allows the public to access information held by any federal agency unless it comes within one of the specific categories of matters exempt from public disclosure. While both Congress and the federal courts are exempt from FOIA regulations, a limited common-law right to the public records of Congress and these courts still remains. Each state also has a state FOIA law.
- *Small Claims Court.* The lower state court that hears disputes involving small sums of money, the amounts of which are determined by each state individually (usually between $1,500 and $3,000). Ordinarily, the plaintiff and defendant in the dispute are heard before a judge, not a jury. Often, the parties represent themselves "pro se" or "pro per" (the same thing) and court procedures and rules of evidence are more relaxed (see Chapter 17, for more information).
- *Federal district court.* Where you and your employees will slug out any legal disputes pertaining to federal employment laws (see Chapter 18).

- *Paper trail.* An all-time favorite term and sometimes an obsession of most attorneys. Think of the trail in *Hansel and Gretel,* only instead of crumbs, visualize lots of documents, correspondence, and notes—paper substantiating and allowing you to find your way back to the beginning of a problem. Documenting every aspect of your history with employees and customers will help you immensely should you need to initiate action, defend yourself, or prosecute a claim. It may even help you to avoid court altogether because you have the goods. Thus, the paper trail is useful both as a sword and a shield.

- *Notice.* A key legal concept. To give notice is to let someone know ahead of time. The concept behind notice is to give people ample opportunity to respond to an issue appropriately and in a timely fashion. Surprise attacks are not appreciated or countenanced by the law.

## BASIC LEGAL RESEARCH

- *Business Law,* by Christopher Dungan and Donald Ridings (Barron's). A good resource for all kinds of information about your rights as a business owner.

- *The Consumer's Guide to Understanding and Using the Law,* by Daniel Johnson (Better Way Books). Basic guidelines to legal principles and your rights in a whole host of situations, not just business.

- *Your Rights in the Workplace,* by Henry H. Perritt, Jr. (Practicing Law Institute). Another source for finding out your legal obligations to your employees.

- *Your Right to Government Information,* by Christine Marwick (Bantam Books). The American Civil Liberties Union Handbook, which can provide you with additional information about the Freedom of Information Act.

- *Summary of Freedom of Information and Privacy Laws of the Fifty States,* by Wallis E. McClain (Washington DC, Plus Publications). A summary of state information laws.

## KEY RESOURCES

- *Federal Office of Information.* For more information on FOIA, contact the Federal Office of Information; (202) 466-6312.

- *The National Technical Information Service.* This organization sells report from government-sponsored research. Write to 5285 Port Royal Road, Springfield, VA 22161.
- *The National Archives.* Publishes material explaining how to make use of its resources. Write to National Archives, Eighth and Pennsylvania Avenue NW, Washington, DC 20408.

## COURT COACH® SUGGESTS

1. *Look very carefully at your interviewees for any position, even the most menial.* If the interviewee smells bad, looks rumpled, and has permanent bad hair, consider, do you want to fire this person someday because he or she has not bathed? What you see is what you get! Do not be dazzled solely by IQ and a dynamite resume—those broken nails and scruffy shoes count, too.

2. *A sad reality: Most small businesses traditionally operate on the old-fashioned principle: My word is my bond.* In the next millennium, you need to be more self-protective and write things down. Computers are a substantial aid. But whether inputting information into a computer or making a handwritten notation to keep in your file (it need *not* be lengthy), the important thing is "to do it" *and* to do it at the time of the event in the ordinary course of business. Materials prepared after the fact as a defensive strategy have less probative value (they are viewed more suspiciously as self-serving documentation of your version of the facts).

3. *Great legal phrases: To defend your rights; moral turpitude; and egregious.* Don't you love the sound of those phrases. The terms literally sound "evil."

4. *Be the leader in setting the office tone by "sharing the grunt work," if need be.* Take out the trash to the dumpster when overflowing, and offer to get your secretary a cappuccino if you are going out for a break.

# 15

# BUYING AND SELLING (OR GETTING FRIENDLY WITH THE UNIFORM COMMERCIAL CODE)

## COMING AND GOING:
## YOUR LEGAL STATUS AS A
## PROVIDER AND A CUSTOMER

Every small business owner wears two hats, simply by virtue of the nature of running a company. You are a provider of goods and/or services to customers, and you are someone else's customer as well. What follows in this chapter can be read from your perspective as a consumer and/or a merchant.

Just as your customers have legal protection against shady business practices, so do you. And, conversely, the laws that apply to you as a provider of goods and/or services also apply to the folks with whom you are on the receiving end of a business transaction.

## LET THE SELLER BEWARE (OR CAVEAT NON-EMPTOR): THE CUSTOMER IS ALWAYS RIGHT!

Our unofficial advice to you, as a small business owner who wants to remain in business, is to let the title of this section be your motto. Trust us, you will save yourself a lot of legal hassles. As a provider, when you take the virtuous high ground of "I'm right, therefore I will stand my ground," you are bound to lose—if not dollars—then customer loyalty at the least.

Customer relations is a delicate balance, between your right to be paid and the customer's right to satisfaction. Be sure and weigh the possible dollar loss now against lost sales in the future, not to mention the loss of a potentially valuable source of advertising—word of mouth—forever.

## The Uniform Commercial Code: Legal Protection for You and Your Customers

The UCC, Uniform Commercial Code, is your bible to all kinds of rights and responsibilities in the following commercial transactions: sales of goods, commercial paper, bank deposits and collections, letters of credit, bulk transfers, warehouse receipts, bills of lading, investment securities, and secured transactions. Buy a copy at a legal bookstore, skim through it, and keep it handy (right next to your other legal bible, *Black's Law Dictionary*). The language is clear, the outline straightforward; you will be able to read and understand the provisions, as well as find them quite useful (e.g., Article III on Sales will figure prominently, especially if you are in retail). However, in reaching a legal conclusion about how to proceed in a given situation, be sure to check with a commercial law attorney because unraveling the UCC statutes that apply to your particular situation can be quite complex.

This is not to say that you can't take any action to diffuse an irate customer without consulting an attorney. Let's say a customer swears up and down that you shipped defective goods that were also damaged in transit and were not received on time. You can use the UCC to find out what the customer's legal rights are; what your legal rights are; and at least predicate your discussion on legal principles instead of ire. The first line of defense is a logical, sane, legally justifiable reply, on the phone, in person, or in writing. But, again, be careful to check with an attorney before you inadvertently write something that undermines your legal position. When in doubt, buy 30 minutes of an attorney's time to have an expert look over your handiwork before sending a letter.

## Unfair Trade Practice Laws

As you'll find out soon enough if you continue to peruse this chapter, the state and federal governments have devised a cache of consumer protection laws that you, as a small business owner, must comply with. In your state, the legislature might afford additional protection to the customer through state consumer protection laws. For example, the statute in Connecticut is called CUTPA for Connecticut Unfair Trade Practices Act. These consumer protection laws are aimed at stamping out *any* unfair or deceptive business practice in advertising, pricing, delivery of service, product quality, refunds, and credit to name a few. Basically, customers are entitled to get what they paid for.

It's important to be aware—and make your employees aware—of these consumer protection laws (see Basic Legal Research at the end of this chapter). A customer can sue you even if the violation of consumer rights was unintentional. And judges and juries are infinitely more sympathetic toward unsuspecting buyers than uneducated sellers, since ignorance of the law is no excuse for breaking it.

With this kind of legal power—where an unfair trade practice claim can generate attorneys' fees and treble damages to the claimant—next to a disgruntled employee, a dissatisfied customer is your worst nightmare.

## The Bottom Line

When a customer asks for a refund, always consider that a loss of several dollars, or even of several hundred dollars, may be a wise business investment for more reasons than one. You avoid two nasty possibilities: either a lawsuit or haggling—in a letter, on the phone, and sometimes in your place of business in front of other customers. As a daughter once instructed: "Never pick an argument with a fool; no one will know the difference." Even if your customer is not a fool, and chances are that is true, most lawsuits are about just such seemingly ridiculous incidents, which can mushroom into a full-blown lawsuit over which you have no control.

Hence, consider the possibility that one disgruntled customer can domino the loss of several other customers who don't know who is at fault. Take a cue from a large company like Nordstrom's, a department store chain based in Seattle, Washington. This retail business has thrived in difficult times by offering excellent customer service. We can vouch for that, having tested out Nordstrom's public relations in both Seattle and Portland, Oregon. Their service includes a most important ingredient: having a pleasant, downright cheerful staff of employees who treat the customer like a real, live person (even if the customer is wrong). Truly amazing! (As you can see from our enthusiastic praise, it certainly is true in customer relations as in life, "What goes around, comes around.")

Another consideration is that even if you choose not to cheerfully refund a dissatisfied customer's money (or at least offer an exchange of goods) and resolve the dispute, the customer can always stop payment on the check or refute the credit card charge. Either way, you don't get paid. But one way, the consumer walks away angry and primed for a fight; the other way, the person walks away feeling that you're a fair business owner and may even sing your praises to friends (that old valuable commodity, word-of-mouth advertising!). If the customer feels that you were selling the item in question in "good faith" (it was in working condition to the best of your knowledge), you may avoid being named in a lawsuit that names the manufacturer as responsible in the chain of distribution.

## WARRANTIES

A warranty is your guaranteed promise to the customer that your product or service is of a certain quality and will retain that quality. Usually a written warranty, full or limited, (only covering certain aspects of the product) is provided by the manufacturer of a product. But even so, if you are selling a product or supplying goods, you are legally bound to a standard of "good faith and fair dealing" with your customers. This means that, to the bets of your knowledge, the products/services you are providing are in good condition and working order. In other words, you are not a fly-by-night shyster.

Two types of warranties cover both the quality of the product, and the liability of both the manufacturer and the seller:

1. *Express warranty.* The terms of the warranty are written in contract form, affirming that the goods purchased will do a specified function or serve a specified purpose. If you own a washer or dryer, it undoubtedly came with one of these.
2. *Implied warranty.* Even without a written express warranty, the buyer is guaranteed by implication that the seller is providing usable, safe goods of a certain level of quality. The merchant is responsible for selling goods that are "fit for the ordinary purposes for which such goods are used."

## Avoiding or Limiting the Liability of an Express or Implied Warranty

A written or verbal disclaimer can modify a warranty obligation. Most commonly, the seller can disclaim in part by providing a limited warranty covering only certain aspects. The buyer then purchases subject to the disclaimer.

However, the simple written notification "sold as is," or even "sold without warranty of any kind" still does not necessarily absolve you from all responsibility should something go wrong. In addition, some states have passed laws that make it extremely difficult to disclaim any implied warranty. The reason: to protect consumers from unscrupulous practices and to make sure manufacturers and sellers pay strict attention to and avoid putting unsafe or hazardous products into the marketplace. In the much talked-about McDonald's hot coffee settlement, an elderly woman collected millions for burns suffered by scalding hot coffee. Apparently, the liability here was less for the injury and more for putting an unsafe product in the marketplace, coffee that was purposefully hotter than the competition's and that the company apparently knew could cause injury. Looking at the size of the judgment, one could conclude that any attempts to disclaim liability met deaf ears.

Just like McDonald's, you do not want negative publicity of this ilk. All of a business owner's positive good-faith efforts may be forever tarnished by one huge blot of bad publicity or a public lawsuit. And, all lawsuits are a matter of public record, available in the courthouse records for anyone who requests the file.

## State and Federal Laws Regarding Sales and Warranties

Important regulations for the selling and buying of products in interstate and intrastate commerce are contained in the federal laws and state laws as well. For your state regulations, see your state's commercial law section of the statutes. The federal laws covering sales and warranties can be found in:

- *The Uniform Commercial Code (UCC).* This complex set of laws, *inter alia* (among many other things), says that the buyer has a right to return the goods purchased if they do not meet the standards put forth by the seller and manufacturer.
- *Magnuson-Moss Warranty Act.* Supplements state laws in requiring full disclosure of warranty terms in clear language

when the seller or manufacturer provides a written warranty. It covers consumer products costing over $10 that are used for personal, family, or household purposes.

## REPRESENTING YOUR BUSINESS TO THE PUBLIC: ADVERTISING, PRICING, PACKAGING, AND MERCHANDISING ARE REGULATED, TOO

The Federal Trade Commission (FTC), with its headquarters in Washington, DC, and regional offices throughout the United States, has federal jurisdiction over unlawful advertising, pricing, merchandising, and packaging. In addition, each state has a consumer protection agency and attorney general to watch out for consumers' rights. You should get acquainted with the following federal statutes if you, as a manufacturer or seller, provide goods and/or services either wholesale or retail:

- *Consumer Products Safety Act.* Prohibits the sale of harmful products and outlines product safety standards.
- *Child Protection and Toy Safety Act.* Forbids the sale of toys that are known to be dangerous.
- *Fair Packaging and Labeling Act.* Requires a label disclosing the ingredients of all packaged products.
- *Antitrust Laws.* The following principal antitrust laws protect trade and commerce from unlawful restraints, price discrimination, price fixing, and monopolies: Sherman Act (1890), Clayton Act (1914), Federal Trade Commission Act (1914), Robinson-Patman Act (1936), the Miller-Tydings Act (1937), and Celler-Kefauver Act (1950).

It hardly needs saying, but unfair advertising, packaging, and otherwise misrepresenting your business and its products to the public is also a poor business practice. Again, your intent may not be to make fraudulent claims to consumers or malign the competition, but if you inadvertently do either, ignorance of the law is no defense in a court of law.

### How to Stay out of Trouble with the FTC

Follow two basic rules of thumb when sending your message out to the public: (1) Say *exactly* what you mean; and (2) Don't promise what you can't deliver with 100 percent certainty. So, if you want to sell your remaining stack of women's sweaters quickly, you might advertise "Women's Sweaters, Marked down 20%, Limited sizes and colors. One-day sale only, Saturday, March 1."

Carefully avoid the following advertising pitfalls:

- *Ads containing exaggerated or false statements.* If it's not the best thing since sliced bread or the "best" or the "only," don't say it. A favorite ploy at touristy establishments is to hang a banner outside that reads "$.99 for Margaritas"; once inside, the customer discovers a whole list of conditions and limitations in small print on the beverage menu, such as "from 5:00 to 6:00 P.M. on Mondays, Tuesdays, and Wednesdays."
- *Products priced to undercut the competition unfairly.* Here, the federal antitrust laws come into play.
- *A "loss leader"—merchandise actually sold at a loss to attract customers—can backfire if the supply runs out, and you do not provide a rain check for the customer to purchase the item at the reduced price when it is in stock.* In other words, you cannot play the "bait-and-switch" game.

Consumers with complaints can go to the FTC or the state attorney general's office. The most common consumer complaints registered with the FTC and State Attorney Generals' offices involve deceptive pricing—"sales" that don't really provide any savings, and "free" products that come with a hidden price tag. You can take several precautions to avoid any confusion over what you think you're offering consumers and what they think they are buying.

### Do Offer Free Items for Free

If you offer something for "free," make sure the small printing contains no hidden costs. You may not advertise free socks in letters 2 feet tall, with microscopic print explaining that consumers need to buy $100 shoes to get them.

### Do Offer Sale Items on Sale

A "sale" item should reflect a bona fide discount from the manufacturer's suggested retail price, or your regular price. You can't mark up the price two weeks prior to a sale in anticipation of advertising a sale, or mark and "slash" the price simultaneously to create a false sense of savings. For example, Filene's Basement, in Boston, has sales tickets that state the discounted price *and* the expected discounts as of certain dates.

## If You're Comparing Your Product with the Competition's, Tread Softly

Just saying it doesn't make it so. Double-check your facts and substantiate that your product or service really does produce twice the results at half the price before putting it in print.

## Beware of False Promises

Don't make promises inadvertently that you can't deliver. If quantities are limited, or the product is only available in certain sizes or colors, say so in your ad. That way, you'll have fewer disappointed—and potentially angry—customers who have made the trip to your store for naught. Or, if your restaurant offers a prix fixe dinner, offering one glass of Dom Pérignon champagne to each diner, reserve the right to substitute the house bubbly for Dom Pérignon when your supply of the more expensive champagne runs out. Your customers understand this reality, but are not so understanding of being ripped off without notice.

# Play It Straight: No Games!

We probably have all been victims of the same game—bait and switch—where we thought, for example, we were buying a SWATCH watch at an incredible bargain, only to find on arriving home that we had purchased a SWITCH nonbrand knockoff. The moral? If you say it's swordfish, it had better not be shark. This is the cardinal rule for not only staying out of trouble with the FTC, but also for building up a loyal clientele of customers who trust you.

For your further education, here are some other "games merchants play" to avoid.

## For You, My Friend, I'll Make a Deal

Don't give potential clients the age-old spiel, "My usual charge is $250 per hour, but for you I'll only charge $150." It's most embarrassing when the person talks to another customer and finds out that, in actuality, you usually do charge $150. It is also probably illegal under any one of a number of these consumer-oriented laws, especially if this is your usual modus operandi. A practice *not* adopted in the ordinary course of business by your competitors may be viewed as unfair and thus illegal.

## Playing Dumb

Certain unscrupulous service providers will pretend that they don't know the answer to a customer's question so that they can go "do some research" and come back with the answer five minutes later. This is generally not impressive to busy consumers, merely irritating. Even if customers do feel that you've gone through some special effort on their behalf, if you do it to charge more, there's probably a viable claim of deceptive practice.

### Playing Smart

This is equally as irritating as playing dumb, and may be equally as troublesome legally. Merchants or service providers who go on and on about the performance capabilities or the benefits of a product and have little or no knowledge of the actual realities will eventually trip over their tongue. Think electronics, insurance policies, stocks and bonds. Think of refunds at any rate, and a dissatisfied customer and all the legal hassles that can bring, as described previously. Think of claims of churning the account, fraud, undue pressure, and the like.

We could go on and on. But the bottom line is, stay on the right side of the customers and the right side of the law. The legal standard for judgments of right and wrong is the "reasonable person" standard. Thus, if what you are saying offends your customer, this legal standard *and* the tilt in the law toward protecting the consumer rather than the supplier of goods and services mean that playing fast and loose could easily come back to haunt you. Like the monkeys, do no evil, see no evil, hear no evil.

## AN OUNCE OF PREVENTION RATHER THAN THE OUCH OF A LEGAL CURE

The recipe for success for an entrepreneurial business and for successfully avoiding legal trouble with customers is simple, really. Customer service is your top, number one priority. A satisfied and loyal clientele will not resort to legal remedies, even when you are legally liable.

Providing the best customer service, then, without going broke or running afoul of the law, will be your most effective shield against legal liability. Develop customer service policies that make sense for your particular business and draft your own customer relations statement. As food for thought, consider how your style and business requirements can be met regarding these issues:

- Check "acceptance" requirements, including identification via a picture ID card such as a driver's license.
- Your payment policy and the conditions of payment, including payment in full, installment plans, late charges, interest on outstanding balances.
- Credit cards, if any, that will be accepted, and procedures for implementing card company requirements.

- Return policies, such as the conditions for a refund.
- Charges for bounced checks.
- How to handle suggestions and complaints.
- Whether your company offers any guarantees or warranties.

## KNOW YOUR KEY TERMS

- *Uniform Commercial Code (UCC)*. Uniform comprehensive law governing commercial transactions, adopted by all states except Louisiana.
- *Services*. Any labor or assistance that you offer on a pay-for-hire basis.
- *Goods/Products*. As defined in the UCC: "All things . . . which are movable at the time of identification to the contract for sale other than the money in which the price is to be paid, investment securities and things in action" UCC § 2-105(1).
- *Unfair deceptive trade practice*. Defined differently in different instances, generally a fraudulent or dishonest practice in trade or commerce.
- *Warranty*. A written or oral guarantee to consumers of goods or services that their purchase meets a quality standard. If the quality is inferior, customers are entitled to satisfaction—replacement or repair.
- *Disclaimer*. A written statement eliminating or modifying the warranty or other obligations. For example: "product sold as is."

## BASIC LEGAL RESEARCH

- *Uniform Commercial Code (American Law Institue and the National Conference of Commissioners in Uniform State Laws*. This is "the" official text of the comprehensive modernization of various statutes originally approved in 1952 and amended from time to time thereafter.
- *Antitrust Analysis,* by Phillip Areda (Little, Brown). A complete overview of antitrust laws.
- *Consumer Action Guide,* by Barbara Kaufman (Nolo Press). Includes an overview of warranties and federal warranty legislation.
- *A Business Person's Guide to Federal Warranty Law.* A publication written by the Federal Trade Commission that can be ordered

through the U.S. Government Printing Office, Washington, DC 20401; (202) 783-3283.

---

### KEY RESOURCES

- *The state attorney general's office.* Here's where you can get pamphlets about consumer rights and your legal responsibilities to your customers in the eyes of the state, and ask questions and make complaints.
- *State and local professional or trade organization.* Check out what your peers are doing in terms of customer service policies, and credit and finance procedures.
- *The Federal Trade Commission.* The main office address is Sixth and Pennsylvania Avenue NW, Washington, DC 20580; (202) 326-3175. Call and find out what services they can supply to your small business.

---

### COURT COACH® SUGGESTS

1. *Observe the competition's interesting business practices.* Learn from your peers and participate in the most sincere form of compliment by emulating their successful customer relations policies: clever posted notices (witty quotes and poems) regarding customer policies such as extra charges for returned checks; return policies that make sense and are customer friendly; suggestion procedures that actually elicit customer suggestions.

2. *Make your clients like you, and they'll be less likely to sue.* This is a big part of customer relations. Some companies in the trucking industry put a telephone number on the back of their large trailers and encourage travelers to comment on the truckers' driving. This is a show of good faith, just as asking "How can we serve you better" goes a long, long way to creating good faith in your clients. A client's goodwill may be the best defense against a problem escalating into a lawsuit.

3. *Purchase a copy of the Uniform Commercial Code if your business is involved in any way with sales, commercial paper, bank deposits and collections, documents of the investment securities, or secured transactions.*

4. *Above all else, remember: The Customer Is Always Right!*

# 16

## COLLECTING YOUR MONEY (CASH, CHECKS, AND CREDIT CARDS)

### MONEY MAKES THE WORLD GO 'ROUND—AND YOUR BUSINESS!

Up until now, we've been focusing on the customer's legal rights, and how a business owner must not infringe on them. But now it's time to take a look at the other side of the coin: the seller's rights. As a seller, your major concern, besides providing your customers and clients with what they request, is making and collecting your money. The first and cardinal rule of business is to stay on top of the cash flow. More money "in" than money "out" each month means you turn a profit. The reverse means you may soon be out of business.

### A SHORT AND SWEET COURSE ON GETTING PAID IN A TIMELY MANNER

The concept of expecting prompt payment for quality products or good services sounds simple enough. But this will probably be the greatest source of headaches and financial woes for you as a small business owner. Almost any business owner, freelance writer, lawyer, doctor, or Indian chief will tell you how they must wait, not 30 days, but 60 days, 90 days, and sometimes many more—and sometimes never, for payment.

You need to rely on prompt payment from your customers so that you can, in turn, pay your creditors in a timely manner. On the other hand, you don't want to strong-arm or harass your customers for money they may not have, and thus run afoul of the consumer-oriented collection laws. The balance between collecting your money and keeping your customers is fragile, requiring the finesse of a tight-rope walker.

Have you ever heard the wonderful song in *Les Misérables,* "Master of the House," lauding the scoundrel innkeeper who "cooks the books" (does not account properly), perhaps by skimming cash off the top? The IRS will definitely disapprove of this recipe for financial chaos, and in corporations and partnerships, your colleagues can hold you accountable, too. Hence there are almost no problems associated with cash transactions, except that you should account for it accurately.

## CASH

Your best bet is cash on the barrelhead. Wouldn't that be lovely? The beauty of any cash-and-carry business, which is how Court Coach® operates, is that you can put that income to work for you earning more money in the bank or in investments immediately. You can pay off your own debts and eliminate late charges on your statements. And, if you choose, you can create customer goodwill by offering a discount for cash. While checks need to clear a bank, and credit card charges need to be recorded and posted to by financial institutions, this is not true of cash. The money is yours; your client or customer will not stop payment or charge back; end of story.

As you can plainly see, we love cash! But there is a downside to dealing in greenbacks. Record keeping is more difficult, and there is always the temptation to pocket said cash rather than declare it as income. Although many people would consider you a fool not to pocket "some cash," this is a strict legal no-no. The Court Coach® says: Play it safe and sleep easy. After all, you don't want to get in on the wrong side of the bed with the IRS. They'll give you a slab mattress and a rock for a pillow if they catch you in an audit and you can't account properly for the discrepancy between your cash in and cash out.

One more warning about cash: In cash businesses like bars and restaurants, employees have the unfortunate reputation of stealing the owner blind if the owner is not on-site. Hire trustworthy people and watch out for the razzle-dazzle employee extraordinaire who may have great skills but no character.

## CHECKS

While not as problematic as credit, checks come with their share of risks. In fact, about 450 million bad checks are written each year, even though intentionally passing a bad check is a crime with criminal penalties (fines and/or jail).

Let's look a little more closely at different kinds of checks, since these are options at your disposal:

- *Personal checks.* An individual's own check drawn on that person's own bank account.
- *Cashier's checks.* A bank's own check drawn on itself and signed by the cashier (hence the non de plume) or some other authorized bank official. The bank lends its credit to the purchaser of the check to make it available for immediate use.
- *Certified checks.* A check drawn on a depositor's personal account that has been stamped by a bank official with the words "accepted" or "certified." The bank's certification warrants that sufficient funds are on deposit and have been set aside, that the bank is holding money to pay the check and is liable to pay the proper party, the payee on the check.

### What Can Go Wrong with Checks

With checks, there are a litany of things that can (and often do) go wrong. Here's a laundry list of some of those things:

- Insufficient funds to cover the amount of the purchase.
- A fictitious account that never existed or has been closed.
- Forgery, in which case the bank will refuse payment.
- A person endorsing a check on behalf of a business, as an agent, who doesn't have the authority to do so.
- Stop payment orders.

### How to Bounce Back from Bad Checks

So what can small business owners do to protect themselves against bad checks? Here are some suggestions:

- Once burned by a client, refuse to accept a personal or corporate check. Insist on "good funds," a bank or certified check, credit card, or cash (or C.O.D.).
- Ask for a corroborating signature.
- Require an ID photo before accepting a check.
- If not inscribed on the check, make sure you have a motor vehicle license number, and home or business phone number. (Note: Some states do not allow you to require a customer's phone number.)
- Have a check-writing policy. Example: No work is performed until a check has cleared the bank. If work must be done on an expedited basis, then only good funds are accepted: certified check, money order, cash. Regarding checks over a certain minimum amount (as much as you are willing to lose), have a limitation policy (e.g., checks over $100 must be certified).

And, what happens when a disgruntled customer pretends to pay you with what appears to be a perfectly good personal check, only to dash to the bank or place a call directing the bank to "stop payment" on that check?

We recommend the following protective maneuver: Dash to your bank and, instead of depositing the check, endorse it and ask for cash. To shortstop any sleight-of-hand tricks by a potential deadbeat, have the check certified by the customer's bank, even if the customer complains about a charge for this service. Another option is to request a cashier's check, especially if the check is for a large sum of money and you need the funds immediately.

Some bad checks are written unintentionally and bounce unexpectedly; a simple phone call to the embarrassed customer will rectify the situation. But many times, your recourse will entail hauling the delinquent debtor into small claims court—if you can locate the person (see Chapter 17). So, once again, your best plan of action is preventive medicine. Consider incorporating these additional protective procedures into your customer service policies:

- Accept only checks drawn on local bank accounts.
- Charge a processing fee for bounced checks; $10 to $20 is a normal charge for processing a check returned from the bank for insufficient funds. Give your customers notice of this charge in your customer policy statement posted near your cash register for handy reference.
- Make a photocopy of all checks for your file.

- Be wary of issuing a refund or substitution on any item before the check has cleared.
- Be wary of accepting checks written for more than the purchase price as a regular practice. Remember: You are not the bank or the ATM machine. This practice makes a mess of your books and records.

## Accepting Checks Made Payable to the Customer (Third-Party Checks)

Exercise extreme caution when accepting checks made payable to your client or customer, not you (you can learn a little law now). Since a check is a negotiable instrument, a check made payable to someone other than you—your customer's paycheck for instance—can be negotiated to you. When the payee endorses the check by signing her name on the back, that person has converted the check into what is called "bearer paper." This means that the check is just like cash and anyone can use it as such.

Now, if your customer also adds the words "made payable only to Jane Doe," and you are Jane Doe, you are still left relying on an unknown third party, the maker of the check (in this case, your client's employer), to have sufficient funds to cover this check. A little risky, wouldn't you agree?

When payment is in dispute, you need also to think twice before accepting a check that does not cover full payment. An attempt at a quick "buy-off" is irritating to put it mildly. It can be sabotaged somewhat by placing below your signature endorsement on the back "No accord and satisfaction."

You've now taken a legal position that "Yes, I cashed this check," which means *ordinarily* that there is an "accord," or meeting of the minds, and that you both agree that the dollar amount of the check satisfies a debt in full. But, in this instance, you are alerting the maker (the person who wrote the check) that you took your money as a partial payment but do not agree that the debt is fully satisfied (this is definitely a favorite Court Coach® tip).

## CREDIT

In a perfect world, everyone would be able to pay for every purchase with cash. But, just as you will most likely depend on credit to pay your suppliers, you can offer personal credit to special customers who will need the option of "the float," forestalling payment of their bills for more than the traditional 30 days. You can also personally offer the option of a payment schedule, in which the customer pays a percentage of the total charge on a monthly basis. But becoming the bank by financing your client is the least desirable option.

## To Offer Credit or Not to Offer Credit

A much better option than offering credit yourself is to let the banks and finance companies that offer credit cards do the work for you. Even as a small, one-person operation, you can offer the benefits of a credit card acceptance for customers and avoid the headaches of collection.

Most major credit cards offered through banks (e.g., Visa, MasterCard) and charge cards offered through private finance companies (e.g., American Express, Discover) charge a small start-up fee and 3 percent per purchase accompanying each business transaction. This is a small price to pay compared with the potential risks, ranging from no payment at all to the expense and time involved when you become "the bank" by extending credit through your business. Financing your customers' transactions can mean waiting 90 days to collect an account receivable. In other words, let MasterCard do the collection job for you.

If you do decide to offer credit through your business, you'll need to implement a well-organized system of accounts, send out bills and past-due notices, and deal with the issue of charging interest. Since there are almost no all-cash businesses any more, more than likely, you'll need to become acquainted with your state laws about extending credit and collecting debts, as well as the following federal statutes:

- *Fair Debt Collection Practices Act (16 USC § 1692–16920).* Prohibits the use of deception, harassment, and other unreasonable tactics in attempts to collect past-due accounts.
- *Fair Credit Billing Act.* Protects consumers from unfair credit billing practices.
- *Fair Credit Reporting Act.* Requires that credit reporting agencies keep accurate records. Consumers have the right to receive a copy of their credit report on request to review for accuracy and obsolescence.
- *Consumer Credit Protection Act (Truth in Lending).* Terms and interest charges must be fully disclosed to consumers who buy on credit.

- *The Truth-in-Lending Act.* States that a seller who extends credit must disclose credit terms, including finance charges. This law also covers credit cards. The liability of a cardholder is limited to $50 after notifying the creditor that a card has been lost, and billing a customer for unauthorized charges is prohibited.

The best defense against credit collection problems is, of course, a good offense. Several ways to head off credit collection problems at the pass and ensure that a customer's credit is good are:

- *Have new customers complete a credit application or information sheet* (see Chapter 1 for more information).
- *Run a credit check with a credit reporting agency.*
- *Have a credit collection policy and write it down.* You can incorporate your credit policies and collection procedures (see next section) into your customer service policy. Make your customers aware of your policies.
- *Consider charging interest if credit payment isn't paid with a certain time limit (usually 30 days).* This can be a powerful motivator for customers to pay off their credit bills in a timely manner. But most states have a ceiling on the interest you can charge, as defined in the state credit statutes.

Be extremely careful about the interest you charge for late payments, as a rate that smacks of usury may well constitute an unfair trade practice under your state's Unfair Trade Practice statute or other consumer protection laws or the state's credit statute (for information about collecting outstanding debts via small claims court, see Chapter 17).

## Developing a Collection Procedure: The Cornerstone of Your Business Foundation

Chances are some of your customers will pay their bills late, especially if you are not superdiligent about outstanding accounts receivable. Others won't pay at all. A sound collection procedure is invaluable in making the process of extracting your money from tightly clenched fists less time consuming and cumbersome.

Time is of the essence when collecting debts. According to a recent report from the Commercial Law League of America, collectibility of debt drops dramatically as time goes by. While 94 percent of debts owed for one month are collected in full, that figure drops down to 74 percent after six months, and only 27 percent of debts overdue for a year get collected.

Several procedures can strengthen your collection policy.

### Monitor Your Accounts

Put in place a bookkeeping technique that makes it easy for you to spot delinquent accounts. One effective method is to separate accounts according to where they are in the billing process. New accounts, accounts 30 days past due, accounts 60 days past due, and so on, would all be separate files for easy access.

### Use Duplicate Invoices

Send a duplicate invoice, indicating the account is past due, 30 days after the initial invoice was sent. You may also want to indicate on the invoice that a service charge will be tacked on for accounts 60 days past due. Your state may have laws regarding what percentage of the debt can be charged as a finance fee, but it's typically 1 percent to 5 percent.

### Make Wake-Up Calls

If there's no response after a few weeks, give the customer a "wake-up call"; a chance to rectify the situation. A concerned and understanding, yet firm, phone call may be appropriate at this point. You can inquire if the customer has a problem paying the bill and, perhaps, suggest setting up a payment schedule if necessary. Don't be afraid to put the customer's feet to the fire and get a time frame as to when you can expect to see your money in hand (e.g., by the "close of the business day on Friday, May 31, 1996").

### Use Demand Letters

After 60 days elapse, send out a form letter demanding payment. This letter should warn the customer in a friendly tone that, while you value his or her business, you will be forced to forward the account to a collection agency if the bill is not paid in another 30 days.

### Still No Money after Ninety Days?

Now you are at a fork in the road where you can pursue your civil remedies or take the route to criminal prosecution. Civil remedies include:

- *A lawyer's letter.* This is a letter written by your attorney on letterhead outlining the facts and circumstances surrounding the bad debt; the actions taken by the seller or provider to resolve the situation amicably; and the legal options now available:

lawsuits, turning the debt over to a collection agency, attachment and garnishment of wages or property. The point of this letter is to give the debtor one last opportunity to avoid the unilateral decision on the part of the business owner to pursue any one of these other options. It also signals to the debtor your serious resolution to be paid. You are now out-of-pocket.

- *A collection agency.* You may choose to bypass the lawyer's letter and go straight to a collection agency, which has the power to place the debtor on a "bad credit" list, jeopardizing the debtor's credit rating. Note that the collection agency takes a substantial percentage of the debt owed, which will cut down on your profits considerably.
- *Resolution in court proceedings.* See Chapters 17 and 18 for details.

## KNOW YOUR KEY TERMS

- *Accounts receivable.* The dollars you expect to receive.
- *Accounts payable.* The dollars you owe to others.
- *C.O.D.* Cash on delivery. Have cash or a check ready when the UPS truck turns in the driveway.
- *Check.* A negotiable instrument, defined by the Federal Reserve Board, in part, as a "draft or order upon a bank" that must contain the words "pay to the order of," signed by the maker, which contains an unconditional promise to pay a sum certain to the payee in money.
- *Due and owing.* A debt is often said to be "due," meaning it is payable under law. A person is primarily bound to pay, whether or not the time for payment has, or has not, arrived.
- *Collection procedures.* The methods by which you turn accounts receivable into a healthy bank account for your business.
- *Inter alia.* A Latin term that means "among other things." It is shortcut legalese to convey the idea that there are "lots of something"—provisions, spices on a shelf, or whatever—and you want to single out or focus on just one or two of them.

## BASIC LEGAL RESEARCH

- *State statutes.* To find out the law in your state regarding collection policies, visit the law library and look up your state statutes under Collection of Debts, or Consumer Protection.

- *Financial magazines.* Publications such as *Worth, Inc., Kiplinger's Personal Finance, Bloomberg Personal,* and *Money Magazine* are excellent sources of information on money and banking.
- *Financial newspapers.* The *Wall Street Journal, Barron's,* and the *New York Times* (the Money section of the Saturday edition, in particular) are terrific resources.

## KEY RESOURCES

- *Collection agencies.* These collection specialists, found in your yellow pages, typically charge fees ranging from 10 to 30 percent; and you give the agency exclusive right to collect the debt for a contracted time period (such as six months). The same arrangements are common when hiring an attorney who specializes in debt collection.

## COURT COACH® SUGGESTS

1. *More on partial payment checks.* Another backstop if there's a good-faith dispute about how much is owed to you and you receive a partial payment check as full payment is to write the words "Under Protest" along with your endorsement of the check.

   The states allowing a creditor to cash a disputed full payment check and still go after the debtor include Alabama, Delaware, Massachusetts, Minnesota, Missouri, New Hampshire, New York, Ohio, Rhode Island, South Carolina, South Dakota, West Virginia, and Wisconsin. Check your state statutes to see if your state has recently modified.

2. *Be very careful about posting customers' names who have written bad checks or have outstanding debts.* Forms of embarrassment such as framing bad checks or posting a list of the names of people with delinquent accounts are unwise and may certainly be illegal. Check your federal, state, and local ordinances before publicizing someone's account status. A posted notice of debt might be construed as a common-law tort of defamation of character, or an unfair trade practice.

   For example, in Connecticut, it is a violation of Consumer Protection Regulations to ". . . display a list of, pictures of, or other information about consumer debtors who allegedly refuse to pay debts which could identify any consumer debtor to the general public" (*Conn. Agencies Regs.* 36-243c-5).

4. *Do have an internal memo system naming customers whose checks have bounced, and a follow-up procedural policy.* The next check may bounce as well. What will you do?

5. *Shop around for credit cards you will accept in your place of business—they're not all the same.* Consult with the credit card representative and ask questions about anything you don't understand or agree with. Also, read every single solitary line of credit card contracts, and make sure you know what your rights and responsibilities are.

6. *Be aware of "charge backs."* Even if you're using a third-party credit card company, yes, the customer can still withhold your money. The customer can contact the credit card provider and refuse to pay a disputed charge. The credit card financial institution then battles it out with your bank and your money is in limbo for what can be quite a long time. This applies to services as well as goods.

7. *A Court Coach tip® on looking good, feeling smart.* Some additional nifty legal terms relating to money and debts:

   *Commercial paper.* A blanket term for various instruments such as bills of exchange, bank drafts, promissory notes, and bank checks. It also includes short-term notes issued by corporations to borrow money.

   *Negotiable instruments.* A negotiable instrument is commercial paper that meets certain requirements of the Article 3 Uniform Commercial Code. It must be a writing signed by the maker or drawer; it must contain an unconditional order to pay a sum certain in money; payable on demand or at a certain definite date and must be payable either to the bearer or order; and it must not contain any other promise, order, obligation, or power given by the maker or drawer.

   *Accord and satisfaction.* An accords agreement by the parties to discharge a claim by accepting a settlement "satisfaction."

8. *A Court Coach® tip for getting quick payment:* If you have already provided a service, and you have given your customer notice of your policy, there is no legal reason you can't shorten the traditional 30-day payment policy or have a payment policy that requires payment on completion of a project, task, or service. If you deliver goods or supplies, you have the option of C.O.D., cash on delivery.

9. *Look up your state statute regarding damages allowed for bad checks and see what you stand to gain by going to court.* Many states allow for two or three times the amount of the check, not to exceed a certain limit ranging from $500 to $1,000. Some allow for attorney fees as well (see Appendix D for a chart of state bad check laws).

# 17

---

# THE SMALL
# CLAIMS COURT

## WHAT IS SMALL CLAIMS COURT AND WHEN MIGHT YOU FIND YOURSELF THERE?

We hope that you will not find yourself in Small Claims Court, either looking for money as a Plaintiff, or defending a nonpayment as a Defendant. The many reasons that you might find yourself in Small Claims Court are outlined in this chapter. Courts, like Small Claims Court, exist for the specific purpose of providing a remedy to you. They are part of your state system and something your tax dollars support. Therefore, use this court to protect yourself or to make sure that you are not trampled on financially by your debtors.

The most important thing to know about your state's Small Claims Court is the limit on the amount of money you are allowed to collect there and the kinds of lawsuits that may be brought there. The state legislature changes these amounts on a regular basis; consequently, you do need to call your Small Claims Court to inquire about the dollar limit. For example, in Connecticut you cannot recover on a debt in excess of two thousand dollars ($2,000.00), but you can also recover some minimal court costs in addition to the two thousand dollars. You may want to proceed in Small Claims Court even if your debt is more than two thousand dollars because the procedure is simple and you can probably proceed comfortably *pro se.* Hence, on a debt of $2,600.00, you could recover only the maximum in your state, and you would have to write off the balance of the debt.

You can find the address and phone number for your Small Claims Court listed in your local telephone directory. The clerks are there to assist you so ask questions freely. However, they may be few in number, depending on how much money your state is able and willing to pay on that portion of the judicial system. This may determine how much help you may receive. Very often Small Claims Courts have excellent written materials and brochures that will give you a good, brief outline of how to proceed.

Most of the lawsuits you may encounter as a small business owner—either as the plaintiff or the defendant—can probably be resolved in Small Claims Court, as opposed to a higher court where there might be either a judge or a jury (with the exception of discrimination charges). Small Claims Court, sometimes called "the people's court," is quick, easy, and all the rage. In California alone, 481,506 plaintiffs filed small claims suits during fiscal year 1992–1993. Typical cases include auto repair, property damage, rental deposits, and small business disputes.

This informal forum was set up to settle personal or business disputes involving limited sums of money (see Appendix G for list of state ceilings for small claims suits, usually $1,500–$3,000). State law sometimes prohibits attorneys from appearing in Small Claims Court, and it is usually economically unfeasible to hire an attorney to handle a small claims case.

This leaves the defendant (party being sued) and plaintiff (party suing) left to their own devices in front of the judge. No jury is involved. And even if attorneys are allowed, as a pro se, you will appear more in need of the protection of the court and will arouse the judge's sympathy—especially if your adversary is represented by an attorney.

For several reasons, it is advantageous to take a case to Small Claims Court rather than to a higher court with concurrent jurisdiction. First of all, it takes less time for your case to actually come to trial (about 30–60 days versus years possibly). And once you arrive in court, the evidencing rules and the standard of proof are more lenient in Small Claims Court, as there is no jury involved and oftentimes no attorneys representing either party. However, according to your state's rules, you may be able to have a small claim heard in a higher level civil court with either a judge or a jury, and you may be able to remove the case to higher court if you are the one being sued (see Court Coach® Suggests for good reasons to remove your case).

## ASSESSING YOUR CASE

The following are the main criteria to use when deciding whether or not to sue:

- Do you have enough evidence to prove your case?
- Is there enough money at stake to make it worth 10 to 20 hours of your time?
- Can you collect your money if you win, or is your opponent "judgment proof" (a polite word for "broke")?

Keep in mind that Small Claims Court as a place to get even is highly overrated. (Actually, using any court to vent your anger is a bad idea.) If a person or business doesn't actually have the assets to pay you, do you really want to take the time filing paperwork, lining up witnesses, collecting evidence, and going to court—only to find that you can't collect any money? Another equally frustrating scenario is that the judge will allow the defendant to pay you at a minimum statutory rate, like $60 per month, and you'll be faced with keeping tabs on the debtor for this small fee for many months to come. You may want to weigh the satisfaction of more immediate closure against whatever money is involved.

So, the big question is: How do you determine if your debtor is solvent? It's much easier to determine if a business is solvent than an individual. If the supplier who sold you defective widgets has a storefront and cash register, you can probably collect your judgment one way or the other. The sheriff will actually visit the store and take your money out of the cash register if need be. But if an unlicensed carpenter whose office is his truck and whose mattress is his banker put your window display shelves in backward, you're probably out of luck.

To help you discover evidence of a "deep pocket," some states have a legal procedure called citation to discover assets, by which the defendant is ordered to provide information regarding assets under penalty of perjury.

A final note when deciding whether or not to take your case to Small Claims Court: Consider that more than 50 percent of small claims cases are won by plaintiffs by default—that is, the defendant doesn't show up. You win hands down just by presenting your side of the story. Keep in mind that if you are the one being pursued, by suppliers or outside contractors for example, the same rule applies (show up or pay up).

Before you file suit, you should send a letter, or a letter with your invoice attached, *demanding* payment to the individual or company you are planning to sue. This is called a demand letter. It will not only alert the other person as to your serious intent, but may also resolve the issue before you have to go to Small Claims Court. Your demand letter should state the facts about your claim, what happened, and why you think you should be paid. At the end of the letter, it is a good idea to put the receiver on notice by making a statement similar to the following: "Unless I receive a check for (specified dollar) amount within fourteen days from the date of this letter, I will bring action in Small Claims Court to recover."

## WHAT TO DO ONCE YOU'VE DECIDED TO SUE

OK, so you've decided it's worth your while to sue . . . What now? First off, you need to figure out whom you will sue. The Court Coach® rule of thumb here is: Make as many people liable as possible. Name your debtor, the debtor's spouse who works in the business, and their business to make sure the debtor can't transfer money to a bank account you will find it difficult to touch. Many times, someone who knows a lawsuit is in the offing will divert funds, so the more bank accounts you can tap into the better.

When suing a company or corporation, make sure that you know the legal name of the business and who owns it. You can verify this information by checking the county clerk's records, or calling the office of the secretary of the state.

### Filing a Complaint: The Paperwork That Gets the Ball Rolling

To start your small claims case rolling, the first formal step is pay a fee to the court clerk (usually about $15) obtain and fill out a "complaint" form that states whom you're suing, for how much, and why (see Figure 17–1). Write down the facts accurately, since the judge will later read this statement as the initial procedure in assessing the validity of your suit. Also keep in mind that you may not be afforded a chance to amend your complaint.

After filing your complaint at the local courthouse, the court clerk will draft a "summons," a document giving the defendants notice of the suit and the details as to where and when the court hearing will be held (see Figure 17–2) and mail in with the complaint. At the same time, the court will also supply you with notification of the hearing's place, time, and date. If you are suing more than one debtor in a single claim, each additional summons issued costs another $15 or so, depending on the fee schedule of the state in which you live.

## Figure 17–1

**SMALL CLAIM AND NOTICE OF SUIT**
JD-CV-40  Rev. 10-82
C.G.S. § 51-15, 51-195L, 52-549a,b,c
Pr. Bk. § 547 et seq.

STATE OF CONNECTICUT
**SUPERIOR COURT**
SMALL CLAIMS SESSION

For Court Use Only

DOCKET NO.

RECEIPT NO.

Hearing required if defendant defaults   ☐ YES   ☐ NO

CONTINUANCES

TO:
Defendant #1.

Paul Doe
16 Elm Street
New Haven, CT  06510
Telephone: 922-2222

IND  PART  CORP
☒   ☐   ☐
("X" ONE)

1.
Defendant #2.

IND  PART  CORP
☐   ☐   ☐
("X" ONE)

ATTY. FOR DEF.

2. YOU ARE THE DEFENDANT AND **YOU ARE BEING SUED** BY THE FOLLOWING PLAINTIFF(S):

| NAME, ADDRESS AND TELEPHONE NO. | NAME, ADDRESS AND TELEPHONE NO. | ATTORNEY FOR PLAINTIFF (Name, address, telephone and juris no.) |
|---|---|---|
| John Smith<br>32 Oak Lane<br>Hartford, CT  06106<br>Telephone : 866-6666<br>("X" ONE) ☒ IND. ☐ PART. ☐ CORP. | ("X" ONE) ☐ IND. ☐ PART. ☐ CORP. | |

THE ABOVE PLAINTIFF(S) **CLAIMS YOU OWE** ➡ PLUS COSTS, FOR THE FOLLOWING REASONS:

AMOUNT NOW DUE
1,000.00

Here please state briefly and clearly the basis of your claim.

(Include any relevent dates and addresses.)

☒ "X" here and complete the Military Service Affidavit below if the defendant(s) is/are an individual(s) or partnership. *The undersigned, being duly sworn, deposes and says that the above amount now due is now due from the defendant(s) to plaintiff(s) in accordance with the above claim.*

| SIGNED (Plaintiff or Plaintiff's Attorney) | TYPE IN NAME OF PERSON SIGNING AT LEFT | TITLE OF PERSON SIGNING |
|---|---|---|
| DATE ENTERED | SUBSCRIBED AND SWORN TO BEFORE ME ON (Date) | SIGNED (Clerk, Notary, Comm. of Sup. Ct.) |

**MILITARY SERVICE AFFIDAVIT**

The undersigned deposes and says: ☐ that no defendant in this action is in the military or naval service of the United States, and that, to the personal knowledge of the undersigned *(state facts showing defendant is not in such service and state source of knowledge of these facts)*:

☒ that the undersigned is unable to determine whether or not the defendant(s) in this action are in the military or naval service of the United States.

SIGNATURE AND TITLE _____

Subscribed and sworn to before me:

ON (Date) _____    SIGNED (Clerk, Notary, Comm. of Sup. Ct.)

| ANSWER DATE | SMALL CLAIMS TELEPHONE NO. | COURT LOCATION |
|---|---|---|
| | 789-7465 | Superior Court G.A. 6<br>121 Elm Street<br>New Haven, CT  06510<br>SIGNED (Clerk) |

☐ WITHDRAWN   ☐ DISMISSED   ☐ TRANSFER TO REGULAR DOCKET

**JUDGMENT** (For court use)

JUDGMENT FOR: ☐ PLAINTIFF ☐ DEFENDANT
AFTER DEFAULT: ☐ WITH HEARING IN DAMAGES ☐ WITHOUT HEARING
AFTER HEARING BY: ☐ COMMISSIONER ☐ JUDGE
☐ MAGISTRATE
☐ BY STIPULATION (Agreement) ☐ SETTLED ON _____ Date

| | | |
|---|---|---|
| Damages | $ _____ | Entry Fee $ _____ |
| Interest | $ _____ | Service $ _____ |
| Atty. Fees | $ _____ | Subpoena $ _____ |
| TOT. DAM. | $ _____ | Photocopy $ _____ |
| | | TOT. COST $ _____ |

☐ SEE OTHER SIDE

SC
DOCKET NO

| WEEKLY PAYMENTS OF | COMMENCING (Date) | DISPOSITION DATE | SIGNED (Judge or Clerk) |
|---|---|---|---|
| $ | | | |

## Figure 17–2

036754

**SUMMONS**
**CIVIL** *(except family actions)*
**JD-CV-1 Rev. 1-87**
GEN. STAT. 51-346, 51-347, 51-349, 51-350, 52-45a,
52-48, 52-259
PR. BK. 49, 63, 66

**SUPERIOR COURT**

**"X" ONE OF THE FOLLOWING:**
*Amount, legal interest or property in demand, exclusive of interest and costs is*
a. ☐ less than $2,500
b. ☐ $2,500 through $14,999.99
c. ☐ $15,000 or more

d. ☐ *Claiming other relief in addition to or in lieu of money damages.*

**INSTRUCTIONS**

1. Prepare on typewriter: sign original summons (top sheet) and conform copies of the summons (sheets 3 and 4).
2. If there is more than one defendant, prepare or photocopy conformed summons for each additional defendant.
3. Attach the original summons, with computer sheet attached (page 2), to the original complaint, and attach a copy of the summons to each copy of the complaint. Also, if there are more than 2 plaintiffs or 4 defendants prepare form JD-CV-2 and attach it to the original and all copies of the complaint.
4. After service has been made by officer, file original papers and officer's return with the clerk of the court.
5. The party recognized to pay costs must appear personally before the authority taking the recognizance.
6. Do not use this form for actions in which an attachment, garnishment or replevy is being sought. See Practice Book Section 49 for other exceptions.

TO: Any proper officer; BY AUTHORITY OF THE STATE OF CONNECTICUT, you are hereby commanded to make due and legal service of this Summons and attached Complaint.

| JUDICIAL DISTRICT OR G.A. NO. | AT *(Town in which writ is returnable)* (Gen. Stat. 51-346, 51-349) | RETURN DATE *(Mo., day, yr.)* |
|---|---|---|

| ADDRESS OF CLERK OF COURT WHERE WRIT AND OTHER PAPERS SHALL BE FILED (Gen. Stat. 51-347, 51-350) | CASE TYPE *(From Judicial Dept. code list)* |
|---|---|
| | Major        Minor |

| PARTIES | NOTE: *Individual's Names:*<br>*Last, First, Middle Initial*  NAME AND ADDRESS OF EACH PARTY | ☐ Form JD-CV-2 *attached* |
|---|---|---|
| **FIRST NAMED PLAINTIFF ►** | | |
| Additional Plaintiff | | |
| **FIRST NAMED DEFENDANT ►** | | |
| Additional Defendant | | |
| Additional Defendant | | |
| Additional Defendant | | |

**NOTICE to each DEFENDANT**

1. You are being sued.
2. This paper is a Summons in a lawsuit.
3. The Complaint attached to these papers states the claims that each Plaintiff is making against you in this lawsuit.
4. To respond to this summons, or to be informed of further proceedings, you or your attorney must file a form called an "Appearance" with the Clerk of the above named Court at the above Court address on or before the second day after the above Return Date.
5. If you or your attorney do not file a written "Appearance" form on time, a judgment may be entered against you by default.

6. The "Appearance" form may be obtained at the above Court address.
7. If you believe that you have insurance that may cover the claim that is being made against you in this lawsuit, you should immediately take the Summons and Complaint to your insurance representative.
8. If you have questions about the Summons and Complaint, you should consult an attorney promptly. The Clerk of Court is not permitted to give advice on legal questions.

| DATE | SIGNED *(sign and "X" proper box)* | ☐ Commissioner of Superior Court<br>☐ Assistant Clerk | TYPE IN NAME OF PERSON SIGNING AT LEFT |
|---|---|---|---|

**FOR THE PLAINTIFF(S) ENTER THE APPEARANCE OF:**

| NAME AND ADDRESS OF ATTORNEY, LAW FIRM OR PLAINTIFF IF PRO SE | | TELEPHONE NO. | JURIS NO. *(If atty. or law firm)* |
|---|---|---|---|

| NAME AND ADDRESS OF PERSON RECOGNIZED TO PROSECUTE IN THE AMOUNT OF $250 | SIGNATURE OF PLAINTIFF IF PRO SE |
|---|---|

| NO. PLFS. | NO. DEFS. | NO. CNTS. | SIGNED *(Official taking recognizance; "X" proper box)* | ☐ Commissioner of Superior Court<br>☐ Assistant Clerk | RECEIPT NO. | *For Court Use* |
|---|---|---|---|---|---|---|
| | | | | | FILE DATE | ☐ No<br>☐ Fee |

**IF THIS SUMMONS IS SIGNED by a CLERK:**

a. The signing has been done so that the Plaintiff(s) will not be denied access to the courts.
b. It is the responsibility of the Plaintiff(s) to see that service is made in the manner provided by law.
c. The Clerk is not permitted to give any legal

advice in connection with any lawsuit.
d. The Clerk signing this Summons at the request of the Plaintiff(s) is not responsible in any way for any errors or omissions in the Summons, any allegations contained in the Complaint, or the service thereof.

| I hereby certify I have read and understand the above: | SIGNED *(Pro se plaintiff)* | DATE SIGNED | DOCKET NO. |
|---|---|---|---|

**ORIGINAL**

**SUMMONS, Civil**

## Serving the Papers

To "serve your papers," or summons and complaint, means to give the defendant actual notice that a day in Small Claims Court looms in the future. Every state has its own rules on how papers must be served and we have described the procedures we practice. Check with your court for information about their procedures. Certified mail with a return receipt requested is a common method. If your state requires that the papers be served in person, or if the defendant refuses to sign for the letter, you can hire a private process server or the sheriff to deliver the papers for you ($25 to $65).

## Answer and Counterclaim

After you've given the defendant(s) notice of your intention to sue (the proverbial slap in the face with a glove), your opponent has an opportunity to contest the claim or counterclaim in a written answer to the court. For example, if you sue a customer for withholding payment for goods delivered, the debtor may very well turn around and sue you in a counterclaim alleging shoddy performance or defective goods.

In the best-case scenario, the defendant will realize that you mean business and will send you a check, or call you to settle the dispute out of court and save everyone some time and money. If this happens, you need to notify the court by phone, letter, or in person that you are withdrawing your lawsuit. In the very likely case that doesn't happen, though, read on.

## Preparing for Your Day in Court

Whether you're the plaintiff or the defendant, there are certain things you need to do to prepare for your day in court. Make no mistake, your day in Small Claims Court isn't going to be anything akin to "L.A. Law." In fact, it probably isn't even going to have the dramatic impact of "The People's Court." You've got a few minutes of the judge's time to make your case—so you'd better be well organized and prepared to use every second wisely. Plaintiffs typically spend about 10 to 20 hours preparing for their three minutes in the limelight.

If you are suing a business, use its legal name. To find out if it is a corporation, registered to do business in the State, you may call or write the Office of the Secretary of State, for the proper "corporate name." If the business has no office in your area, the Secretary of State's office will help you get the name of the company's "agent," that person who receives legal papers for the corporation in Connecticut.

If you determine that the business you wish to sue is not a corporation, you should call the Town Clerk in the town where the business is operating. The Town Clerk will provide you with the full name and post-office address of the person conducting the business, or in the case of a corporation using a trade name, its full name and principal post-office address.

Suing has become somewhat of an American pastime, consequently many states require that you make a stab at settling your dispute out of court. The most common method is writing a "demand" letter, which should politely and briefly outline the circumstances of the outstanding payment due (see Figure 16–1, in Chapter 16). This may be enough to show your debtor that you mean business. It's also an excellent piece of evidence, outlining your case concisely for the judge, should you wind up in court.

One of the most common mistakes made by plaintiffs is not having enough evidence and witnesses, or having evidence organized haphazardly. As one former Small Claims Court judge said, What you drag through the door with you will usually determine whether you win or lose. You want to document all the significant points of the story you're going to tell without going into overkill.

Another important point to remember when preparing for court is, Practice makes perfect. You need to plan how to tell your story succinctly and where to present key pieces of evidence because the judge is going to get impatient and interrupt your story if it takes too long to tell. When you get tired of practicing in front of the mirror, you might want to rehearse with a business-savvy person you know who can act as a "mock judge," or work with an attorney on an hourly fee consultation basis (discussed more later in this chapter).

If possible, carve out an hour or two to actually visit the courtroom where you'll be presenting your case. For one thing, often this is a good way to combat the butterflies that will no doubt be residing in your stomach on your court date. By calling the courthouse and finding out the name of the judge assigned to small claims on your court date, you will afford yourself the opportunity to observe the judge's style and demeanor. Remember, the judge is your only audience—an audience of one—so focus on persuading the only person who counts.

## YOUR DAY IN COURT

Start your day in court off right by bringing your court calendar notice with you so that you will at least find the right courthouse. Your first order of business on entering the courthouse will be going through a metal detector, so leave the gold chains and belts with metal buckles at home. Usually a sheet of paper called the court calendar is tacked to a prominent wall somewhere near the entrance to help you find the courtroom. This will list all cases by the name of the plaintiff and defendant, as well as the courtroom assignments.

If you are totally confused and lost, grab a friendly looking court personnel clerk, bailiff, or lawyer and plead ignorance with a smile. Now that you've found the courtroom, sit down, relax, and get yourself psyched.

At the appointed hour, the court clerk or judge will read a list of cases to be heard. Do show up on time, as your case may be dismissed or thrown out of court if the plaintiff isn't there. Either the plaintiff or defendant may request that the hearing be adjourned to a later date. If there are valid grounds for the request, it may be granted at the judge's discretion, but not if the judge sees it as a stall tactic.

Next, you and your opponent may be asked to forgo presenting your case before the judge and submit your controversy to arbitration instead. Or, the judge may ask all litigants to step outside and just try to settle the case on their own one last time. These requests represent efforts to save both your time and the court's, as most Small Claims Courts often have limited judicial resources and dozens of cases on the docket each day.

The arbitration hearing is the same as that held before a judge, except that the arbitrator is usually an attorney or ex-judge. The major advantage of arbitration is that instead of waiting hours for your case to wend its way before the judge, you will usually be able to proceed to your hearing in a matter of minutes and be done with the matter—one way or the other!

The plaintiff always has the option to testify first, which can be an advantage or disadvantage depending on how you look at it. When the plaintiff presents a solid case, that's a tough act for the defendant to follow. Then again, the defendant has the advantage of hearing the plaintiff's argument before telling the other side of the story and can modify that story to persuade the judge in his or her favor (which is not to be confused with telling lies). Either way, the person with the most convincing evidence to support his or her case and most credible demeanor usually wins.

## Courtroom Etiquette

Whether you're the plaintiff or defendant, you have the rather daunting task of presenting a persuasive case to a judge (or arbitrator). Above all else, remember that the judge is basically a reasonable person similar to you and me who seems like she or he just happens to be sitting on a wooden throne, wrapped in a black shroud. If you truly have reason to collect a judgment and can tell your story in a comprehensible manner, the judge can be your greatest ally.

Following the unwritten rules of courtroom etiquette can indeed make or break your case. Here are a few simple rules that can make your day in court run smoothly.

### Dress for Success

Show up on time. Remember, the judge's first impression of you sets the mood for the hearing. A suit isn't absolutely necessary, but don't go before the judge in jeans and a sweatshirt.

### Make Sure You Get to Court on Time

Being prompt is a sign that you respect the judge's time. Not to mention that you'll probably be calmer if you have time to sit down a few minutes before your hearing to collect your thoughts and review your paperwork. Allow time to find a parking space and get lost finding the coatroom, bathroom, and courtroom.

### Keep Your Nonverbal Demeanor Neutral

Don't be defensive and aggressive. No matter how much irritation and aggravation the other party has put you through, don't bring your emotions into the courtroom—either verbally or nonverbally. Your tone of voice, facial expressions, and body language as observed by the judge—even when you are simply listening—all speak to your authority as a credible party who deserves to be believed.

### Speak to the Judge in a Respectful and Professional Manner

Don't try to be glib or joke with the judge. Just answer any questions politely and honestly. An occasional "Yes, Your Honor" doesn't hurt either (never "Yes, Ma'am," as this may be perceived as condescending).

### Always Stand Up When Addressing the Court

Even if it is just to answer "Yes" or "No" or to make a simple objection ("I object!").

### Start with the End of the Story to Get the Judge's Attention

Begin with a sentence similar to this: "The defendant owes me $_____ pursuant to our contract, and he did/didn't pay on _____ the date stated in the contract." Then elaborate on the important details.

### Keep Your Story Short

Stick to the point (take about three minutes) to avoid interruptions. Remember, you're dealing with a judge who has probably heard hundreds of similar cases and wants to resolve your case as quickly as possible to attend to everyone on the crowded schedule that day.

### Anticipate What the Other Party Is Going to Say

Be prepared to present proof that supports your side of the story in a logical manner. Assume that the other party is going to skew the truth in his or her favor by skipping some details, minimalizing important facts, or even distorting the truth. When this happens, the worst thing you can do is engage in a heated debate, trading accusations with the other party in front of the judge. The best-case scenario is presenting strong evidence backing up your version of the story and telling the truth!

## LEARN FROM A SEASONED PRO, WITHOUT PAYING HIGH-COST ATTORNEY FEES

Although attorneys are generally not allowed, or needed in Small Claims Court, you may want to buy an hour or two of consultation time to increase your chances of a win. In the following instances, you can do some of the footwork yourself and use an attorney as an advisor:

- Check out the law yourself and have the attorney verify what you've found, as well as add any important facts you've missed.
- Organize your evidence ("the case file") and have the attorney review it to make sure everything's in legal order. We will explain how to organize the case file a little later in this chapter.
- Practice presenting your case with the attorney as mock judge.

## Mock Court: Practice Makes Perfect

It's not just your evidence that's important in court, but how you present it. Go over your story until you get it down pat, and then go over it again. You may even want to request that your mock judge interrupt you with questions.

While engaging in your mock court session, it may be helpful to practice using legal terms and politically correct phrases that may sound foreign to you. Here are some phrases that may bolster your confidence by making you sound more professional in court:

- When the judge asks you a question, answer, "Yes, Your Honor," or "No, Your Honor," whenever possible.
- When the judge admonishes you, gives you a direction, or cautions you, say, "Yes, Your Honor."

- If the judge is argumentive, demeaning, or angry, say, "Yes, Your Honor," or better yet, nothing at all.
- When you want to get the judge's attention, and interrupt your overexcited, perhaps ranting, adversary, say, "Your Honor, if I may be heard."
- Never, ever, ever argue with the judge!
- When the judge excuses you and says you may go, say, "Thank you, Your Honor," and wait until the judge leaves the bench before you leave.
- If you would like to thank the judge, do so "on the record" by saying, "Your Honor, for the record, I'd like to thank you for your attention." It *never* hurts to say thank you.

## ORGANIZING YOUR PAPERWORK LIKE A LAWYER'S CASE FILE

This section may well be worth the price of this book, because we are going to reveal a secret that virtually every successful attorney has learned: how to organize a case file.

Organizing the information as an attorney does is a key to keeping your case running smoothly and efficiently and presenting it well in court. We will include various forms and techniques for you to use in setting up the following materials in an orderly file:

1. Notes.
2. Correspondence.
3. Pleadings and motions.
4. Billing information.
5. Discovery materials.
6. Miscellaneous.

From these materials, you will learn to construct the following elements that are crucial to winning your case:

1. Fact chronology.
2. Cast of characters.
3. History of the case.
4. Court presentation.

The Court Coach® suggests organizing your files the way we organize our files. In an accordion file, there are individual file folders, some of which are color coded, as follows: blue folder for "Attorney's

Notes," green folder for "Correspondence," yellow folder for "Pleadings," and orange folder for "Billing." Additional folders are added as needed for "Retainer Agreement," "Client Information," and other discovery information.

The trick is to organize this file (which can be purchased from any stationery store) before you talk to an attorney—or, better yet, before you begin even thinking about bringing a lawsuit. In each folder, order your papers in reverse chronological order so that you can file the most recently received letter on top without mixing up the previous correspondence.

## File 1: Chronologize Your Facts

Go back to your correspondence and notes that you have kept, including phone messages, internal memos, and information on your computer disk, and draft a chronological history of the case. Start with the earliest date possible to create a logical sequence of events leading up to your face-off with the defendant in court. For example, you may want to start this tracking process with the original contract (if any exists) or the first invoice.

By the end of drafting the history of the case, you will have before you a fact-based scenario that will be the basis of your script in court. Your job is to present these facts to the judge in a cohesive manner. Remember: The judge's sole interest is in the facts of the case—not your theories or your feelings, but the facts.

## File 2: The Cast of Characters

Here's a Court Coach® tip, applicable to any business or personal project, that will save you hours of time. On a large index card or a piece of paper that will not get lost among the paperwork (or better yet, on your computer), list the cast of characters involved in your case.

The cast of characters is a compendium that lists the name, address, phone number, and fax number for everyone involved in this case, including the court clerk and the judge. When you have to go through a secretary or receptionist to contact a character involved in your case, find out the name of this person and add it to your list.

## File 3: The Case History

In your third folder, you have been keeping every document and piece of paper that you have either filed in court or received from court. It is important to have a cover sheet and to log in the date on the document and the date received. When you are preparing your script for court, this case history (together with your cast of characters and your history of the case) will make assembling your presentation a simple task. Court Coach® suggests that you purchase a "Date Received" stamp if you are involved in a legal case. Also have stamps "FILE" and "DRAFT," which can be found easily at your local stationery, office products, or shipping store.

## Using the Case File to Prepare Your Script for Court

Your first step when preparing your script for court, is to review your cast of characters, chronology, and history of the case. Assemble all your original discovery documents that are evidence of your claim (e.g., all the bills and notices that you have sent), and think very carefully about what you want to say to the judge regarding this material. Make it simple.

Take out a legal pad and outline your presentation as follows:

1. Relief requested.
2. Facts presentation.
3. Production of documents supporting your facts.
4. Law that applies to your situation and supports your position, either statutory law (statutes) or case law (cases by name). If possible, give the judge "a case to hang her [his] hat on," by finding in your research another situation with a set of facts similar to yours and a conclusion that is the result you wish to obtain. Then sit down and you are done.

Some attorneys will outline exactly what they are going to say, and they will outline any questions that they might ask the other person if that is allowed on cross-examination. Certainly, you can do the same, although the Court Coach® suggests that you will have a stronger presentation if you just write down three or four main points and make these points forcefully.

If you do have any burning questions for cross-examination, write those down as well. Be brief and be confident because you know the facts better than anybody else and you are there to be a presenter of the facts and not necessarily to argue the law.

# COLLECTING YOUR JUDGMENT

Once you receive a judgment in your favor, don't breathe a sigh of relief quite yet. The next crucial step is collecting your money. We're sorry to inform you that this can be a long and fruitless process. Up to 45 percent of all winners in Small Claims Court never see a dime of their judgment, often because the defendant simply doesn't have the money.

This may be a good time to repeat our caution at the beginning of the chapter: Find out your debtor's financial status before filing a lawsuit. If you can't collect a judgment because your debtor is judgment proof (broke), don't bother venting your anger through the court process.

But let's assume that your debtor is fluid and has plenty of money to pay the judgment. Your first step in trying to collect your judgment is to send a collection note requesting your money pursuant to the judge's order within a given period of time.

If a collection note doesn't prove productive, it's time to call your local sheriff, a collection agency, or a collection attorney willing to pick up the case at this late date. For a small fee paid each time you engage the sheriff's services (for example, $25 in California), the sheriff will attempt to collect your money.

You may think you can relax when you have a judgment in your favor. The bad news is that you have to execute on the judgment which involves a whole series of additional steps in order to actually obtain cash in hand. Once again, check with your court personnel or your state's written materials or consult an attorney specializing in collections. When collection on a judgment is not forthcoming, the collection process can become complicated and we recommend that you consult an attorney for assistance. However, if you want to go it alone, take a look at the Nolo Press Publication, *Everybody's Guide to Small Claims Court*, by Attorney Ralph Warner, to discover the issues. You will have to find out the rules you need to follow in your particular state. The legal procedures you may need to follow include writs of execution, levy, garnishment, and examination of the judgment debtor.

---

## KNOW YOUR KEY TERMS

- *Pro se or pro per.* Self-representation (without an attorney).
- *Small Claims Court.* The municipal court where cases involving sums under an amount determined by the state are heard before a judge, without a jury. Often, the parties represent

themselves pro se, and in some states attorneys are not permitted. Rules of evidence are usually relaxed, as is the standard for "guilt beyond reasonable doubt."

- *Defendant.* The party being sued, who is the alleged debtor.
- *Plaintiff.* The party lodging the complaint and filing the lawsuit.
- *Evidence.* Any documents, photos, or props that you can use in court to help prove your case.
- *Burden of proof.* The burden of moving the facts and evidence along shifts from plaintiff to the defendant as the trial proceeds.
- *Standard of proof.* The amount of proof that is needed in a case to win a judgment. The standard of proof in Small Claims Court is more relaxed than for the state and federal courts.
- *Witness.* Any person who can shed light on your case, and help prove your side of the story, whom you informally request to appear or formally request by delivering a subpoena.
- *Concurrent jurisdiction.* The authority by two separate courts to hear the same case.
- *Judgment.* The judge's decision about how much money the defendant is legally bound to pay you (unless, of course, the person doesn't have it).
- *Judgment proof.* A reference to a defendant who is unable to pay the judgment due to lack of funds. It's best to find out this information up front and bypass the hassle of filing a lawsuit and going to court, only to walk away with nothing but increased frustration and anger (and, as we all know, you can't take that to the bank).

## BASIC LEGAL RESEARCH

- *Where to find your local Small Claims Court.* Call the local county courthouse, listed in the blue pages under Government Offices, and ask to speak to the clerk of the Small Claims Court. This court may well have a special pamphlet or instructions on how to file, process, and prosecute or defend a small claims action.
- *Collect Your Court Judgment,* by Gini Graham Scott, Stephen R. Elias, and Lisa S. Goldottas (Nolo Press). Offers 19 ways to get paid when you win a lawsuit.
- *Everybody's Guide to Small Claims Court,* by Ralph Warner (Nolo Press). A step-by-step guide to preparing and presenting a case in Small Claims Court.

## KEY RESOURCES

- *Private process servers.* These people hand-deliver the court summons to the defendant if face-to-face delivery is required by your state. Your local sheriff or county clerk can give your some references.
- *Local sheriff's office.* You can call or visit and ask pertinent questions about putting the paperwork you have for them in order.
- *Collection agencies.* Found in the yellow pages, these services may be helpful in collecting your judgment for you.
- *State Bar Association.* Often, the Bar or one of its committees, may have prepared materials on small claims inquiries.

## COURT COACH® SUGGESTS

1. *Do some detective work on your own to assess whether a debtor will pay up if you drag the person to court and win.* If you have a driver's license number, you can use it to glean some valuable information. The local Department of Motor Vehicles may be able to verify data such as the license owner's proper name and address, if the person has any recorded driving violations, and whether or not the person owns the car (the information provided varies according to state law). A phone call to the local department of property services will tell you if your debtor is a homeowner. Or look in the white pages of the local telephone books. Your public library will have them, too.

2. *Court and litigation is not real life.* Remember, your job in court as a pro se, like any attorney, is to *persuade.* The courtroom is a theater where a drama unfolds, and you and all the other parties—the witnesses, the defendant—are players for an audience of one: the judge.

3. *Beware of a fraudulent conveyance.* First of all, what is it? Just like it sounds, this is what occurs when a potential debtor conveys property to another person, knowing that a debt is owed or that a lawsuit to collect a valid debt is imminent or in process. Hence, if the debtor transfers title to her house to her spouse, even if your lawsuit is still in the wings, that conveyance may in the future be deemed "fraudulent" and set aside (meaning it didn't work and no property interest was transferred). Note

further that what is good for the goose is good for the gander. If you are the debtor, a transfer to avoid a valid debt may be adjudged illegal.

4. *The Three (Courtroom) C's.* Always remember the Three C's:

   Be cool. Keep your emotions under control and your wits about you.

   Be courteous. The politer the better!

   Be contrite. If you are in the wrong, express genuine regret and state the real reason for your failure.

   Remember, the judge is supposed to be objective and reasonable, *and* if you have a bona fide defense position and state your position *courteously* and *coolly*, the judge will factor this position in when rendering judgment.

5. *If you are the defendant, consider filing a motion to have your case heard before a jury in a higher court.* If you are being sued, rather than suing, you may want to remove your case to a higher court to take advantage of a jury trial,

6. *Remember that even a small money settlement against you could set a precedent for other similarly situated individuals.*

7. *Regarding judgment: "Splitting the baby" is the norm (a variation on "throwing the dog a bone").* Believe it or not, most judges are reluctant to make one person the "big winner." If you really deserve to win it all, hands down, you may come away disappointed if the judge gives some credence to your opposition's position (whether you are the plaintiff or defendant). So be forewarned that, even though you deserve every single penny, you may not receive it.

   Somehow, from time to time, the notions of objectivity and fairness get translated into the old cliches: "No one is all right or all wrong," and "We want everyone to go away a little bit happy and a little bit sad." The invariable result is that the losing party gets a bone—a small token—to placate him or her, even though the person may not really deserve a scrap of any kind. The best attitude to take if you win a case and your opponent is thrown a bone is to be content that you made an educated effort and it was successful.

# 18

---

# HAVING YOUR DAY
# IN COURT

While the majority of small business collection matters takes place in
Small Claims Court, almost all other civil litigation involving small
business matters takes place in trial courts, either state or federal, and
appellate courts on both levels as well.

This chapter will aid your comprehension of the state and federal
court system. It is not meant as a tallyho for you to represent yourself
in court armed with false bravado and this book. This chapter is
meant to:

- Give you a feel for the types of cases that may take you, as a
  small business owner, to a state or federal court;
- Remove the veil of mystery surrounding the state and federal
  court system and thus to boost your understanding of and confidence in the judicial process.
- Encourage you to participate actively if you bring or defend a
  claim in court—you can cut down on attorney fees, maintain
  control of your life and your business, and feel right about the
  outcome.

# AN INTRODUCTION TO THE STATE AND FEDERAL JUSTICE SYSTEM

Before we talk about how to take your case to either a state or federal court, let's examine what exactly those "courts" are. As you've probably gathered by now, there are two different systems of law.

While the details of this dual structure of courts can be complex, the basic concept to keep in mind is simple: The two separate justice systems—the state courts and the federal courts, operating side by side—hear matters involving the two respective bodies of law (for more information on the differences between state and federal laws, see the Introduction to this book).

Most state legislators take their cue from the federal laws passed and tailor those general federal laws to suit the specific needs of the citizens in their particular state. For example, the Congress passed a Family and Medical Leave Act, and many state legislatures have expanded on that Act. Both federal and state laws will be applicable to you, as a small business owner, and you must comply with them.

## State System

The state judicial system, which hears cases dealing with laws passed by your state legislature and common-law cases not meeting federal jurisdictional requirements.

A case involving state law will only go to Small Claims Court if it falls under that court's jurisdiction, that is, "power or authority" to hear cases. Small Claims Court, a special kind of state court in the civil division, have jurisdiction to hear cases about money damages only up to a certain limit. In Alaska and Utah, the jurisdictional amount is $5,000; in Minnesota, it is $7,500; and in Mississippi it is $1,000. Some Small Claims Courts also have jurisdiction over cases not involving money damages, for example, eviction. Further, some can offer other kinds of relief in addition to an award of dollars: rescission, resolution, reformation, and specific performance.

All other cases involving the civil law of the state, and all criminal law cases, go to your state's trial court, usually called Superior Court. The easy way to figure out whether you should be in state court is to ask yourself, "Is this a situation about a claim for dollars and the dollars are more than the jurisdictional limit allowed in my state?" If the answer is "yes," you should definitely be in the (trial) court of your state.

You need to look at the cause of action (problem) and the remedy or relief you are asking the court to give you. There are many possibilities besides money damages. Hence, you may need to go to your state court for any of these reasons, wrongs committed against you, for which you want relief:

**Injuries to persons, including death injuries**
Personal Injuries
Wrongful Death Actions
Nonfatal Injuries to Others

**Deception**
Fraud
Affirmance of the Contract
Rescission of the Contract
Innocent Misrepresentation
Nondisclosure
Nonpecuniary Loss

**Duress, Undue Influence, Unconscionability Injury to Tangible Property Interests**
Misappropriation of Money
Injuries to Personal Property
Injuries to Real Property

**Injuries to Intangible Business and Relational Interests**
Destruction of a business
Inducing Breach of Contract
Diversion of Benefits
Infringement of Patents and Statutory Copyrights
Diversion of Trade

**Defamation and Business Disparagement**
Personal Defamation
Invasion of Privacy

**Breach of Contract/Unenforceable Contracts**
Contracts of Sale of an Interest in Land
Contracts for the Sale of Chattels
Construction Contracts
Employment Contracts
Contracts Unenforceable Because Not in Writing
Contracts Unenforceable Due to Impossibility or Frustration
  of Purpose
Contracts Unenforceable Because of Lack of Capacity to
  Contract
Agreements Unenforceable Because of Illegality

For all of these causes of action, your state court has remedies. When it comes to relief, a discussion of that topic must wait for another day. We strongly recommend that you consult an attorney if you are preparing to proceed in Superior Court. If you do not want total representation, perhaps you could request your business attorney to work with you on a consultation basis, to "unbundle" the services, or, for a small fee, you could call Court Coach® for a referral (203-838-7001).

## Federal System

The federal judicial system deals with the federal laws passed by the Congress; administrative law of the federal agencies; common-law cases meeting federal jurisdictional requirements; and cases involving a federal question under the U.S. Constitution or a treaty.

## GETTING TO FEDERAL COURT

You need certain criteria to qualify for taking a case into federal court. Basically, the federal court only has the power to hear two kinds of cases:

1. *Cases involving a federal question, rising out of the U.S. Constitution, a treaty, or a federal law.* In a business context, this affects civil rights issues covered in the Constitution, or laws pertaining to federally regulated aspects of business, including bankruptcy, patents, copyright, and trademarks. These laws are applicable to you no matter what state you live in.
2. *Diversity jurisdiction involving amounts over $50,000.* As we mentioned before, a state has jurisdiction over its citizens. But what happens when the plaintiff and defendant are from different (diverse) states, which may have different standards for the same law? You are allowed to use the federal court system because the controversy is "between a citizen of the state where the suit is brought, and a citizen of another state."

Let's say, for example, that Lou's Prefab Houses is a company that manufactures homes in Boise, Idaho. Lou lands a huge contract with Mountain View Development and must complete 10 homes by a given deadline in the contract. Lou's supplier, Jack's Lumber, in Tacoma, Washington, accidentally routes the lumber order to Des Moines, Iowa, by mistake. Consequently, Lou does not receive the shipment in time to make his deadline, which costs him a penalty of $60,000.

Obviously, Lou is going to sue Jack for his loss, but it's not quite so obvious which court they'll land in. If both the defendant and plaintiff were from Idaho, they would go to the state court in Idaho. But since the parties operate businesses in two different states, with two different sets of laws, the fair and legal thing for these two disputing parties to do is take their case to a federal court. The only way around this would have been for Lou to have stipulated in his contract with Jack the state court in which legal matters were to be resolved.

## The Hierarchy of the State Justice System

To simplify a justice system that took hundreds of years to evolve, in just a few short pages, let's begin by explaining the elements of the state justice system. As you can see in Table 18–1, the setup of the state courts mirrors that of the federal courts (to clarify the hierarchy, refer to Table 18–1 frequently as you read this chapter).

As a *small* business owner (emphasis on the small) you'll probably find yourself in state court as opposed to federal court if a legal dispute arises. Most lawsuits, including business litigation, are heard in the state courts because a state has primary jurisdiction over its citizens. There are three state laws that all citizens in a given state are subject to:

1. *The "statutory" laws* that have been enacted in your state's legislature over a long history of time, and that often take their lead from federal laws that are passed.

2. Common-law  cases. As we discussed in the Introduction to this book, case law arises out of common-law concepts, for example, a tort or a contract. From decisions made by judges and juries over a long period of time creating precedents, a body of case law has emerged.

3. Your state's Constitution.

Now, it gets a bit more complex. The concept of *states' rights,* such an essential element of the U.S. Constitution, allows each state to develop its own system of courts, involving the several levels illustrated in Table 18–1. Consequently, not all states have exactly the same levels or names for their state system. The various levels are usually as follows, from lowest to highest:

1. *State trial court.* This is the starting point for civil and criminal cases. A judge, and sometimes a jury if so chosen, determines the result based on a presentation of evidence.

**Table 18–1**    The State and Federal Court System

| | State Level | Federal Level |
|---|---|---|

**Level 1.   Trial Courts**
(Your civil or criminal case's starting point)n

| | | |
|---|---|---|
| Court name | Superior Court (or NY Supreme Court) | District Court |
| Judge or jury? | Either a judge or jury of your peers will hear the case, depending on the claim and your choice. | |
| Your recourse | If you don't like the court's decision, file a timely "appeal" and proceed to Level 2. | |

**Level 2.   Appellate Courts**
(The intermediate court)

| | | |
|---|---|---|
| Court name | Not all states have an intermediate court. If they do, it's simply called the Appellate Court. | 9 Circuit Courts (each court has jurisdiction over certain states) |
| Judge or jury? | In both courts, your case will be heard by a panel of judges. | |
| Your recourse | If you don't like the court's decision, file another appeal and proceed to Level 3. | |

**Level 3.   Supreme Court**
(The buck stops here)

| | | |
|---|---|---|
| Court name | Supreme Court, except in New York, which calls it the Court of Appeals. | U.S. Supreme Court (located in Washington, DC) |
| Judge or jury? | A panel of judges. | 9 Justices (appointed by various Presidents of the United States and confirmed by the Congress) |
| Your recourse | Nada. You've had your last bite at the apple. | |

2. *Appellate court.* Sometimes an intermediate level court is available, where either the plaintiff or defendant can take the case if dissatisfied with the results reached at the trial level. Not all states have an intermediate appellate court. Note that prosecutors cannot dispute trial court decisions.
3. *Supreme court.* This is the highest state court. Decisions made here, by a panel of judges, are final. The buck stops here.

## THE LITIGATION PROCESS: HOW THE ENGINE WORKS

Now that you have a grasp of the legal definitions and body structure that make up the legal system, let's explore the litigation engine—how we get this thing to work!

Regardless of whether your case is going to be heard in state or federal court, here's how the system works (this is the way Court Coach® explains it to clients to cut through the legal mumbo-jumbo): When you have a problem, you have a "complaint" about something. Because we are a nation of law, you have "standing"—the right to sue via a "summons" (a written notice) the person you are having the dispute with into a neutral territory called "the court." Here, there is supposed to be an objective third party to decide who wins or loses.

This objective third party will be a judge, and sometimes a jury. After hearing each side's story and reviewing the evidence supporting each version of the truth, the judge and/or jury will make their decision a judgment or order if before a judge, and a verdict when a jury is involved. The judge can order one of the following to rectify the situation:

- The defendant or plaintiff must do something.
- The defendant or plaintiff must refrain from doing something.
- The plaintiff is awarded or denied a judgment of monetary compensation.

A final word about the way in which evidence is presented to the judge and/or jury. This depends on whether the case before the court is a civil or criminal matter:

- *Criminal case.* Evidence is presented by a prosecutor, who represents the state, and the defense, either a (free) public defender or a private defense attorney.
- *Civil case.* Evidence is presented by the plaintiff and defendant, who are represented by attorneys or pro se (self-representation).

Chapter 17 provides definitions for additional legal terms and information pertaining to your day in court. The same basic concepts about presenting or defending your case apply, regardless of which court your case is being heard in.

## Step 1. Getting the Cast of Characters on Board

The plaintiff and defendant have the opportunity to have their respective sides of the story heard by a judge or sometimes a jury in a court of law. Once the summons and complaint is served, everybody is on notice that a lawsuit is in progress. Then the cast of characters must be assembled and brought on board, prospective attorneys (if any), co-defendants, and witnesses.

## Step 2. The Discovery Phase

Here's your opportunity to (1) assemble all your paperwork and (2) find out, through document requests, subpoenas of documents, depositions, and written interrogatories, any and all relevant information. This is the fun part when you get to discover the other side's secrets. You get to read people's diaries and day timers, subpoena checking statements, registers and financial records of every ilk. You are entitled to dig out all the information—hidden or not—that you deem is necessary to bring your case properly into court.

If you are on the receiving end of this (the defendant), there are defensive maneuvers to protect yourself from revealing trade secrets, confidential records and communications, and irrelevant data unrelated to the case. Examples of legal ways to oppose your adversary include a motion to preclude, restraining order, and injunction.

The central rule for discovery decorum is, while discovery is broad, it can't be overly burdensome or meant to harass, or irrelevant. In a commercial dispute, your personal life (e.g., your marital status or sexual orientation), is probably completely nondiscoverable. Confidential exchanges of information—such as between a fiduciary/client, priest/penitent, doctor/patient, attorney/client, or therapist-counselor/client—is usually protected by privilege, meaning you or the professional will not be required to reveal this information.

The courts do not look favorably on "fishing expeditions," during which you ask wide-ranging questions in the hopes of finding some damaging evidence.

# Step 3. Court Time (Let the Games Begin!)

Depending on the court's backlog (number of cases on the docket scheduled to be heard), you will now enter the final phase of dealing with the court directly—live and in person. In many court systems, there may be intermediate steps before you arrive at actual full-blown trial. This is the judicial system's attempt to cut down on the backlog and expedite resolution by providing mechanisms to help the disputants settle somewhere along the way. The following are the most common intermediatory methods (your state may use different terms for these procedures, so inquire).

**Status Conference**

The judge is apprised of what's happening and what needs to happen to move the case along. The judge has the power to direct you, or your attorney, to do whatever needs to be done to move to resolution, such as finish answering interrogatories, schedule a deposition, or even set a trial date. This is an informal conversation, usually, in the judge's chambers and your attorney, not you, will appear if you are represented.

**Pretrial Hearing**

Both sides informally present their evidence before the judge. After listening to both sides, the judge gives a "thumbnail" reaction of how the case might be decided given the bare-bones evidence presented. The judge will also provide a range of judgment (dollar figures) if the dispute involves damages. Keep in mind that there are no witnesses at pretrial hearings, and things can change dramatically once an actual trial is underway and witness credibility is brought into play.

You can also brief the facts and the law for the judge's consideration in a pretrial memo. In the case of a pretrial hearing or memo, the judge will probably encourage the two sides to come up with a settlement—or at least a range of figures—agreeable to all.

If you are going before a judge in a pretrial hearing, or are writing a pretrial memo, you'll need to put together a legal animal known as "a brief" (a summary of your case). Your first step is to find cases that support your own (see Introduction to this book), so here let's touch on the structure.

Remember, only bare-bones evidence is proffered in the brief. Open with a short presentation of the facts as you see them, and then offer a few cases to support your position. Make sure your attorney reviews your brief if you write it yourself.

### Four-Way Conferences

The attorneys and their respective clients can meet anywhere along the road. This is where you put your cards on the table in an informal atmosphere outside the courtroom (well, maybe not all your cards; see Chapter 7 for points on negotiation). While discussing your earlier and present settlement proposals, you will no doubt discover whether there is any possibility of settling this case out of court.

You certainly will want to do this preliminary assessment to flush out the opposition's position before going to court. You may be able to get a handle on the strengths and weaknesses of the other party's case, and evaluate the "sympathy factor" that your opponent may illicit in court. The sympathy factor has nothing to do with who's right and who's wrong, but it has been responsible for many a jury being swayed one way or the other.

### Masters Hearing, Court Referees, Magistrate Court, Mediation, Arbitration, or Other Alternative Dispute Resolution

As the date for the trial grows ever closer, the court will probably become more diligent in its effort to avoid an expensive trial. Depending on the state and the charges, all sorts of quasi-judicial alternatives to court are available.

For example, in Connecticut, a Masters hearing takes place before three attorneys who will give you a nonbinding decision based on their combined expertise. In other instances, a court referee (sometimes a retired judge) or a legal magistrate will hear your case and give you a binding decision.

These alternative dispute resolutions may be optional, or they can also be mandated by the court as a pretrial requirement. The irony of the legal system is that, not just the Court Coach, but almost any lawyer and most judges would tell you to avail yourself of any one of these alternatives to avoid the emotional and economic costs of a trial.

## YOUR DAY IN COURT

Please take what follows with this qualification: We are describing the Court Coach's personally developed perspective on what the courtroom is all about and how to prepare for trial. This point of view is Shakespearean—all the world's a stage, and men and women merely players. In this case, the stage is the courtroom, where a drama enfolds; this is your story, scripted by you, with a cast of characters chosen by you.

## Structuring Your Script

First off, let's examine the role of a lawyer, whose job it is to script this performance so that the desired ending is achieved (you win). A lawyer's job is persuasion, not truth. The lawyer in court is an advocate and, as an advocate, takes a position, marshaling certain facts to support that position. A good advocate draws a picture for the court and convinces through (1) careful and thorough preparation, (2) orderly presentation, and (3) a clear articulation of the previously determined position.

If you are acting as your own lawyer, you need to proceed in exactly the same manner. But first, you need to put the right frame around your thinking: You are a dramatist presenting a short play to the court, your audience of one, if a judge, or a few, if a jury of your peers. In structuring your play, think like a playwright, using three steps:

1. Beginning (your opening statement).
2. Middle, a presentation of the facts through testimony of witnesses and documents put into evidence.
3. End, a request for relief, summation of the law, and a statement of how this play should end (you prevail, of course). Called closing argument.

Before you do anything else, you need to decide on your theme. Start off by putting yourself in the place of the audience (the judge or jury) and consider what will keep their attention.

Let's say your case involves wrongful termination and your position is that you did not wrongfully terminate. An obvious theme might be: "I am a really good guy and respectable businessperson who wouldn't act in such a negative manner, and this employee was nothing but trouble." Now you have your theme, you want to present individual vignettes or scenes all supporting and reinforcing this theme. Anything else is extraneous so throw it out. Possible scenes might include the following evidence:

- Evidence showing you are a good guy:
  Employment history.
  Profit/loss in business.
  Employee loyalty.
- Evidence that the plaintiff is a poor employee:
  Past work history.

Performance evaluation.

Negative supervisors' reports.

Your witnesses and your documents should be marshaled, one by one, to underscore and reinforce your theme.

Even if you have a lawyer take you to trial, discuss this approach and work with your lawyer by fully providing the supporting information (witnesses and documents).

## Presenting Your Script to the Court

We discussed some of the principles of courtroom etiquette and presenting yourself professionally before a judge in Chapter 17. Here's a refresher course, with a few extras thrown in that apply especially to the more formal atmosphere of a higher court.

### Keep It Simple

In a real effort to keep things simple, one lawyer in a major litigation used his child's grade-school science book to explain a complicated engineering principle!

### Play It Straight

Sarcasm, negativity, cynicism, attacks, even wit and humor, are risky business. Play it straight until you hit the big leagues.

### Listen to the Judge

One judge reported recently that he tries to tell lawyers and "propers" (another term for pro se litigants) appearing before him exactly what he wants to hear after he has listened for a while. And very often, the lawyer or "proper" cannot refocus his or her thinking and insists on following the prepared script. This particular judge has been known to excuse himself from the courtroom, saying to continue speaking but that he won't be listening until the lawyer reaches the issue the judge wants to hear about.

### Observe the Judge

Ask the judge for guidance and what would be helpful for the court to hear. Do not ignore that the judge's eyes are glazing over or that the judge's words and demeanor indicate a loss of patience. This would be a good time to ask for guidance.

### Focus on the Relief You Want

What are you asking the court to grant? What do you want the court to do for you that the court has the power to do? This should be the only reason you are in court—not to get even, humiliate, or exact revenge.

We discussed the kinds of relief the judge can order in a civil case (noncriminal) in Chapter 17. The additional relief the judge can order in a criminal case is prison time for the offender.

**Plead Your Case Well**

Your good performance is most important in obtaining the relief you want. Knowing how to present yourself in court and what "court" really means can turn this nerve-racking day into a day of great personal triumph (see Chapter 17 for insider tips on preparing yourself for court).

## UNDERSTANDING COURT DECISIONS (OR, HOW CASE LAW IS BORN)

In the Legal Primer in Appendix L, we introduce you to the state and federal court reporters. As you now know, those books—with all the written decisions handed down from the highest courts of these two court systems—are called case law.

It's important to be able to research these decisions, as they will affect how the judge and/or jury view your case. These decisions interpret the statutory law and are binding on all. They set a precedent that must be followed by either all state or all federal courts until later changed, or overruled, by the same high court, usually the supreme court of the state or the U.S. Supreme Court.

Here's an illustration of how the decisions in a case traveling through the federal court system may become "the law." Let's say, Robert "Bobcat" Jones [hereinafter known as "Bobcat"] is a 73-year-old janitor at Large Corporation, Inc. [hereinafter referred to as "Large Corp."], in Big City, Montana. Bobcat habitually refers to himself as an "old codger," but sues his employer for age discrimination when the CEO of Large Corp. starts referring to Bobcat habitually as a "funny old codger" and lets him go because of an economic recession and a cash-flow emergency.

The Montana District Court hears the case and rules that Large Corp. is, in fact, guilty of age discrimination as it is defined by federal law. But Large Corp. disputes the court's ruling, arguing that legitimate reasons prompted the firing. Large Corp. argues that the court has misinterpreted the law and files an appeal.

After hearing the facts of the case, the panel of three judges on circuit court of appeals overturns the district court's decision and rules that Large Corp. is not guilty of age discrimination. But Bobcat begs to differ and files yet another appeal, landing the case in the U.S. Supreme Court after it accepts Certiorari.

Ultimately, the Supreme Court does not side with Bobcat, and agrees with the court of appeals ruling in Large Corp.'s favor. The written decision of the panel of nine judges on the Supreme Court, as you know, is the law of the land—what they say, goes. And so, another case is reported in the reporter and becomes binding precedent, and anyone can now read the history of the case, the reasoning behind it, and the decision on *Jones* v. *Large Corporation, Inc.,* v. *Jones* (1995).

## LEARN BASIC RULES OF WRITING SO THAT YOU PASS MUSTER IN THE COURTS

If you're representing yourself in court, the first step in presenting yourself professionally (like a lawyer) is to be able to write professionally (like a lawyer). We cover this topic briefly in Appendix L, but here are some rules for legal writing.

### Lawyers Write in Declarative Sentences

Fine, but what's a declarative sentence? These are the sentences we learned in grade school; they go like this:

| **Jane and Dick** | **saw** | **Spot.** |
|:---:|:---:|:---:|
| Subject (nouns) of sentence | Simple predicate (verb) of sentence | Object (noun) of sentence |

Keep doing these in short paragraphs and you are almost home.

### Break Up Your Writing with Interrogatory Sentences

Every once in a while, in a brief or memo or letter, ask a question, an interrogatory sentence, recognized by the question mark (?) at the end. In the law, interrogatories are a discovery document asking lots of questions that await an answer. So, if you draft a set of interrogatories, you will be using this format.

### Avoid Exclamatory Sentences

In briefs or other legal documents, sentences that end with an exclamation point (!) almost never exist (we're cool), but they are fun to include in a letter from time to time.

### Use a Tried-and-True Format to Outline Your Thinking

The following format works for writing just about anything— from legal documents to magazine articles:

- *ISSUE:* Whether Large Corp. fired Bobcat due to his age or for a legitimate business purpose.
- *ANSWER:* Depending on who you are, Bobcat or Large Corp., you will respond: "I was fired because I was getting old and they were paying me too much and could hire a younger person for less" or "We fired Bobcat for a legitimate business reason."
- *EXPLANATION OF ANSWER:*

  *Statutory Law.* The same law applies to both Bobcat and Large Corp., and the law states x, y, and z. Large Corp. says they complied and Bobcat says they did not comply.

  *Case Law.* The cases that present facts similar to this case where the court "held" for your position (depending on whether you are Bobcat or Large Corp.) on this issue.

### Write in Short Paragraphs
Remember, keep it short and to the point.

### Understand Basic Legal Shorthand
The following shorthand is commonly used in legal writing. Use these symbols and abbreviations and you'll look like a pro:

| | | | |
|---|---|---|---|
| ¶ | denotes "paragraph" | **b.f.p.** | bona fide purchaser |
| | also denotes "plaintiff" | **br.wrt.** | breach of warranty |
| Δ | denotes "defendant" | **b.o.p.** | burden of proof |
| **K** | contract | **s.o.l.** | statute of limitations |
| **c/a** | cause of action | **o.o.p.** | out of pocket |
| **stat.** | statute | N | negligence |
| **j/d** | jurisdiction | **pun** | punitive |
| **inj.** | injunction | **p.f.** | prima facie |

**[hereinafter "Bobcat"]** a shortened reference to someone or something you are going to name over and over. The first time you use the shortened form, bracket it, and put it in quotation marks. Use the word in quotes as quoted consistently throughout.

---

## KNOW YOUR KEY TERMS

---

- *Federal Court.* A system of courts (district court, circuit court of appeals, Supreme Court) that was created by Article III of the

United States Constitution or by Congress. These courts oversee the federal laws adopted by Congress, rights under the Constitution, and federal common laws determined by decisions made in the federal courts.

- *State Court.* The court system that oversees each state's constitution and laws adopted by the state legislature, and common law derived from the cases tried in state courts in towns throughout the state.
- *Deposition.* A questioning, usually at an attorney's office, where a party or a witness under subpoena is asked questions under oath in the presence of a court reporter, who transcribes the questions posed by the attorney and the answers and responses of the deponent.
- *Subpoena.* A legal document requiring a person to appear as a witness at a trial or deposition.

## BASIC LEGAL RESEARCH

- *Trial Advocacy in a Nutshell*, by Paul Bergman (West Publishing). Covers the fine points of handling a trial.
- *How and When to Be Your Own Lawyer*, by Robert W. Schachner (Avery). Legal nuggets of knowledge about the court systems, as well as other self-help legal tips.
- *The Federal Courts and the Federal System*, by Bator, Mishkin, Shapiro, and Weschler (University Casebook Series). The book that law students use to learn about this subject.
- *A Practical Guide to Legal Writing and Legal Method*, by John C. Dernbach and Richard V. Singleton II (Fred B. Rothman) and *Legal Writing—Sense and Nonsense*, by David Mellinkoff (Scribner's, New York). Helpful basic reference books. And have your attorney review and edit all your written materials, including correspondence.

## KEY RESOURCES

- *Make friends with the law librarian.* Or at least start up a conversation with a law student in the lobby.
- *Media.* Learn from court TV, CNN, articles on court cases. Educate yourself by observing, absorbing, and comprehending.

Osmosis works too! Remember to read reported court cases with a questioning mind. And when you don't understand a term, turn to a resource like *Black's Law Dictionary.* Or nab your friend the lawyer at lunch and ask for an explanation or an opinion.

---

## COURT COACH® SUGGESTS

1. *Take advantage of the Choice of Law provision in any interstate contract you enter into.* This provision guarantees that, should a lawsuit ensue, it will be settled in a particular state's court. Do your research and find out the difference between your state's commerce laws and those of the state in which the other party does business. You may very well find some legal loopholes or small details that would give you an advantage in the courts of one state or the other. The statute of limitations for prosecution also differs from state to state.

2. *Ah, yes! The sweet smell of discovery.* The simplest way of having the opposition produce the "paper" documents you want is to make a "request" pursuant to the state or federal discovery rules. A much harder way is subpoenaing documents by a sheriff or other process server. Ask your attorney what rules apply to discovery.

3. *Consider all forms of information the opponent has that may be useful in discovery.* In our technological age, don't forget that you are entitled to lots of different kinds of information, including documents, computer printouts, videotapes, and even E-mail. Consider all of these—and request any and all that you may need.

4. *Hidden tape recorders, eavesdropping, and the ubiquitous answering machine: Legal or illegal evidence?* This is a tricky form of discovery, and you really need to check with an attorney about what is legally permissible to do and/or what evidence the court will allow in.

5. *Hiring a private investigator is an option.* Experience has taught the Court Coach® that this may be the fastest way, and sometimes a cheaper way, to obtain information. Private investigators are especially adept at finding missing persons through public records. And, much to our amazement, their image has improved. Many private investigators come from the ranks of police detectives on early retirement. Count on spending upward of $50 per hour.

6. *Why avoid going to trial?* It's expensive, it's nerve-racking, it's time consuming, and it will not, unequivocally, produce a better result than an agreement negotiated between two reasonably sane people committed to fairness. Also, however, be forewarned that dispute resolution alternatives are not necessarily a panacea. The problem is that while you may be perfectly sane, reasonable, and fair, your adversary may be none of these, in which case you will not be able to reach a *fair* settlement. Despite your own good intentions, your ship will inexorably find a port of call at the nearest courthouse.

7. *When writing a brief for a pretrial hearing, give the judge a case to hang his [her] hat on.* This old legal saw lets you visualize how to win. The case, a prior decision, is a peg that stands for the principle you are relying on and has facts similar to your own. The more these facts resemble your own, the better, since this gives the judge an opportunity to simply agree with the decision of a previous court.

# Part III

# CLOSING DOWN A SMALL BUSINESS

# 19

## HOW TO CLOSE UP SHOP GRACEFULLY

### LIQUIDATING YOUR BUSINESS WITHOUT DECLARING BANKRUPTCY

If you need to close up shop because you are not profitable and are accumulating debt, or you simply want to retire, we have some helpful suggestions in this chapter about how to get out with your credit rating intact. The following are several options to consider when you want to close up your shop without burning your bridges with creditors (without filing for Chapter 7).

### LIQUIDATING YOUR BUSINESS THROUGH A SALE

While this has the same end result as filing a Chapter 7 bankruptcy, liquidating your business to repay debts doesn't come with the same negative side affects: *i.e.,* a bad credit rating and going to court. When considering liquidation, there are three primary considerations:

1. Do you really want to sell your business?
2. How much are you willing to sell your company for?
3. How do you want to sell your business?

The following sections will discuss these considerations.

## Do You Really Want to Sell?

Before you make a decision to sell your business, make sure you know what you're going to do with the rest of your life. Here's a little anecdote to illustrate what can happen if you make a move too quickly.

There once was a dapper gentleman (no names) who ran a well-established business during the recession of the late 1980s. He felt forced to sell his enterprise because of personal expenses and slightly sagging sales (even though the company was still viable). The aftermath was that this poor chap was left with a considerable void in his life—no job. He realized, too late, that he might have been better off hanging onto his business—which eventually picked up again—than left unemployable, and with no money to send his kids to college.

## What Is Your Selling Price?

Once you've decided to put your business on the market, you need to set a price. Even if you use a broker or other professional intermediary, you still need to have an educated idea of the price range you're willing to accept. Consider these factors:

- The location of your company.
- The potential profitability of your particular industry.
- How quickly you need to sell.
- How much you initially paid, and what the local real estate market has done since then.

## How Will You Market the Company?

Your answers to the first two questions will help you decide how to market your company: on your own, through a broker, or through a lawyer or other professional for a finder's fee.

### Option 1. Do It Yourself
This method is definitely not for everyone. Sometimes, it's worth every penny you pay to have an intermediary do the legwork

and negotiating. There are several things to consider when deciding whether or not to skip the broker's fee, or finder's fee, and sell your business yourself:

- *Assess the salesman in you.* Do you really want to, and can you, sell the company on your own? If you're not comfortable with the wheeling and dealing required, then a middleman may actually do a better job and earn every penny of the commission on the sale price.
- *Evaluate the time commitment.* Consider how much time you will need to devote to selling your business versus the time you need to spend managing and running your business to keep current and profitable before the sale. It may take weeks or months of marketing efforts, meeting with prospective buyers and deal making, to complete a sale. Consider who's going to actually mind the store during this time if you're tied up.
- *Determine how much money it will cost you to market your business.* Advertising your intention to sell will be an investment that varies depending on how wide a scope of potential sellers you want to attract. If your business is located on a busy street, a "For sale" sign in the window may be all that's warranted. On the other hand, you may want to canvass the community and advertise in local newspapers and trade publications.

If you're a good salesperson and have the time, you may at least make an initial stab at selling your business yourself to increase your profit margin on the sale. If time permits, you may want to try networking—spreading the word informally—before you spend money advertising. Consider the following options:

- Attend industry conferences where potential buyers might be present.
- Let your intentions be known to associates, suppliers, and competitors.
- Ask your lawyer, banker, accountant, and other service providers who deal with entrepreneurs on a regular basis if they could refer potential buyers to you.
- Spread the word among local merchants. You never know, the local grocer may have a brother who's been looking for just the right business in which to invest his honed skills and considerable capital, and your establishment is a perfect match!

If selling your business yourself doesn't pan out or you find your time really could be put to better use, you can always go to Plan B: Hire a broker or other professional for a finder's fee. The finder's fee, like a broker's fee, is a percentage of the sale price your business brings in. You may be able to offer a finder fee that's lower than the percentage of the sale that a broker commands (10 to 12 percent), because the broker usually has to give part of his take to the firm that employs him. Even if you find a potential buyer yourself, you still might want to engage the services of a business broker to negotiate the deal and coordinate all the legal and financial details.

From a legal point of view, before making *any* verbal or written offers, make sure you understand that "an offer" + "an acceptance" = "a contract" (see Chapter 7). If you tell someone verbally or in writing that you want to sell your company for, let's say, $400,000 and the other person agrees to that price (either verbally or in writing), you've "sold your business." Congratulations!

Hence, you can see the importance of writing down all the conditions of the sale—not just the sale price—so that the buyer and seller are clear as to their obligations. To paraphrase the Godfather, you may have said, "Make me an offer I can't refuse," but don't be blinded by the light of the sale price alone.

### Option 2. Hire a Broker

The best way to locate a reputable broker who's familiar with your industry is to query your associates and others in the industry. A local trade association may be able to give you some referrals. Your banker and accountant may also be able to suggest brokers they've dealt with before.

Before hiring a broker, be very clear about exactly what it is you want done. The services of a business broker might include:

- *Locating potential buyers.* It can take quite a bit of time to find interested, and qualified, buyers for your company—especially if you don't know where to look. An experienced broker will know how to locate potential buyers, and what questions to ask to make sure that interested parties have the financial wherewithal to complete a sale. You do not want to spend six months working out a deal only to discover your potential buyer had more wishful thinking than money.
- *Setting a realistic asking price for your business.* It's hard to put a price on the company you've nurtured since its conception. Having an outsider appraise the market value of your company, backed up by data on what similar companies have sold for recently, may be a good idea. Of course, you're not obligated to accept the price that the broker suggests.

- *Negotiating the terms of the sale.* Brokers work on commission, a percentage of the sale price, so it's in their best interest to get as high a price for you as possible and make the sale as quickly as possible.
- *Handling the paperwork and coordinating the details of the sale.* Working with the accountants, lawyers, mortgage company, and anyone else involved with the sale.

Always get the names and phone numbers of several references who can attest to the broker's competence and professionalism. Entrusting a broker with the sale of your company may be a great relief, but only if you are confident in your choice. Here are some questions to ask brokers before hiring one:

- How long have they been a broker?
- What kind of training do they have?
- Have they successfully sold companies in your industry before?
- Have they worked with companies your size before?
- Do they have contacts to locate possible buyers?
- How do they plan on marketing your business?
- Can you reserve the right to find your own potential buyers and sell your business yourself without having to pay the broker a commission?

### Option 3. Other Middlemen

A broker's not the only, or necessarily, the best way to go if you want to use a middleman to sell your business. There are many other professionals who may have the skills needed to market a business and negotiate a sale quickly and smoothly, including attorneys, accountants, and bankers for a finder's fee or other compensation. And so if you know a reputable real estate lawyer, for example, who is also a born salesperson, you may want to approach this individual about selling your business.

## PREPARING TO SELL YOUR BUSINESS WITHOUT LEGAL SNAGS—NO MATTER WHO'S SELLING IT

Whether you sell your business yourself, or use a middleman, certain practical and legal considerations will aid in a swift and efficient sale. First off, make sure your existing records, including income tax and sales tax returns, are in good order so that you, and the potential buyers, can realistically assess the value of your business. These records should include:

- Statements showing that all back taxes are paid. If you can't pay your back taxes, you may need to sell your business at a bargain price.
- Financial statements for every year your company's been in business, preferably prepared by a CPA.
- A list of your liabilities. These will also be deducted from the market sales price.
- Schedules of revenues and expenses for every year your company's been in business.
- Evaluations of the business inventory, equipment and goodwill. "What is goodwill?" you may ask. Read on!

## Placing a Value on Goodwill

Goodwill is a term that deserves your considerable attention. Goodwill is the advantage or benefit acquired by an established business, secured by the patronage of the public. This goes "beyond the mere value of the capital, stocks, funds or property. . . ." Paying for the goodwill of a business is paying for:

- Good employee relations.
- High employee morale.
- A well-established business name.
- Satisfied customers.
- Reputation.

All these goodwill components should translate into "greater than normal earning power" for your business. So, for example, if your business has been run with superior managerial skills, or has a strong client base that the competition doesn't have, this can be a very valuable asset to a potential buyer.

But how do you put a dollar value on goodwill? Here's where your learned and trusted legal professional comes in handy, as this is a completely negotiable commodity between a buyer and a seller. Capitalizing excess earnings is a good starting point. (This means you can determine how much the business is earning over and above a similar business.)

## Another Consideration for Corporations

If your business is a corporation, you need to decide the viability of offering capital stock (while other investors also maintain ownership of stock) or the assets of the business (the whole enchilada). There are pros and cons on both sides.

If you sell the stock, the corporation continues its legal existence. Consequently, the corporation's leases, contracts, and the name of the corporation all remain in existence as well. But so do all the corporation's liabilities, which could be a bad thing for the buyer. By far the most common situation when a corporation is involved is for the buyer to purchase the assets, dissolve the corporation, and start a whole new company.

If you sell the assets and not the stock, it's the buyer's responsibility to comply with the Bulk Sales Act. This state law requires that creditors be notified when merchants sell the major part of their business inventory (the bulk of their inventory). This can include equipment as well. The seller must furnish a list of existing creditors on request from the buyer. We strongly suggest and urge that a business law attorney handle this somewhat complicated transaction.

## Covenant Not to Compete

Like goodwill, this is another intangible concept. If, as the seller, you agree to enter into a covenant not to compete (which is legally binding as long as it is limited in time and the geographic area covered), you can increase your sale price as this asset has a price tag on it. If you are going to retire, this may make sense.

---

**KNOW YOUR KEY TERMS**

---

- *Business broker.* A professional who, for a percentage of the sale price, hooks up potential buyers with business owners who wish to sell their company.
- *Finder.* A matchmaker one who secures mortgage financing for a borrower or who locates a particular type of business acquisition for a corporation or individual; finds and brings together a securities insurer and an underwriter or two companies in a merger; one who locates a particular type of executive or professional for a corporation.

- *Finder's fee.* The dollars charged by the finder for bringing together the happy couple. However, a lawyer, broker, or individuals usually negotiate the terms of the contract and officiate at the sale ceremony.

## BASIC LEGAL RESEARCH

- *Research all laws that might hold up or sabotage a sale:* zoning; real estate; commercial law relating to your type of business. Uniform Commercial Code and banking laws may apply. Look at the bankruptcy law as a possible option, too.
- *Depending on your form of business, you need to look at your state's law closing down a sole proprietorship or corporation, or dissolving a partnership.* Review your contracts and leases.
- *Give notice of and terminate all of your contracts and leases according to the terms.*

## KEY RESOURCES

- *The local Small Business Association.* Look this organization up in the phone book; the people there may be able to hook you up with a broker, or maybe even a buyer for your business.
- *Word of mouth.* As we've stated throughout this chapter, this is your best resource for selling your business.

## COURT COACH® SUGGESTS

1. *If you do decide to sell your business, be sure that you have enough funds to keep it up and running during the time it takes to find a buyer.* Otherwise, you may be forced into exactly the situation you're trying to avoid—filing for bankruptcy!
2. *Make sure the broker you use to sell your business is not too "hungry" for a sale.* As we mentioned before, brokers work on commission, so they have two objectives: (1) to make a sale as quickly as possible; and (2) to get as much money as possible for the property being sold. Unfortunately, a broker who needs cash fast may be tempted to sell your company as quickly as possible in lieu of holding out for a better price. You should

make sure you know how much your company is worth, and make it clear to the broker what you're willing to settle for.

3. *When hiring a broker, leave yourself an escape hatch by limiting the contract to 30 days.* The usual contract period with a broker is 30 to 60 days. By sticking to the short end of this range, you let the broker know it is essential to do the job quickly and effectively. If the 30-day period expires and the business is still on the market, you can either extend the contract or sever the relationship cleanly if the broker isn't living up to your expectations.

3. *Here is a formula for setting a price for your business.* Most businesses sell for 2 to 2.4 times the cash flow. To calculate the cash flow, take the net income and add back depreciation and other noncash items, such as the amortization of intangible assets like customer relations and employee loyalty.

5. *If selling your business yourself, consider flexible financing.* This could be a good deal if you want to sell quickly and get some cash, and the buyer wants to own a business but doesn't have all the necessary funds. One example would be to offer to spread the payments out in a monthly financing plan, in exchange for the buyer paying an extra fee.

6. *When negotiating with the buyer, be sensitive to the other party's needs.* Remember our "negotiation dance" from Chapter 7? You need to let the other party lead sometimes to avoid stepping on that person's toes.

# 20

# AVOIDING BANKRUPTCY IN THE CASE OF SUDDEN DEATH OR DISABILITY

Nobody wants to think about sudden death or disability, let alone make plans for these somber realities. But, protecting your business assets is essential so that everything you've worked hard to build won't come crashing down. The worst thing that can happen if you do plan for death and disability is that you beat the grim reaper and retire to Arizona long before you or your heirs might need to implement these best-laid plans.

In that case, you've spent a minimal amount of time and money to achieve great peace of mind for yourself, your family, and your employees. On the other hand, if you live by the theory that these potentially disastrous events just happen to "the other guy," you may inadvertently wind up leaving behind a legacy of legal and financial chaos.

This chapter will dance you through, as quickly as possible, the four most important safeguards for your business enterprise's continued health after you are peacefully pushing up the daisies or physically unable to remain at the helm.

256

# THE FIRST SAFEGUARD: DISABILITY INSURANCE

There are two forms of disability insurance: Social Security disability insurance, provided by the government, and disability insurance plans provided by private insurers. As a small business owner, you should be aware of how much disability coverage Social Security actually provides, and what your options are for additional disability coverage.

## Social Security Disability Insurance

The Federal Insurance Contributions Act (FICA) requires employers to withhold a specified percentage of employee wages, to contribute a matching sum on all earnings up to a statutory maximum amount (approximately $40,000 annually at this time), and to send these dollars off to the Internal Revenue Service for all employees, including the boss. These funds are used to pay, among other things, Social Security disability insurance.

The same concept of building up a stake in the Social Security system through taxation applies to you as well as your employees if your business is incorporated and you receive a paycheck as a corporate officer. If you work for yourself, as a sole proprietor or a partner, your Social Security contribution is covered by a self-employment tax (see Chapter 10).

Only bona fide independent contractors and nonstatutory employees at your place of work do not have to pay in and be covered by matching employer contributions. But then they must rely on private disability insurance paid out of their own pockets without matching employer contributions, or pay on their own to the government.

Unlike the workers' compensation program, which pays out degrees of benefits in accordance with the degree of disability a worker suffers, Social Security disability insurance coverage is an all-or-nothing deal. Either you can work to some degree, even though it may not be to your full capacity, or you can't. You only receive disability benefits in the latter case (total disability). Also, unlike workers' compensation, Social Security disability insurance covers off-the-job as well as work-related accidents.

The following are some other key stipulations of Social Security disability insurance:

- *The sum of all your disability payments can't exceed 80 percent of your earnings averaged over a calculated period of time before you become disabled.* This sum includes workers' compensation and private insurance.

- *Benefits are only paid to workers and their families when the worker has accrued enough work credits to qualify.* This is determined by the worker's age and number of years of employment covered by Social Security. Workers accrue one quarter of work credit for each $570 per year earned in covered employment, with a maximum of four quarters per year.

- *You must have earned a minimum of 20 quarters of the required credit within 10 years immediately preceding the time you became disabled.* However, there are exceptions to this rule, such as if you are disabled by blindness or you are disabled between the ages of 24 and 31.

- *You must be able to prove, through medical records or doctors' reports, that you have a disability that has lasted, or is expected to last, at least 12 months.* In addition, you must be able to prove that this illness or injury prevents you from any gainful employment—not just the job you previously held or the profession for which you were trained.

We have heard many horror stories of the difficulties people have had in trying to qualify for Social Security Insurance (SSI) benefits. Remember, this is a government agency, complete with myriad rules and regulations. To simplify the process of qualifying for Social Security benefits, the Social Security Administration has developed the following list of conditions that it considers disabling:

- Diseases of the heart, lung, or blood vessels that have resulted in serious loss of heart or lung reserves as shown by X-ray, electrocardiogram, or other tests; and, in spite of medical treatment, there is breathlessness, pain, or fatigue.

- Severe arthritis which causes recurrent inflammation, pain, swelling, and deformity in major joints so that the ability to get about or use the hands is severely limited.

- Mental illness resulting in marked constriction of activities and interests, deterioration in personal habits and seriously impaired ability to get along with other people.

- Damage to the brain or brain abnormality which has resulted in severe loss of judgment, intellect, orientation, or memory.

- Cancer which is progressive and has not been controlled or cured.

- Diseases of the digestive system that result in severe malnutrition, weakness, and anemia.

- Progressive diseases that have resulted in the loss of a leg or that have caused it to become useless.
- Loss of major function of both arms, both legs, or a leg and an arm.
- Serious loss of function of the kidneys.
- Total inability to speak.

Keep in mind that while injuries and ailments on this list will probably not be challenged by the local Social Security Administration office, other conditions not listed will be considered on a case-by-case basis. Remember, too, that you always have the option to appeal a denial of your disability benefit request and be scheduled for a hearing before an administrative law judge.

## Disability Insurance Plans through Private Insurers

As we mentioned in Chapter 6, disability insurance is a necessity for small business owners who are typically the glue that holds their businesses together. Statistically, an executive at age 30 has a 48 percent chance of being disabled for 90 days or more before reaching the age of 65. And remember, Social Security disability insurance only kicks in if you can prove you're disabled for life.

The type of disability policy you buy depends on what you're willing to spend, how much coverage you need, and the insurance company you select. A good starting point is to find an insurance agent you can trust, if you don't already have one. Shop around and be choosy. This is your life and the livelihood of your business we're talking about.

After you've found an agent you're comfortable with, you'll want to calculate how much coverage you need by adding up your costs of living and subtracting any income from investments, royalty payments, Social Security, or spouse's earnings.

Next, you'll need to submit an array of information about yourself and your business to the insurance agent, who will compute the monthly premium for your disability policy based on factors such as:

- Your age and gender.
- Whether or not you are a smoker.
- What type of business you own.
- What percentage of time you spend in the office, as opposed to in the field.

- Whether you work at home or in an office building.
- Whether you have any employees or work alone.
- Your yearly gross income.

Other factors determining the amount of your payment for disability insurance include:

- *The amount of time after becoming disabled you wish to wait until receiving benefits.* You usually have a choice of 30, 60, 90, or 120 days after injury. The longer you can wait for your benefits to kick in, the lower your premiums.
- *The length of time benefits will be paid after you become disabled.* Your choices here range from one year up until you're age 65, or even for life. The shorter amount of coverage time you opt for, the lower your premiums. If you opt for coverage only up to age 65 instead of lifetime, you can cut your premium costs in half.
- *The amount of benefit coverage you want if you should become disabled.* You're entitled to up to 75 percent of your gross yearly income. The more coverage you opt for, the higher your premiums will be.

And perhaps the most important consideration comes last—can your cash flow support a monthly disability payment? If you are a woman of childbearing age, this qualified "disability" can cover related pregnancy complications forcing you out of the workforce, either before or after childbirth, and may be worth the coverage at that time. Also, man or woman, if it's a choice between an apartment rental of $800 or $1,000, or a car payment of $200 or $400, go with the disability insurance coverage as essential before upgrading your lifestyle.

A final caveat about disability insurance for sole proprietors: The solo nature of this class of business owners makes disability insurance especially important, but equally difficult to collect. You may be stuck in a Catch-22 because there's nobody to take over the daily operations of your business in the case of disability, and there's also nobody to verify that you're actually unable to work.

"There's a lot of fraud when it comes to disability insurance, especially among people who work by themselves," says Al Applestone, an insurance broker based in Seattle, Washington. "Your doctor can verify that you have a physical condition that prohibits work, but unless you have an employee or someone you rent office space with who can verify that you're actually not working, your chances of obtaining a reasonably priced disability plan are slim." Make sure that you have an unbiased, reliable source who can verify that you're actually not working before approaching an insurance agent to do your bidding with the insurers.

## THE SECOND SAFEGUARD: BUSINESS LIFE INSURANCE

While most people understand the importance of protecting their loved ones against financial ruin by purchasing life insurance, many small business owners feel that extending this same philosophy to protecting their business is a luxury they can't afford. As with disability insurance, buying business life insurance is an investment in peace of mind that you will hope you never have to use.

But in the event that you die prematurely, you or other principals, partners, family members in a family-run business, stockholders in your corporation may very well require "key person" insurance on your life to keep the company solvent while your replacement is found or the enterprise is restructured to run without you, or the temporary dip in cash flow by the dollars you generated is replaced by the proceeds from this life insurance. It may very well mean the survival of your business, whether new or long established. Those left behind will be grateful to have been spared financial chaos by your business acumen.

While planning your estate through a will, living trust, or other estate planning documents is essential (see following section), life insurance can act as a safety valve to provide your business with quick cash while your estate is being executed. The beneficiary (in this case, your business) can cash in the policy without going through the red tape, costs, and delays associated with probate court, which is the legal body that oversees estate planning laid out in a will. Life insurance is also excluded from the insured's personal taxable estate and can significantly reduce the taxes your loved ones inherit along with your estate.

In small companies run by one or a few principals, where these individuals have spouses and children at home, it is almost a given that each person have enough life insurance to support the widowed spouse and family. Otherwise, the surviving spouse will want either to maintain family income by participating in running the business or to have the remaining firm members cash them out of the company's interest. The company left behind will have to have sufficient capital or loan power to liquidate the deceased's interest, not an easy thing to accomplish, especially in sudden death.

Purchasing a life insurance policy for your business is similar to buying a policy for any other beneficiary. You have four basic choices:

1. *Whole Life.* You are covered for the face amount of the policy throughout your lifetime. So, for example, you might purchase $200,000 worth of whole life insurance, paying premiums of $150 per month. There is a limited cash surrender and loan value, as the premiums are spread out over the course of your entire estimated lifetime. This means that you can cash the policy in and receive some cash back out of your investment of premiums, and you can borrow against the policy, too. Contrast this with term insurance (see item 4).

2. *Limited Payment Life.* As with whole life, you are covered for the face amount of the policy throughout your lifetime. But premiums are paid for a set number of years, at a higher rate than whole life. This policy has a substantial cash surrender and loan value because of the higher premiums.

3. *Endowment Life.* Premiums are paid for a set number of years, until the accumulated cash value equals the face amount of the policy. You then receive the face value of the policy in a lump sum (endowment).

4. *Term Life.* This policy entails the lowest premiums because you are paying solely for insurance protection; no cash reserve is accruing. Consequently, the policy has no cash surrender value or loan possibilities. All you receive is the face amount of the coverage, say $200,000, if you die while the policy is in effect and you have not disqualified yourself by, for example, committing suicide.

## THE THIRD SAFEGUARD: ESTATE PLANNING

This section is not meant to be an all-inclusive guide to planning your estate, but rather an explanation of how your business fits into the overall scheme. The first question you need to ask yourself is, "Do I want my business to continue operating?" If the answer is "Yes," you'll need to outline the provisions for passing on your business, or the shares you own in your business, in the most expedient manner possible so that the business can continue to operate without interruption.

Three issues are involved with planning your estate so that your business can continue to operate:

1. Who will run the business?
2. How can probate costs and delays be avoided?
3. How can estate taxes be reduced?

## Who Will Run the Business?

This question is at the crux of your estate planning. Dealing with it effectively can help to avoid a messy court battle involving your surviving beneficiaries and business associates. No matter how you decide to transfer ownership—to one or several family members, a partner, or key employees—make sure that everyone who is affected by this decision knows about it while you're still around to mediate any disagreements.

You'll also need to make sure that whoever will take over the helm for you is up to the task. Even though you may want your husband to be the primary beneficiary to benefit financially from the business you've built, in reality he may not have sufficient knowledge of your industry to qualify as the best person for the job. Also consider your candidate's relationship with your employees and business partners. Any personal differences will most likely magnify in your absence.

If your business is a partnership or corporation, this question of who will assume your place in the company, or whether that is possible legally, will be governed by the partnership agreement or corporate bylaws (see Chapters 3 and 4 for more information on partnerships and corporations). For example, surviving principals of a corporation usually reserve the right to purchase ("buy out") the shares of a deceased principal from the estate. In this case, the corporate bylaws should also address how the shares are valued, and how the money is to be paid to the deceased principal's heirs.

## Avoiding Probate Costs and Delays

Placing the assets of your business in a living trust is the most common way to avoid probate, whether you're a sole proprietor, partner in a partnership, or principal in a corporation. A living trust is a legal document that fulfills the same function as a will, to transfer your property and assets to your heirs, without the help of probate court.

Before we get into how a living trust works, let's define some of the key legal elements of this animal:

- *Grantor.* This is the person who sets up the trust (you).
- *Trustee.* As the grantor of the trust, you will be the trustee during your lifetime, given that you remain mentally competent. This means that only you have the power to make changes in the trust, or gain access to the trust assets. On your death, a successor trustee whom you've named in the trust will take over the management and execution of the trust estate.

- *Trust estate.* This includes all the assets and property that you transfer to the trust.
- *Revocable.* Most living trusts are revocable, which is to say that you can make any changes (add or remove items, alter the beneficiaries) at any time.
- *Beneficiaries.* The people or organizations (such as your business) that you designate in the trust as the recipients of the trust's assets on your death. You are the beneficiary while you're alive.

Now, we'll get back to how a living trust works. While the property in the trust is legally yours while you remain alive (you still pay taxes and any outstanding debts attached to it), on your death the living trust becomes a legal separate entity that now owns the assets in it.

So, how does the trust help your heirs sidestep probate court? On your death, the trust assumes the same role that probate court does: A holding place for your assets until the estate is executed. This separate entity you have created and given your assets to now legally owns all these assets. Once the trustee dispenses the trust estate to the beneficiaries, the trust ceases to exist. All this takes place in a matter of weeks, as opposed to the months that probate court typically takes to execute a will.

In regard to your business, the most common way for a business to be transferred to a living trust is to incorporate and transfer your stock into the trust. The trust then outlines how the stock is to be divided among the beneficiaries. In the case of a solely owned company, you can also use the trust to outline how you would like your business to be managed.

If corporate bylaws or a partnership agreement is involved, this document should specifically state that each partner or principal is permitted to transfer his or her interest to a living trust. In return, the living trust must adhere to the specifications of the partnership agreement or corporate bylaws.

## Reducing Estate Taxes

Contrary to commonly held belief, living trusts do nothing to reduce estate taxes (or "death taxes," as they are often called). There are both federal and state estate taxes, to be paid, and the amount you pay will depend on the state in which you live and the value of your estate. All estates valued at more than $600,000 are taxed by the federal government, according to the size of the estate (the larger the estate, the larger the tax). In addition, a number of states also impose estate taxes.

Lest you have the uneasy feeling that your estate will be eaten up by taxes, fear not. The federal government has designed a number of tax law deductions and credits (exemptions) that allow you to leave a good deal of your assets to your heirs unscathed by estate taxation. These include:

- *Unified credit.* Allows the first $600,000 of property to pass on to heirs tax-free. Any tax-free gifts given during your lifetime will be subtracted from this $600,000.
- *Marital deduction.* Exempts all property left to a surviving spouse who is a citizen of the United States.
- *Charitable deduction.* Exempts all property left to a tax-exempt charity.

In addition, several federal estate tax rules for small businesses can reduce your taxes:

- Estate taxes assessed against the value of a small business can be deferred five years and then paid in 10 annual installments. The final payment is due 15 years after the owner's death.
- Tax breaks are permitted for corporate stock redeemed to pay estate taxes assessed against a family business. Your attorney can clue you in on the specifics if this rule applies to you.
- Real estate used in a family business can be valued for estate tax purposes at its value for the present use, rather than at its highest potential value. Again, ask your attorney for the stipulations for this rule if it applies to you.

## Gift Taxes

Another way to reduce estate taxes is through gifts. Saving the best news for last, often the optimal time to remove wealth from your taxable estate is before you have accumulated it. How? If you have incorporated, you can give your children part of the stock, keeping always a majority share yourself. And, since they will own it at the time of your death, there will be a minimal gift tax, if any, if you did this when the business started and at a time when the value of the stock was likely to be negligible. Note, too, that you can also make lifetime gifts to your children (and any others) of $10,000 per year to each completely free of federal gift taxes.

## THE FOURTH SAFEGUARD: BUY-SELL AGREEMENTS (HOW TO PASS THE BATON TO THE NEXT RUNNER WITHOUT ANY GLITCHES)

A buy-sell agreement is unquestionably a de rigueur requirement of any business enterprise involving more than one principal. If you have one or more partners or business associates, you will want to draft for an attorney to review or have your attorney draft a buy-sell agreement to avoid the following problems that could ensue on your demise or disability, or if you simply want to kick up your heels, put on your loafers, and sell your interest in the business. Why?

- Your surviving family members might not find a buyer for your interest, or might have to discount your interest significantly to attract a potential buyer.
- Again, your survivors might be faced with a significant death tax on your interest and little cash with which to pay it.
- As for others in the business with you, where does your death or disappearance leave them in terms of management and ownership? What will happen to the business if your spouse or child wants in but your partners want them out?

The solution we favor is to have a buy-sell agreement funded by key person insurance on the owners so that in the event of death, the other owners can collect the proceeds and buy out your interest in the business. The other circumstances short of death should be covered by thoughtful alternatives planned ahead of time by consultation and negotiation with all principals and owners.

---

### KNOW YOUR KEY TERMS

- *Sudden death.* For legal purposes, a reference to premature death. Planning for sudden death is essential so that your business can continue to operate and maintain its financial flow.
- *Disability.* For legal purposes, any illness or physical injury that renders you incapable of earning an income.
- *Will.* A legal document that outlines how you want your estate to be distributed.
- *Living Trust.* A legal document that allows you to avoid the costs of probate by transferring all the assets from your estate to a trust while you're alive. On your death, the beneficiaries of

the trust will receive the assets without going through probate court.

- *Estate.* Your property and other assets to be distributed to the beneficiaries of a will or trust on your death.
- *Probate.* The legal process in which a court oversees the distribution of property outlined in a will.
- *Estate taxes.* Taxes imposed on the property of a person who dies.

## BASIC LEGAL RESEARCH

- *Social Security, Medicare and Pensions,* by Joseph L. Matthews with Dorothy Matthews Berman (Nolo Press). Provides a complete explanation of how to use these federal government agencies to your best advantage.
- *Plan Your Estate,* by Denis Clifford and Cora Jordan (Nolo Press). Has information for the do-it-yourselfer about writing a will, creating a living trust, avoiding probate, protecting your business, and more. It includes sample estate plans as well.
- *The Complete Book of Wills and Estates,* by Alexander Bove (Henry Holt). Another fine guide to estate planning.

## KEY RESOURCES

- *The Social Security Administration.* Offices of this federal government organization are located in most major cities. The phone number can be found in the government pages of your phone book.
- *The Medicare information line.* After you've been collecting Social Security benefits for 24 months, Medicare coverage kicks in. For more information on Medicare, call (800) 952-8627.
- *The Internal Revenue Service.* Your local IRS office, listed in the government pages of your phone book, can supply you with pamphlets on estate taxes, gift taxes, and more.

## COURT COACH® SUGGESTS

1. *If you're a sole proprietor and want to reduce your self-employment taxes, talk to your accountant about the possibility of incorporating*

*your business and electing S corporation status.* This conversion may allow you to receive some corporate earnings in the form of dividends rather than a salary, thus reducing your self-employment taxes.

2. *Make sure your disability insurance policy is both "noncancellable" and "guaranteed renewable."* This means that the insurance policy can't be terminated after you become sick or make a claim. The company must renew the policy as long as you remain current on your payments, although it can raise the rate.

3. *If you're incorporated, look into buying yourself a workers' compensation policy.* This can be a low-cost form of disability insurance for work-related disabilities.

4. *Cut down on the costs of estate planning by drawing up your own will using self-help books or software, and paying an attorney to look it over.* Nolo Press publishes *Simple Will Book, WillMaker 4.0* software, and *Nolo's Law Form Kit* for wills for the do-it-yourselfer (valid in all states except Louisiana). Also available are *Wills: A Do-it-Yourself Guide* (HALT), *Will Builder* (Sybar Software), and *Will Power* (Jacoby & Meyers).

5. *Even if you use a living trust to avoid probate, it's still essential to write a will.* There are many reasons to prepare a will including disposing of property and assets not transferred to the trust as you wish, naming a personal guardian for your children, and as a backup tool in case you inadvertently leave something out of the trust.

6. *Check your Social Security records every few years.* Everybody makes mistakes, even the government. You can get a free postcard form for this, or to report any changes in your name (such as when you get married), at your local Social Security office.

# 21

## THE BANKRUPTCY DECISION: WHAT TO DO WHEN YOU HEAR THE FAT LADY PRACTICING HER SCALES

### INTRODUCTORY COURSE IN BANKRUPTCY

If you find yourself in the predicament of many entrepreneurs and small business owners who have accumulated greater debt than their bank accounts can support, then bankruptcy is your legal shield of protection from creditors. The U.S. Bankruptcy laws allow individuals and businesses who find themselves in this unfortunate financial predicament the opportunity for a clean slate and fresh start, either by wiping out debt or by reorganizing debt so that it can be paid off within the financial means of the debtor.

Historically, the idea behind bankruptcy was to keep the wheels of commerce rolling and the economy growing. So, instead of throwing debtors into prison, where debts were certain to remain unpaid, we developed these laws as an alternative. The major hitch is that in exchange for this clean slate, you may be refused credit for up to 10 years and lose the majority of your assets as well. But at least you will not spend years languishing in jail; and forewarned and forearmed, you can hope that your next commercial attempt will put dollars in your pocket and contribute to the gross national product.

Companies, large and small, fail and are forced to file bankruptcy for many reasons: growing too rapidly, lack of focus on key markets, a weak business plan, undercapitalization, poor financial planning and management. Poor management alone can easily torpedo an otherwise successful business with inadequate record keeping, failure to pay attention to outstanding accounts receivables, and failure to establish efficient working procedures that eliminate nonproductive downtime and duplication of efforts. It is only fair to recognize that forces outside your control also may affect your business: acts of God, nature, war, serious illness, and economic downturns caused by recessions and stock market crashes.

One thing is certain: Filing for bankruptcy is one of the hardest decisions an entrepreneur ever has to make. To help you recognize when to file bankruptcy, and how to do so with as little damage to your financial position and credit rating as possible, this chapter will address the following questions:

- *What are the pros and cons of bankruptcy, and how can I overcome the negative association I have of bankruptcy and failure?* First of all, you shouldn't make bankruptcy synonymous with failure. While to speak of filing bankruptcy leaves a nasty taste in many entrepreneurs' mouths, it can be a soothing relief from the hot breath of audacious creditors at the nape of your neck. Shame is nothing but a waste of valuable energy. Just get on with it.

- *What are the bankruptcy options for my company?* We'll define— in plain English—Chapter 7, Chapter 11, and Chapter 13. We'll also review the positive and negative aspects of each.

- *When is the right time to file bankruptcy?* You don't want to file without exhausting all your remedies to stay alive. But if hanging on too long means that you'll be shut down by creditors or the IRS, or even thrown out in the street by an eviction process, you've waited too long. Your company will have a negative net worth and will be extremely difficult to sell.

- *Are there steps I should take to prepare for bankruptcy before actually filing?* The answer to this question is an emphatic, *"Yes!"* This is perhaps the most important aspect of bankruptcy for you to consider, from the first day you open your doors for business. Optimism is what fuels entrepreneurs to succeed, and planning for bankruptcy may at first seem incongruous with the chutzpa it takes to embark on a business venture. But having a sound, well-written bankruptcy plan may mean the difference between closing up shop for good and bouncing back from a financial mishap should one occur.

As you read the following pages, keep in mind that bankruptcy is an extremely complicated area of the law; this chapter in no way provides a complete guide to filing bankruptcy. Our intent is to present an introduction to the Bankruptcy Code so that you have a base of knowledge from which to speak when talking to your bankruptcy attorney.

There are slews of bankruptcy attorneys out there; shop and compare and you'll undoubtedly discover the services of a good lawyer who will become your very favorite hand-holder during this difficult process. Attorneys specializing in bankruptcy are keenly aware that in choosing this area of law they have opted to deal with clients who are not flush with dollars (they deal in volume). We think you'll be pleasantly pleased with the reasonable fees.

## THE MUDDY WATERS OF THE PROS AND CONS OF BANKRUPTCY

Bankruptcy was once a scarlet letter that meant financial and social ruin, as typified in the classic 1940s film, *It's a Wonderful Life*. Uncle Billy loses the Bailey Building Saving and Loan's money, and a panic-stricken George Bailey (Jimmy Stewart) shouts, "Do you realize what this means? It means bankruptcy and scandal and prison!" Back then, there were only 236,000 personal bankruptcies filed during the entire decade, while in 1991 and the early part of 1992, the American Bankruptcy Institute reported that more than one million people—a record number—filed for bankruptcy.

Well, it's debatable whether an angel will save you on Christmas Eve as Jimmy's angel did, but the bankruptcy court might. Bankers, brokers, doctors, lawyers—white-collar professionals who have not been traditionally associated with bankruptcy—are seeking relief from overwhelming debt in the federal courts.

Even former Secretary of the Treasury and Texas governor John Connally and superstar singer Willie Nelson have gone through the bankruptcy process and survived quite nicely (although apparently Willie still has to sing for his supper). In fact, there have been a number of stories in the news lately about high-level executives who somehow manage to keep luxury items and an affluent lifestyle despite declaring bankruptcy.

While there's still a negative stigma associated with filing bankruptcy, it can definitely be "a wonderful life" after the dust settles. Most creditors will warn you of the "10-year mistake," referring to the 10 years a bankruptcy remains on your credit report. But many of those same naysayers will typically grant credit long before that period has passed. A recent study conducted by the Purdue University Credit Research Center, in West Lafayette, Indiana, found that 16 percent of people who have filed for bankruptcy obtained credit within a year, and 53 percent within five years.

So far, bankruptcy sounds like a pretty good deal, but be forewarned: This is where we muddy the waters. Make no mistake, all this is not by way of bidding you a safe journey and fond farewell as you jump on the bankruptcy bandwagon and go on your merry way to the bankruptcy court. Financial experts purport that, while the stigma in filing has significantly diminished, the long-term effects can still be devastating: job discrimination, rental discrimination, lowered self-esteem, lost friends, and family conflicts.

These devastating effects can be much more profound with a Chapter 7 filing. Why? Because you must liquidate your business rather than keeping it operational as under a Chapter 11 or 13 restructuring. This is why prebankruptcy planning can mean the difference between using bankruptcy as a tool to reexamine your goals and business plan, and bankruptcy as sudden death.

## BANKRUPTCY OPTIONS FOR SMALL BUSINESSES

The Bankruptcy Code, a federal law applicable uniformly throughout the United States, provides for three options for small business owners: Chapter 7 (Liquidation of Assets), Chapter 11 (Business Reorganization), and Chapter 13 (Adjustment of an Individual's Debts). Once bankruptcy is filed, your creditors are blocked from trying to collect their debts until after the bankruptcy hearing.

The debtor usually voluntarily files a bankruptcy case, but creditors may also initiate a Chapter 7 or Chapter 11 proceeding by filing an involuntary petition. In either case, filing a bankruptcy case creates an "estate" consisting of all the debtor's property, except in certain cases when property is classified as exempt (you get to keep it). The court appoints a trustee, or board of trustees depending on the type of filing, who oversees distribution of the debtor's assets.

These three major types of bankruptcy filings will be discussed in detail in Chapter 22, but here's a thumbnail sketch of each.

## Chapter 7 Bankruptcy

This is the most common bankruptcy procedure for all kinds of debts. The court-appointed trustee "liquidates" (sells) all the debtor's non-exempt property and pays off creditors according to their priority under law. For example, secured debts are paid before unsecured debts (see section on trustees in Chapter 22 for more information).

The major benefits of a Chapter 7 bankruptcy are:

- It's generally quick, taking an average of 120 days, start to finish.
- Most debts are wiped out (see Chapter 22 on nonexempt debts).
- An "automatic stay" goes into effect on the filing of your bankruptcy petition. Creditors can't call or write you; nor can they repossess or foreclose on your property (this is also true for a Chapter 11 or Chapter 13 bankruptcy).
- It's the least expensive bankruptcy option. The filing fee is $160, and attorney fees start at a minimum of $600.
- You appear before the U.S. Trustee, not a judge, who acts as the interlocutor and asks questions of the debtor.

## Chapter 13 Bankruptcy

This reorganization procedure allows you, the debtor, to design a re-payment plan to repay your debts over a three- or five-year period. The court may also reduce the amount paid to your creditors, so that the business can remain operating instead of being forced into liquidation. Secured debts and nondischargeable debts like alimony and child support will remain in place. (*Note:* This option is available *only* to those with stable income and unsecured debts not exceeding $250,000, and secured debts of no more than $750,000.) Chapter 13 bankruptcy is *not* available to corporations or partnerships (your state laws define what a "partnership" consists of).

Here's how it works: You file a payment plan with the court, which must be approved by a court-appointed trustee (usually an attorney or accountant). If approved, monthly debt payments are made directly to the trustee, who is responsible for distributing the funds to creditors.

Only about one fourth of your disposable earnings goes to creditors, although the specific amount depends on your income level and family financial responsibilities. The real plus of Chapter 13 bankruptcy is the significant degree of protection from creditors and the IRS:

- The IRS can't seize your property while you are in Chapter 13 bankruptcy.
- You have up to five years to pay back debts.
- If you are behind on your house, car, or office space payments, you have up to five year to make up the payments you have missed.
- If you owe on a big-ticket item, such as a car or office equipment, you only have to pay for the value of the item, plus interest, over the three- to five-year period you're in bankruptcy. This can reduce your payments significantly. For example, let's say you owe $15,000 on a car but it's real value has depreciated to $10,000 because it's a year old. You only have to pay the $10,000 over the term of the bankruptcy. The difference is treated as an unsecured debt, and erased.
- Unsecured creditors are paid only what you can afford over the period of the bankruptcy, but no less than what the creditor would have received under the terms of a Chapter 7 straight liquidation bankruptcy. Any unsecured debts remaining after the period of bankruptcy is over are discharged by the court (erased).
- You have much lower costs than if you file a Chapter 11 bankruptcy. The filing cost for a Chapter 13 is $160, while the filing cost for a Chapter 11 is $800. Also, you'll spend more time in court for a Chapter 11, which translates to more money spent on attorney fees.

## Chapter 11 Bankruptcy

Like Chapter 13 bankruptcy, this procedure allows businesses to remain up and running while devising and implementing a repayment plan. Chapter 11 is available to individuals who don't meet the requirements of Chapter 13 (see preceding section), as well as most partnerships and corporations.

There is no court-appointed trustee, but a U.S. government-appointed trustee will oversee the reorganization plan. The debtor submits the reorganization plan to the court, and acts as the trustee for the company's estate. *Note:* There's a hitch—and it's a big one: The reorganization plan must not only be accepted by the bankruptcy judge (as in other bankruptcies), but also by two thirds of the creditors (two thirds in amount of money owed, and more than half the number of creditors to whom you owe money).

This creditors' committee can act as a major obstacle to successful reorganization because your creditors may want you to pay more than the reorganization plan calls for. "Ten cents on a dollar," for example, is discounting an outstanding debt 90 percent. And that may not be acceptable to all the creditors who must sign off on your plan.

The benefits of a Chapter 11 bankruptcy are the same as for Chapter 13, but if you have a choice between the two definitely go for Chapter 13—it's quicker, cheaper, and easier to resolve because your creditors aren't in charge of approving your reorganization plan. If your company doesn't qualify for a Chapter 13 bankruptcy, be aware that the earlier you begin to plan for a Chapter 11, the better your chances of success are.

## PLANNING FOR BANKRUPTCY

Planning for bankruptcy—even if you never need to actually carry out your plan—should be part of your business plan from day one. Many entrepreneurs don't contact a bankruptcy attorney until they've reached a state of financial panic where bankruptcy is looming over their business like a black cloud of doom. At that point it's often too late to salvage your business through other options—loans, refinance, tightening financial management by cutting expenses and/or increasing income, as well as Chapter 11 or 13 bankruptcy.

"You don't want to think about bankruptcy because it seems like admitting failure, so you try to keep the business going—looking for shreds of evidence that things are turning around," says a small business owner who filed for bankruptcy under Chapter 7 twice. "But then when everything finally does go down the tubes, you go with it. There's no time to file for Chapter 11 or 13 and reorganize, so you just say, 'to hell with it,' file Chapter 7 and close the doors for good."

Planning for bankruptcy, even as early as in your business plan, is the best way to avoid finding yourself in a financial squeeze where liquidating your assets is the only way out as in Chapter 7 bankruptcy. But we'd like to see you be able to exercise your right to choose, instead of being forced into a decision that will affect your personal assets and the vitality of your business irrevocably.

## Step 1. Recognizing When to File for Bankruptcy

Filing for bankruptcy, no matter what kind, should be done only after all other options have been thoroughly investigated, including new management, budgeting more stringently, making a deal with creditors (see Chapter 23), and even selling your business outright (see Chapter 22).

Here are some red flags that may indicate that it's time to start considering bankruptcy:

- You are unable to pay your bills and have been unsuccessful at negotiating payment terms with your creditors.
- You can't get a loan with acceptable terms, and your creditors and suppliers will no longer do business with you.
- You can't pay the mortgage or rent on your company's space and your landlord is threatening to evict you.
- You owe back taxes to the IRS and cannot negotiate an acceptable payment plan.
- Your creditors are threatening legal action, and you fear that your business will be shut down and your assets liquidated.

## Step 2. What to Do (and Not to Do) When Bankruptcy Is Imminent

If your financial situation gets to the point where filing bankruptcy in the near future is a real possibility, there are some prebankruptcy steps you should take before filing Chapter 7, Chapter 11, or Chapter 13. The following is a general checklist to consider before filing any kind of bankruptcy:

- Evaluate your creditors and make sure you're on good terms with those who will be critical to your company's survival during a reorganization.
- *Don't* give preferential treatment to some creditors during the three months prior to filing. The payments can be voided by the court, and the money recovered.
- If you are involved in a partnership or corporation and have loaned your business money, don't repay yourself immediately prior to bankruptcy. This could be interpreted as preferential treatment.

- Don't transfer the titles of property or possessions to friends or family to protect your assets.
- Don't amass debts—either by obtaining possessions on credit or cash advances—immediately prior to filing. The law states that if you incur more than $500 worth of debt on luxury goods or services from a single creditor within 40 days of filing bankruptcy, the debt will not be discharged by the bankruptcy judge, and you will have to pay the creditor. This also holds true if you obtain a cash advance of more than $1,000 within 20 days of filing bankruptcy. Remember, bankruptcy protection is offered to give you a fresh start, not to set you up in style while you recuperate. You need to color between the lines and follow the rules.
- Don't voluntarily give up any assets that will cause you hardship or give a creditor undue influence over you. For example, if you need your car to get to work, don't voluntarily relinquish it to a creditor. Buy some time by forcing creditors to obtain a court order to make you do so.
- Don't give creditors postdated checks. If these checks bounce, bankruptcy won't protect you from any fines or criminal charges incurred.
- Don't borrow money from commercial lenders to consolidate your loans. All this does is trade many little problems for one big one. Financial institutions that offer consolidation loans to poor risk candidates (if considering filing bankruptcy, you definitely qualify) generally have a horrendous interest rate. If you can't afford to pay your creditors at the going interest rate, you definitely can't afford to pay back a loan at an even higher interest rate.
- If possible, make sure that all your tax returns are filed if you're behind.
- In the case of a Chapter 11 or 13 bankruptcy, outline the changes you need to make in your business to ensure that the reorganization plan will be successful the next time around.
- If your business is incorporated, make sure that a corporate resolution is recorded to reflect the corporate officers' decision to file for bankruptcy.

## Step 3. Overcoming the Psychological Barriers to Bankruptcy

Throughout history, debtors have been frowned on by society and punished with prison, slavery, torture, dismemberment, and death.

Being seriously in debt, especially the process of filing bankruptcy, still carries a heavy stigmatism—both from society and in the minds of most entrepreneurs, who have poured much of themselves into their business.

"It's very difficult to separate the entrepreneur from his business, because if you're a ground-start entrepreneur you put everything you've got into your company—financial and emotional assets," says a small business owner who has gone through the experience of filing bankruptcy.

To fully take advantage of the Bankruptcy Code, many small business owners first need to overcome the psychological barrier of the shame and guilt that is often associated with filing for bankruptcy so that they can plan effectively. We suggest viewing bankruptcy as a safety valve for keeping your business afloat instead of a way to send your business down the tubes. Everyone has experiences that don't work out as expected, and bankruptcy is a tool that's available to give you a chance to start over.

## Step 4. Consult with an Attorney and Devise a Bankruptcy Plan

When you contact a bankruptcy attorney, you will probably be advised of other issues such as:

- Property law.
- Any exemptions that you may be entitled to as a sole proprietor.
- Your creditor's rights and how those rights may be carried out.
- State laws relevant to and affecting your rights under federal bankruptcy law. (For example, alimony and child support debts are governed by state law as well as by a federal law.)
- What business records you need to assemble. Each bankruptcy case is decided on a case-by-case basis.

Once you're ready to take pen in hand and devise a bankruptcy plan, make sure you utilize the knowledge of a good bankruptcy attorney who can help you assess:

- How much money to put aside for business operations during Chapter 11 or 13 bankruptcy, as well as for attorneys' and accountants' fees, and negotiating deals with creditors before and during bankruptcy.

- The proper timing for a bankruptcy; how to recognize the signs of financial difficulty before you've dug yourself into a black hole of debt too deep to climb out of.
- When to transfer assets so that the transfers will not be set aside and will stand up in bankruptcy court.
- What actions you should avoid taking prior to actually filing for bankruptcy because they may have a negative effect on your case.

It's ironic that you need to put money aside in your operating plan in case you get into financial trouble and need to declare bankruptcy, but this point is key when dealing with a Chapter 11 bankruptcy. That's because while attorney fees may be as low as $600 for a simple Chapter 7, the average attorney fee for a Chapter 13 is $1,500 to $2,000, and filing for Chapter 11 can easily cost $10,000 to $20,000. Attorney fees differ from one attorney to another, even in the same city, although they are usually competitively priced (the moral of this story is, Shop around). As a general rule, attorneys for each type of bankruptcy are paid as follows:

- *Chapter 7.* The attorney will probably require a substantial down payment on anticipated fees for a retainer. This money typically comes from a person's prepetition earnings or assets.
- *Chapter 13.* The attorney may be paid from the approved reorganization plan.
- *Chapter 11.* This procedure may take years to complete, so the attorney will probably require a substantial down payment prior to filing, as well as a monthly retainer.

## Step 5. Devise an Asset Protection Plan

Sheltering your personal assets from creditors can't be a last-minute action when you decide to file for bankruptcy. Generally speaking, transferring assets to protect them from creditors must be done as part of an overall financial plan, while you and your business are solvent (having greater assets than liabilities). Otherwise, the bankruptcy court may rule that a "fraudulent conveyance" was made. This means the court may regard a suspicious transfer as motivated by a lack of good faith and by a specific intention to deprive your creditors of recovery or of collecting a portion of their just debts.

Solvency is something you must be able to clearly document and prove to a bankruptcy judge with a properly audited balance sheet. Before you transfer any assets, make sure your audited balance sheet discloses real and contingent liabilities. This can constitute proof that you have not made transfers expressly for the purpose of avoiding creditors.

In this area of law, as in all other areas, states have latitude in drafting laws as long as (1) state law does not contravene federal law and (2) state law is not less stringent than federal law. States can have more safeguards and requirements as long as the state complies with its own constitution, as well as the U.S. Constitution and other federal laws.

Federal bankruptcy law has an entire section dealing with fraudulent conveyance, and most states have adopted the Uniform Fraudulent Conveyance Act and the Uniform Fraudulent Transfers Act (UFCA). Be cognizant of the following stipulations governing property transfers:

- Under federal law, any transfers that will pass muster must be made at least one year prior to bankruptcy. State laws require transfers to be made from one to six years prior to bankruptcy, depending on the state.
- The debtor can't be insolvent, or become insolvent, when property is transferred to a family member or a trust fund. (This makes sense: You can't turn yourself willfully into a bankrupt by giving away your assets, and then seek the protection of the law.)
- The debtor can't be insolvent, or become insolvent, when money is gifted to children or another family member (same reasoning as preceding stipulation).
- Sole proprietors and partnerships can't become undercapitalized as a result of transferring property or other assets to family members. In other words, you can't transfer assets if you know that you need that money to pay bills.
- The debtor can't transfer property pending a lawsuit. For example, in the case of *McCarthy* v. *Griffin*, the bankruptcy court ruled that Griffin had made a fraudulent conveyance by transferring all his property to his children six weeks after he was sued and his real estate was attached. Even a property transfer in anticipation of a lawsuit might be viewed unfavorably.

## Step 6. File for Bankruptcy

You may now turn to Chapter 22, where the mysteries of filing for bankruptcy are unraveled.

## KNOW YOUR KEY TERMS

- *Bankruptcy.* A "clean slate" method for legally eliminating or restructuring debts and/or reorganizing a business.
- *Creditors.* Individuals and organizations to whom you or your company owe money.
- *Collateral.* Any asset with value (the more liquid the better) that you own in some way and that you agree to "put up" as security to your lender.
- *Secured debt.* Debt that a business has "collateralized" with an asset, essentially giving the creditor a shared ownership of that asset. For example, most financial institutions offering loans will require you or your company to put up property or equipment, business or personal, before they will make the loan. If you default, the collateral may be theirs.
- *Unsecured debt.* Debt that is not collateralized, such as credit cards, some loans from friends and family, most bills for services rendered. The creditor has no security interest in the debtor's property.
- *Chapter 7.* The most common way for individuals and companies to file bankruptcy. All applicable assets are liquidated and a court-appointed trustee distributes the funds to creditors—meaning your business is *closed.*
- *Chapter 13.* One of two reorganization options for financially troubled businesses. This option is available only to individuals (sole proprietors) with less than $750,000 in secured debt and more than $250,000 in unsecured debt. Corporations and partnerships do not qualify for Chapter 13; however the federal bankruptcy law does not define a partnership (see your state's definition). As in a Chapter 7 bankruptcy, a court-appointed trustee oversees the debtor's estate and reorganization plan.
- *Chapter 11.* A reorganization plan devised by the debtor; the majority of the debtor's creditors must approve it as well as the court. Chapter 11 is generally not a good option for small businesses, but it is the only alternative to Chapter 7 for individuals and some partnerships with more than $750,000 in secured debt and more than $250,000 in unsecured debt, as well as corporations.
- *IRS.* We know that you know what IRS stands for! We include it here to point out that if you get seriously behind on your taxes and ignore the IRS, they will shut you down, seize your property and padlock your doors. Filing for bankruptcy can be a means of avoiding this messy situation.

## BASIC LEGAL RESEARCH

- *Personal Bankruptcy and Debt Adjustment: A Fresh Start,* by John Doran (Random House). Focuses on personal bankruptcy. It has a good glossary and the text of some of the bankruptcy laws.
- *The Bankruptcy Kit: Understanding the Bankruptcy Process, Knowing Your Options, Making a Fresh Start,* by John Ventura (Dearborn Financial). A workbook style publication that gives a good overview of the bankruptcy procedures for small business owners.
- *How to File for Bankruptcy,* by Stephen Elias, Albin Renauer, and Robin Leonard (Nolo Press). A guide for filing Chapter 7, complete with tear-out forms.
- *Chapter 13 Bankruptcy: Repay Your Debts,* by Robin Leonard (Nolo Press). Instructions on filing Chapter 13, complete with tear-out forms.
- *The Law Library.* You'll find copies of a number of legal references regarding bankruptcy at the law library, including: U.S. Bankruptcy Law, Uniform Fraudulent Conveyance Act, and Uniform Fraudulent Transfers Act.

## KEY RESOURCES

- *Your district federal bankruptcy court.* This is where all the action takes place, so if you have questions, this is a good place to call. The phone number is listed under Government Offices in the blue pages of your phone book.
- *Law clerks for the federal bankruptcy judges.* If you are stumped about any changes in the bankruptcy laws, particularly in light of the Bankruptcy Amendments Act of 1994, these folks may be able to help you. The operator at the federal bankruptcy court can give you the proper names and phone numbers.

## COURT COACH® SUGGESTS

1. *Keep track of your suppliers and make sure they are in good financial health.* This is one way to keep your business out of trouble. By getting periodic operating statements from major suppliers, or

customers, you can foresee possible problems and prevent their making a major impact on *your* business's finances.

2. *A bankruptcy filing can be a good thing.* It brings you relief from harassment and garnisheement rather than the poverty that some people fear. And the energy spent avoiding your creditors' phone calls and pleas for money can now be directed on more positive goals.

3. *If you don't know anyone who can refer you to a good bankruptcy attorney, call the bankruptcy court in your area for the phone numbers of the local bankruptcy trustees.* These people work in the bankruptcy courts every day and have had a chance to see different attorneys in action. They will usually recommend several attorneys for you to check out.

4. *If you're filing a simple Chapter 7 bankruptcy, you may not need an attorney to represent you in court.* You may be able to cut the cost of your legal fees by bypassing bankruptcy attorneys in favor of a law clinic (e.g., Hyatt Legal Services or Jacoby & Meyers) that can help you fill out the forms and answer basic legal questions for you. Remember, though, I would not advise using  individuals who aren't attorneys and can't offer you legal advice; they can only tell you the bankruptcy laws that are on the books and the steps you need to take to file. If you're in doubt as to whether or not you need an attorney's help, you probably do (for more information on bankruptcy petition preparers, see Key Resources, Chapter 22).

5. *Shop around for an attorney.* Don't allow yourself to feel intimidated or ashamed to talk to an attorney about bankruptcy. Many an attorney scraped through the recession and the decline in real estate, and some are more familiar with bankruptcy than you might think!

6. *A tip for getting your reorganization plan past your creditors if filing a Chapter 11.* Bankruptcy attorney Sam Albom of Norwalk, Connecticut, suggests that offering to pay 12.5 cents on a dollar, rather than the traditional 10 cents on a dollar, will help your reorganization pass the scrutiny of the panel of creditors as quickly as possible.

7. *Check out the judge if you are filing a reorganization plan.* The judge who is reviewing your plan can make a huge difference, as this is the person who has the final veto power of a Chapter 13 or 11 bankruptcy. Try to sit in on some cases to determine the judge's style and what he or she considers passable.

# 22

## THE ABCs OF FILING FOR BANKRUPTCY: WHAT TO DO WHEN THE FAT LADY SINGS

### BANKRUPTCY BASICS: MORE KEY TERMS TO EXPAND YOUR BASE OF KNOWLEDGE

Now that you've read Chapter 19 and are familiar with the concept of bankruptcy, when to use it, and why it's important to plan ahead, you're ready for Stage 2 in the Court Coach® short course in filing for bankruptcy. Before we get into the specific steps involved with filing for a Chapter 7, Chapter 13, or Chapter 11 bankruptcy, let's review a few basic elements and procedures to expand your expertise on bankruptcy.

### THE MAJOR PLAYERS

First off, let's take a closer look at the major players involved in a bankruptcy case. You, your business, and your money are center stage as the curtain rises. Hovering in the background are your creditors, waving past-due notices and possible demand letters hinting at litigation. After you file a petition for bankruptcy, the bankruptcy court judge and possibly a trustee enter stage left. Ready, set, action!

## The Trustee: The Bankruptcy's Gatekeeper

Next to the bankruptcy judge, the trustee is the most important player in any bankruptcy case. In the case of a Chapter 7 bankruptcy filing, this is the person to whom you will turn over all your non-exempt assets and titles after filing bankruptcy. The court-appointed trustee, usually an attorney or accountant, is paid out of the money you owe your creditors. According to the bankruptcy code, up to 10 percent of what you pay your creditors can go to administrative expenses of executing the bankruptcy, which includes the trustee's salary. The trustee's job is to:

- Determine what property is exempt from liquidation (see Bankruptcy Exemptions, later in this chapter).
- Determine what property can be liquidated, and how to carry out that process.
- Determine the value of the property to be liquidated.
- Review your financial affairs to validate that all nonexempt assets are in possession of the court.
- Validate your creditors' claims.
- Hire professionals such as attorneys, accountants, and appraisers to carry out the liquidation.

### Priority of Creditors

As we previously mentioned, the trustee is in charge of redistributing the debtor's "estate," or assets, to creditors in a prescribed order of priority as follows (this applies to Chapter 11 and Chapter 13 bankruptcies as well):

1. Costs of administering, collecting, and maintaining the estate, including attorney fees.
2. Claims arising in the ordinary course of business, after the bankruptcy petition was filed but before a trustee was appointed or an order for relief was made.
3. Claims for employee wages, of up to $2,000 per employee, earned 90 or fewer days before the bankruptcy petition was filed.

4. Claims for contributions to employee benefit plans, of up to $2,000 per employee, arising from services rendered 180 or fewer days before the bankruptcy petition was filed.

5. Claims of up to $900 for certain deposits with the debtor that were to pay for consumer purchases or leases of property or services, if the property or services remain unprovided.

6. Taxes and penalties due in the three years before the bankruptcy petition was filed.

7. Claims of all other unsecured creditors that exceed the money or time limits in the preceding categories.

## Chapter 13 Bankruptcy

In the case of a Chapter 13 bankruptcy, the trustee will not gain control of your assets. You are left to oversee all assets so that you can implement a plan for your business to remain operating. The court-appointed trustee's main concern is overseeing the reorganization plan, and recommending to the court whether or not this plan should be approved. To this end, a trustee and judge will evaluate and approve your plan depending on how you have complied with the following guidelines:

- All paperwork should be properly filled out and filed by the appropriate deadlines.
- The plan must be proposed in "good faith," which is to say that your intention is to pay back all creditors to the full extent of your capabilities.
- Unsecured creditors must receive at least as much as they would have received if you had filed a Chapter 7 liquidation.
- The plan must outline how secured creditors will be compensated; either by the return of collateral or repayment of the value of the collateral plus interest during the application of the plan.
- The plan must outline a schedule of payments that are realistic for you to meet.
- The plan must account for all disposable income.

Once the plan is set forth, payments are made to the trustee (usually on a monthly basis), who then distributes the appropriate funds to your creditors.

## Chapter 11 Bankruptcy

In contrast to a Chapter 13 bankruptcy petition, Chapter 11 allows you to create and implement the reorganization plan for the bankruptcy judge's approval. A trustee is assigned to your case to monitor your business and make sure that you are complying with the terms of the approved repayment plan. A Chapter 11 plan must be proposed in good faith and comply with the following guidelines:

- Classify all claims as "impaired" or "unimpaired" (see Court Coach Suggests at end of chapter).
- Give all creditors (not just unsecured) at least the same amount they would receive under a Chapter 7 liquidation.
- Provide full payment of all priority claims, as listed earlier under Priority of Creditors, over the life of the bankruptcy.
- Provide cash payment of all postfiling administrative expenses at the time the plan is approved.

In the case of any bankruptcy, the trustee has the power to:

- Accept or reject any contracts made between the debtor and creditors.
- Revoke unperfected property transfers (those uncompleted or not fully executed).
- Negate preferential or fraudulent transfers of assets and property (see Chapter 22 for more on transferring assets and property).

## The Creditors

While dealing effectively with creditors is discussed in detail in Chapter 23, their role in the beginning stages of bankruptcy is what we're concerned with here. As you may have gathered, your goal is limit the creditors' role and power to influence the bankruptcy proceedings. An "automatic stay," which is invoked as soon as you file a bankruptcy petition and remains in effect until your bankruptcy case is closed or dismissed, is your legitimate means to this end. This court order provides the following relief from your financial woes:

- Any lawsuits filed against you are stopped.
- Your creditors can't enforce judgments against you, even if they have filed lawsuits against you and obtained a judgment ordering you to pay.
- Creditors can't repossess any of your possessions, including your home.
- Creditors, including the IRS, can't garnishee your wages.
- Any proceedings in the U.S. Tax Court are stopped.

- Any contracts wherein you pay a monthly charge—from the health club to the phone company—can be broken at the discretion of you and the trustee.
- The utility company can't cut off your services, providing that you notify them that a bankruptcy has been filed. (*Note:* the utility can demand a "reasonable" deposit within 20 days from the date you filed your petition.)

The automatic stay will give you some breathing room, but it is not a panacea for all your financial woes. It is merely a temporary measure pending the resolution of your bankruptcy, and there are a number of exemptions on the automatic stay, including:

- Criminal actions, such as writing a bad check.
- Even though the IRS can't collect past-due taxes, it can still audit you.
- While you can use the automatic stay to freeze debts accrued from alimony and child support, the bankruptcy court judge will eventually order you to pay them as part of settling your case. This includes matrimonial obligations construed to be "in the nature of support."
- Creditors have the right to seek relief from the automatic stay if their own financial security is at risk. This is a case-by-case decision made by the judge.

## THE PROCEDURAL RULES OF THE SUBSTANTIVE GAME

We've taken care of the "who you're dealing with" section, now here's the "what you're dealing with." The following rules apply to all kinds of Chapter 7, Chapter 11, and Chapter 13 bankruptcy proceedings.

## Bankruptcy Exemptions: What You're Allowed to Keep

The goal of bankruptcy is for you to clear your debts and make a fresh start; the court does not want to render you helpless or hopeless. Hence, the debtor is allowed to keep certain assets to avoid complete destitution. These "exempt" properties, belongings, and financial resources are beyond the reach of creditors demanding that you satisfy a debt.

There are both state and federal laws that govern bankruptcy (see Chapter 18 for explanation of difference between state and federal laws). The two major types of state and federal exemptions are the "homestead exemption," which refers to personal property used as a residence, and the "personal property exemption," which covers items not used for business valued up to a given amount of money.

Each state has its own exemption laws, which apply only to the citizens of that state. The value of assets and property that is exempt varies from state to state. The federal exemption laws apply to all the citizens of the United States. Some states allow you to choose between the federal and state exemptions when you file bankruptcy, and some states require you to use only the state exemptions (see Appendix J).

The Bankruptcy Code, Section 522(d) a federal law allows exemptions for:

- Equity in a home of up to $7,500.
- Interest in one motor vehicle up to $1,200. A couple filing bankruptcy can each have a car with $1,200 equity.
- Books, tools, equipment, or any other items used expressly for business purposes valued up to $750.
- Prescribed health aids.
- Unmatured life insurance policies, with the exception of a credit life insurance contract.
- Federal and state benefits such as Social Security, local public assistance, veterans', disability, and unemployment benefits.
- Jewelry held primarily for the personal, family, or household use of the debtor or a dependent of the debtor, not to exceed $500.
- Alimony and child support.
- Certain pensions, stock bonuses, and annuities that provide financial security for illness, disability, death, age, or length of service, to the extent reasonably necessary for the support of the debtor and any dependent of the debtor.
- Possessions that are held primarily for the personal, family, or household use of the debtor or a dependent of the debtor valued up to a total of $4,000 (no single item exceeding a value of $200). Examples include household furnishings, clothes, books, appliances, musical instruments, pets, or other items of a personal nature.
- Criminal victim restitution payments, wrongful death benefits, life insurance payments to a dependent beneficiary, and personal injury payments up to $7,500.

- Property worth no more than $400, plus up to $3,750 of any unused portion of the $7,500 homestead exemption.

The simplest way to think of this property exemption business is by the process of elimination: Whatever remains after the exempt property has been determined now falls into the category of nonexempt. That is, it can be considered as part of what is available to be liquidated to pay off nondischargeable debts (the debts the court did not allow you to rid yourself of for one reason or another).

Note that in a Chapter 7 bankruptcy, you may be able to buy back your nonexempt property from the trustee if you offer the trustee a fair price. If the nonexempt property isn't worth enough money to warrant the expense of liquidation, the trustee may opt to abandon the property and you would get to keep it. Chapter 13 bankruptcy also offers a provision for keeping nonexempt property: You can keep your nonexempt property under the stipulation that you pay at least the value of the property to your unsecured creditors.

## Nondischargeable Debts and Denial of Debt Discharge

Now you've come to your principal goal: Some or all of your debt is "discharged," or dismissed by the court, so that it's feasible for you to dig yourself out of a financial hole and start again with a clean slate. Debtors beware: Certain types of debts are considered to be too important to be discharged by bankruptcy. No matter what, you are responsible for paying the following debts, even if all other debt is discharged:

- Alimony.
- Child support.
- Some state and federal government fines and penalties.
- Back taxes owed for the three years prior to filing for bankruptcy.
- Student loans obtained by the debtor within five years prior to filing for bankruptcy.
- Debts you have failed to list in your bankruptcy papers.
- Debts resulting from driving under the influence of alcohol (DUI or DWI), and other criminal restitution obligations.
- Intentional tort claims.
- Debts that weren't discharged in a previous bankruptcy that was dismissed due to fraud or misfeasance (you deliberately deceived the court).

- Claims to assets or property obtained by fraud, false pretense, embezzlement, or misuse of funds.
- Debts exceeding $500 for luxury goods or services purchased within 40 days before the bankruptcy filing.
- Certain cash advances exceeding $1,000 within 20 days before the bankruptcy filing.
- A debt that was not discharged in a bankruptcy hearing occurring within six years of the present hearing.

Take a breather and relax a minute, because things get just a bit more complicated now. The judge may also deny your request for an overall bankruptcy discharge, which is to say that none of your debt is discharged and you must pay your creditors 100 percent of what is owed. In this case, your nonexempt assets are still distributed to your creditors, but you remain liable for the unpaid portion of your debts (as opposed to having the remainder of the debts discharged). This may happen if:

- You have waived the right to a discharge in a written document.
- You have destroyed, concealed, or transferred property and/or records to defraud a creditor.
- You have unjustifiably failed to maintain financial records.
- You have committed bankruptcy fraud (that is, failed to follow the rules or had an intent to deceive).
- You refuse to obey a bankruptcy court order to answer the court's questions or to appear at a scheduled bankruptcy meeting or hearing.
- A bankruptcy court granted you a discharge within six years of the filing of the present petition.
- A prior bankruptcy petition was dismissed within 180 days of filing the present petition.

## Reservation of Right

A bankruptcy court may reserve the right to revoke its discharge decree, if within one year of the hearing, evidence is produced showing that the debtor committed fraud or perjury during the bankruptcy proceedings. There is a clear message here: Scrupulously record and detail all required information, and make sure you have not forgotten any items in your filing.

If you do discover that you've inadvertently left something out—either during the bankruptcy or after your debt has been discharged—

file an amendment to your bankruptcy as soon as possible. This is an amazing break sanctioned by law, and the court will treat this right with great care. Even so, no judge is a "tabula rasa" (clean slate), and it's ultimately up to the discretion of each individual judge to treat this matter according to his or her interpretation of the specific situation. Much may depend on the evidence presented, and the debtor's sincerity in regretting the original omittance.

## FILING FOR BANKRUPTCY: WHERE TO BEGIN AND WHERE TO GO FROM THERE

Once you've decided that you definitely need to file bankruptcy (there's no other option), you'll need to determine which procedure is appropriate for your business and financial needs. To decide which process is most appropriate for your situation consider the following:

- *The financial vitality of your business.* In other words: Is your business worth the fight to save it? Has it ever been, or does it really have the capacity to become, a money maker? If not, Chapter 7 bankruptcy may be your only option.
- *The legal structure of your business.* Sole proprietors have the most options available to them, but if you're dealing with a corporation or partnership and you want to stay in business your only option may be bankruptcy.
- *Your ultimate goal.* If this business is your life's dream and you want to try and work out the kinks you'll be looking at a different filing process (Chapter 11 or 13 bankruptcy) than if you just want to close this episode, pay off your debts, and try again (Chapter 7 bankruptcy).

To ascertain what bankruptcy action is required, the first thing that your attorney will probably ask you to do is fill out a statement of financial affairs. This is a legal requirement whether you're filing a Chapter 7, Chapter 11, or Chapter 13 bankruptcy.

Now, you're ready to file a bankruptcy petition with the Federal Bankruptcy Court and get your case rolling. The following sections describe Chapter 7, Chapter 11, and Chapter 13 procedures.

## Filing for a Chapter 7 Bankruptcy

Chapter 7 is referred to as a "straight bankruptcy," because it is the easiest and most straightforward of the bankruptcy proceedings. This procedure is available to anyone—sole proprietors, partnerships, or corporations—who wants to close up shop and liquidate available assets to wipe out indebtedness (or just John Q. Public who doesn't own a business, but is filing for personal bankruptcy). In any case, the following steps are appropriate.

**Step 1**

*Filing the petition for bankruptcy.* With the help of your attorney, file the bankruptcy petition (see Figure 22–1) and the other required paperwork with the Federal Bankruptcy Court, and pay a filing fee of $160. The bankruptcy petition includes a series of forms ("schedules") that request a litany of information about your financial affairs, including a list of your assets and liabilities and a list of your creditors (see Figure 22–2 for a summary of schedules). How completely and honestly you fill out these forms has a great deal to do with how smoothly your bankruptcy case goes.

**Step 2**

*Automatic stay procedures.* With the help of your attorney, file the petition to invoke the automatic stay of collection actions against you. Immediately following this action, your attorney should send a letter to all of your creditors informing them that bankruptcy proceedings are under way and the automatic stay is in effect. The court will eventually do this also, but it's paramount that creditors get this information as soon as possible, so that you get relief from your debts incurred as soon as possible.

**Step 3**

*Draft your reorganization plan.* During the six to eight weeks after filing bankruptcy, your attorney will prepare for the creditors' meeting. Your attorney will work with creditors to try and smooth out any difficulties that may arise. For example, creditors must be appeased so that they don't challenge the automatic stay and repossess your furniture or kick you out of your office space before you're ready to close down shop.

**Step 4**

*Six to eight weeks after you file for bankruptcy, you and your attorney will attend a creditors' meeting.* This meeting, which takes place at the Federal Bankruptcy Court in your district, is an opportunity for the trustee and creditors to ask you some questions and examine your intentions to repay your debts. The court-appointed trustee, who oversees the meeting, will ask you a series of questions to confirm that you have complied with the exempt and nonexempt ordinances (see Bankruptcy Exemptions Section earlier in this chapter), and ascertain the extent of assets you have that can be liquidated. The trustee will also

## Figure 22–1

| Blumbergs Law Products | Form 1. P1 (11-92) | | Julius Blumberg, Inc. NYC 10013 |
|---|---|---|---|

**FORM 1 VOLUNTARY PETITION**

| United States Bankruptcy Court<br>District of | VOLUNTARY PETITION |
|---|---|
| IN RE (Name of debtor-If individual, enter Last, First, Middle) | NAME OF JOINT DEBTOR (Spouse) (Last, First, Middle) |
| ALL OTHER NAMES used by debtor in the last 6 years<br>(Include married, maiden and trade names) | ALL OTHER NAMES used by the joint debtor in the last 6 years<br>(Include married, maiden and trade names.) |
| SOC. SEC./TAX I.D. NO. (If more than one, state all) | SOC. SEC./TAX I.D. NO. (If more than one, state all) |
| STREET ADDRESS OF DEBTOR (No. and street, city, state, zip) | STREET ADDRESS OF JOINT DEBTOR (No. and street, city, state, zip) |
| COUNTY OF RESIDENCE OR PRINCIPAL PLACE OF BUSINESS | COUNTY OF RESIDENCE OR PRINCIPAL PLACE OF BUSINESS |
| MAILING ADDRESS OF DEBTOR (If different from street address) | MAILING ADDRESS OF JOINT DEBTOR (If different from street address) |
| LOCATION OF PRINCIPAL ASSETS OF BUSINESS DEBTOR (If different from addresses listed above) | ☐ Debtor has been domiciled or has had a residence, principal place of business or principal assets in this District for 180 days immediately preceding the date of this petition or for a longer part of such 180 days than in any other District.<br>☐ There is a bankruptcy case concerning debtor's affiliate, general partner or partnership pending in this District. |

**INFORMATION REGARDING DEBTOR (Check applicable boxes)**

TYPE OF DEBTOR
- ☐ Individual
- ☐ Joint (H&W)
- ☐ Partnership
- ☐ Other _____
- ☐ Corporation Publicly Held
- ☐ Corporation Not Publicly Held
- ☐ Municipality

NATURE OF DEBT
- ☐ Non-Business Consumer    ☐ Business - Complete A&B below

A. TYPE OF BUSINESS (check one box)
- ☐ Farming
- ☐ Professional
- ☐ Retail/Wholesale
- ☐ Railroad
- ☐ Transportation
- ☐ Manufacturing/ Mining
- ☐ Stockbroker
- ☐ Commodity Broker
- ☐ Construction
- ☐ Real Estate
- ☐ Other Business

B. BRIEFLY DESCRIBE NATURE OF BUSINESS

CHAPTER OR SECTION OF BANKRUPTCY CODE UNDER WHICH THE PETITION IS FILED (Check one box)
- ☐ Chapter 7    ☐ Chapter 11    ☐ Chapter 13
- ☐ Chapter 9    ☐ Chapter 12    ☐ § 304-Case Ancillary to Foreign Proceeding

FILING FEE (Check one box)
- ☐ Filing fee attached.
- ☐ Filing fee to be paid in installments. (Applicable to individuals only) Must attach signed application for the court's consideration certifying that the debtor is unable to pay fee except in installments. Rule 1006(b). see Offical Form No..3

NAME AND ADDRESS OF LAW FIRM OR ATTORNEY

Telephone No.

NAME(S) OF ATTORNEY(S) DESIGNATED TO REPRESENT THE DEBTOR

☐ Debtor is not represented by an attorney.  Telephone no. of debtor not represented by an attorney: (      )

**STATISTICAL ADMINISTRATIVE INFORMATION (28 U.S.C. § 604)**
**(Estimates only) (Check applicable boxes)**

- ☐ Debtor estimates that funds will be available for distribution to unsecured creditors.
- ☐ Debtor estimates that after any exempt property is excluded and administrative expenses paid, there will be no funds available for distribution to unsecured creditors.

ESTIMATED NUMBER OF CREDITORS
☐ 1-15    ☐ 16-49    ☐ 50-99    ☐ 100-199    ☐ 200-999    ☐ 1000-over

ESTIMATED ASSETS (in thousands of dollars)
☐ Under 50  ☐ 50-99  ☐ 100-499  ☐ 500-999  ☐ 1000-9999  ☐ 10,000-99,000  ☐ over 100,000

ESTIMATED LIABILITIES (in thousands of dollars)
☐ Under 50  ☐ 50-99  ☐ 100-499  ☐ 500-999  ☐ 1000-9999  ☐ 10,000-99,000  ☐ over 100,000

ESTIMATED NUMBER OF EMPLOYEES -CH 11 & 12 ONLY
☐ 0    ☐ 1-19    ☐ 20-99    ☐ 100-999    ☐ 1000-over

ESTIMATED NO . OF EQUITY SECURITY HOLDERS - CH 11 & 12 ONLY
☐ 0    ☐ 1-19    ☐ 20-99    ☐ 100-499    ☐ 500-over

THIS SPACE FOR COURT USE ONLY

3069-1© 1991 JULIUS BLUMBERG. INC., NYC 10013

© 1991 JULIUS BLUMBERG. INC., NYC 10013

## Figure 22–2

 Form B6 (6-90)

Julius Blumberg, Inc. NYC 10013

**UNITED STATES BANKRUPTCY COURT**                                    **DISTRICT OF**

In re:                                                    Debtor(s)         Case No.                    (If Known)

See summary below for the list of schedules. Include Unsworn Declaration under Penalty of Perjury at the end.

GENERAL INSTRUCTIONS: Schedules D, E and F have been designed for the listing of each claim only once. Even when a claim is secured only in part, or entitled to priorityonly in part, it still should be listed only once. A claim which is secured in whole or in part should be listed on Schedule D only, and a claim which is entitled to priority in whole or in part should be listed in Schedule E only. Do not list the same claim twice. If a creditor has more than one claim, such as claims arising from separate transactions, each claim should be scheduled separately.

Review the specific instructions for each schedule before completing the schedule.

### SUMMARY OF SCHEDULES

Indicate as to each schedule whether that schedule is attached and state the number of pages in each. Report the totals from Schedules A, B, D, E, F, I and J in the boxes provided. Add the amounts from Schedules A and B to determine the total amount of the debtor's assets. Add the amounts from Schedules D, E, and F to determine the total amount of the debtor's liabilities.

| Name of Schedule | Attached (Yes No) | Number of sheets | Amounts Scheduled Assets | Liabilities | Other |
|---|---|---|---|---|---|
| A - Real Property | | | | | |
| B - Personal Property | | | | | |
| C - Property Claimed as Exempt | | | | | |
| D - Creditors Holding Secured Claims | | | | | |
| E - Creditors Holding Unsecured Priority Claims | | | | | |
| F - Creditors Holding Unsecured Nonpriority Claims | | | | | |
| G - Executory Contracts and Unexpired Leases | | | | | |
| H - Codebtors | | | | | |
| I - Current Income of Individual Debtor(s) | | | | | |
| J - Current Expenditures of Individual Debtor(s) | | | | | |
| Total Number of Sheets of All Schedules | | | | | |
| Total Assets | | | | | |
| Total Liabilities | | | | | |

3072 © 1991 JULIUS BLUMBERG, INC., NYC 10013

3072-S  Schedules. 6-91

© 1991 JULIUS BLUMBERG, INC., NYC 10013

examine your financial documents. Your creditors will want to know how you intend to treat their specific outstanding debts.

**Step 5**

*The trustee and your creditors have 30 days after the creditors' meeting to object to any exemptions you have claimed, and 60 days to object to the discharge of any particular debts.* The bankruptcy judge for your case reviews all objections and decides whether or not—and to what extent—the debts must be paid.

**Step 6**

*The creditors listed on your schedule of debts have 90 days to file an adversary proceeding against you.* Some creditors, especially those with secured debts, will feel compelled to file a complaint with the bankruptcy court demanding compensation beyond what the bankruptcy code outlines. For example, let's say you have neglected to pay a supplier for six months, which has caused him financial hardship. If you choose to contest the complaint, you and the creditor will have to face off in front of the judge at a hearing.

**Step 7**

*A discharge hearing takes place about 60 days after the creditors' meeting.* By this point, the trustee has liquidated your nonexempt assets and paid off your nondischargeable debts to the extent possible. The trustee will conduct a final accounting of your case once all available assets are liquidated, and the court will officially close your bankruptcy case.

## Filing a Chapter 13 Bankruptcy

As we discussed in Chapter 21, this reorganization procedure is available *only to individuals, including sole proprietors* (no partnerships or corporations) who meet certain financial stipulations. The steps for filing a Chapter 13 bankruptcy are as follows:

**Step 1**

*Discuss the details of your reorganization plan with your attorney, and possibly an accountant, to make sure that it's legally and financially sound.* At this point, your attorney will probably want to draft a copy of your reorganization plan so that you'll have something concrete to work with (see Figure 22–3 for a Chapter 13 bankruptcy plan form).

**Step 2**

*File the petition for bankruptcy.* With the help of your attorney, file the bankruptcy petition (see Figure 22–1) and the other required

## Figure 22–3

3082   Chapter 13 Plan, 8-91

Blumbergs
Law Products

**UNITED STATES BANKRUPTCY COURT**          **DISTRICT OF**

In re                                Debtor(s)      Case No.            (If Known)

### CHAPTER 13 PLAN

*(If this form is used by joint debtors wherever the word "debtor" or words referring to debtor are used they shall be read as if in the plural.)*

1. The future earnings of the debtor are submitted to the supervision and control of the trustee and the *debtor — debtor's employer* shall pay to the trustee the sum of $          *weekly — bi-weekly — semi-monthly — monthly*     for a period of

2. From the payments so received, the trustee shall make disbursements as follows:

   (*a*) Full payment in deferred cash payments of all claims entitled to priority under 11 U.S.C. §507.

   (*b*) Holders of allowed secured claims shall retain the liens securing such claims and shall be paid as follows:

   (*c*) *Subsequent to — pro rata with* dividends to secured creditors, dividends to unsecured creditors whose claims are duly allowed as follows:

3. The following executory contracts of the debtor are rejected:

Title to the debtor's property shall revest in the debtor *on confirmation of a plan — upon dismissal of the case after confirmation pursuant to 11 U.S.C. §350.*

Dated:                ........................................      ........................................

                               *Debtor*                          *Debtor*

Acceptances may be mailed to........................................      ........................................

                                                   *Post Office Address*

paperwork with the Federal Bankruptcy Court, and pay a filing fee of $160. Follow the same procedure outlined in Step 1 for filing a Chapter 7 bankruptcy. In addition, your reorganization plan may be filed at this time or within 15 days.

### Step 3

*Automatic stay procedures.* With the help of your attorney, file the petition to invoke the automatic stay of collection actions against you (see Step 2 for filing a Chapter 7 bankruptcy).

### Step 4

*Start paying.* You must begin making payments, as outlined in your reorganization plan, 30 days after your plan has been filed.

### Step 5

*Prepare for creditors' meeting.* During the six to eight weeks after filing bankruptcy, your attorney will prepare for the creditors' meeting. As with a Chapter 7 bankruptcy, your attorney will work with creditors to try and smooth out any difficulties that may arise. But at this stage, things get a little more complicated with a Chapter 13 bankruptcy (and *much* more complicated with a Chapter 11). In a nutshell, the attorney must try and negotiate with creditors before the creditors' meeting to minimize objections to your reorganization plan.

### Step 6

*About 40 to 50 days after your petition has been filed, the creditors' meeting will convene at the district bankruptcy court.* In the case of a Chapter 13 bankruptcy, a trustee will again conduct the meeting and ask questions to determine if your reorganization plan is feasible. Your answers are extremely important, as they will serve as the basis on which the trustee either recommends confirmation of your plan or suggests changes that must be made before recommending your plan to the bankruptcy judge.

At this meeting, your secured creditors will ask you questions to help them decide whether they want to (1) file a motion with the court to repossess their collateral; (2) file an objection to your plan; or (3) accept the payment your plan outlines.

### Step 7

*Within 90 days of the creditors' meeting, each of your creditors must file a proof of claim with the bankruptcy court so that the debts you owe them will be included in your bankruptcy.* Secured creditors who fail to meet this deadline may wind up being treated as unsecured creditors and lose their priority standing in your reorganization plan, which means receiving less money. Unsecured creditors who neglect to file a proof of claim in time may forfeit the right to be treated as unsecured creditors and receive no money at all.

### Step 8

*A confirmation hearing takes place in your district's federal bankruptcy court.* The confirmation hearing for a Chapter 13 bankruptcy may take place on the same day as the creditors' meeting, or as much as four weeks later. Assuming that neither the trustee nor any of the creditors object to the plan by this point, the judge will confirm the reorganization plan. If there are any objections, the judge will evaluate them and decide whether or not to approve your plan. If the plan is denied, you may be able to make amendments and present it again at a later date.

### Step 9

*After the reorganization plan is confirmed, the judge will designate a time period (three to five years) in which the debt payments must be made.* During this time, you can petition the court to modify your plan, or convert your case to a Chapter 7 liquidation bankruptcy. After this time period, your plan is considered completed and any debts that aren't fully paid off are discharged.

## Filing a Chapter 11 Bankruptcy

Chapter 11 is not usually a financially viable option for small businesses because of the time and costs involved. If you and your attorney decide that this is indeed the best way for your business to proceed, the filing process falls along the same lines as filing a Chapter 13 with a few extra provisions.

Chapter 11 bankruptcies are more complex than Chapter 13 bankruptcies, though, so the sequence of events after filing the petition and debt schedules isn't as predictable. Basically, the following steps take place.

### Step 1

*Discuss the details of your reorganization plan with your attorney, and possibly an accountant, to make sure that it's legally and financially sound.*

### Step 2

*With the help of your attorney, file the bankruptcy petition (see Figure 22–1) and the other required paperwork with the Federal Bankruptcy Court, and pay a filing fee of $160.* Follow the same procedure outlined in Step 1 for a Chapter 7 bankruptcy. Unlike a Chapter 13 action, your reorganization plan will not be filed at this time.

**Step 3**

*With the help of your attorney, file the petition to invoke the automatic stay of collection actions against you* (see Step 2 for a Chapter 7 bankruptcy).

**Step 4**

*Seek the court's approval to use your cash collateral.* This means that you can use any cash collateral you pledged in exchange for loans, such as, accounts receivable, securities, bonds, and rent income, to keep your business up and running until your reorganization plan is approved.

**Step 5**

*Prepare a disclosure statement and reorganization plan.* This process should actually be set into motion as soon as you've decided to file a Chapter 11—even before you petition the court. You have 120 days after filing to prepare and file these statements with the court. If you don't meet the deadline for your reorganization plan, the creditors will come up with one of their own to submit to the court. This is definitely not a vantage situation for the debtor.

**Step 6**

*Creditors are notified of your filing, and they begin filing their claims of nondischargeable debts.* Creditors can continue to file claims until a date set by the court. Meanwhile, you can object to any of your creditors' claims for the following reasons:

- You disagree with the value of your collateral.
- You disagree with the amount of the debt cited by the creditor.
- You disagree with the classification of a claim (secured or unsecured).

**Step 7**

*A creditors' meeting takes place at your district's federal bankruptcy court.* As we stated in the section on trustees, a government-appointed trustee will oversee the design and implementation of the reorganization plan, but your creditors will be in charge of approving the plan. The reorganization plan must be accepted by the bankruptcy judge and must be two thirds in amount, and more than half in number, of the claims in any particular "class" of creditors (see Court Coach Suggests for explanation of the various classes).

At this meeting, your creditors can object to your business's reorganization plan and/or disclosure statement. They may also object to the way that their claim is categorized in your reorganization plan, the amount of money they will receive, the timing of your payments—and a whole host of other things. In other words: This meeting rarely goes smoothly!

In the case of objections to your reorganization plan, you can either make the stipulated changes before the plan is reviewed by a bankruptcy judge, or disregard the creditors' objections and go for a "cram-down." There are specific circumstances in which a judge will grant a cram-down, or acceptance of the reorganization plan despite the creditors' objections. These circumstances vary from case to case, and your attorney can advise you if your case is a good candidate for this procedure.

**Step 8**

*A hearing is held and the bankruptcy court either approves or disapproves your disclosure statement.* If the court nixes your disclosure statement, you can make some revisions and try again. The court also has the right to dismiss your bankruptcy, and you'll need to resort to a different way of solving your financial problems. Dismissal can occur either before or after your disclosure statement and reorganization plan have been confirmed (see Court Coach Suggests for the circumstances under which dismissal can occur).

**Step 9**

*The creditors vote on approval of your reorganization plan.* In order to do this, each creditor is sent a voting ballot and copies of your disclosure statement and your reorganization plan. If your creditors approve your plan, it will move along to the bankruptcy court for final approval. If your creditors reject the plan, you can either make some revisions and try again or opt for a cram-down.

How the creditors cast their vote will depend greatly on how you are currently operating your business. If they see a substantial turnaround, it is likely to sway them in your favor. But the converse is true as well.

**Step 10**

*The bankruptcy court reviews your reorganization plan, and either approves or denies it.* After your reorganization plan is approved by your creditors and the court, your bankruptcy officially ends as does the court's involvement. All debts except those provided for in your plan will be discharged at this time.

As the debtor in possession, you will be expected to run your business and pay off your debts in accordance with the terms outlined in your reorganization plan. If that doesn't happen, your creditors may petition the court to bring in a private trustee to "help you" oversee your business. You don't want this to happen, as this person will probably be a "bean counter" who has little knowledge of your business or even the industry you're involved in.

---

| **KNOW YOUR KEY TERMS** |

---

- *Dischargeable debts.* Debts that can be dismissed, or erased, by the bankruptcy court.
- *Exempt/nonexempt assets.* A classification of assets used in filing for bankruptcy. Some of your assets are exempt from liquidation (you get to keep them) and some are nonexempt (you need to sell them and use the proceeds to pay your creditors).
- *Reorganization Plan.* A system you devise by which you will repay your debts, to the best of your ability, during a 3- to 5-year period.
- *Good faith.* Refers to the debtor's honest belief in his or her ability to follow the terms laid out in the reorganization plan.
- *Automatic stay.* A blockage that stops the clock ticking on your debts, activated as soon as you file a bankruptcy petition. As of that date, creditors are blocked from hounding you for money or pursuing litigation.
- *Debtor in possession.* The debtor who remains in possession of all assets and is responsible for distributing them to creditors according to the reorganization plan accepted and approved by the court.
- *Disclosure statement.* A statement provided to creditors to help them decide whether or not to approve your reorganization plan. The disclosure statement outlines the following: the financial condition of your business, an explanation of why you're filing for Chapter 11 bankruptcy, a summary of your reorganization plan, a history of your business's success rate, and a summary of the qualification of the management team.
- *Cram-down.* Pressure applied to creditors to gain their acceptance of a reorganization. In the case of a Chapter 11 bankruptcy, the majority of your creditors must accept your reorganization plan. If you feel your creditors are being unreasonable, you can try to get the judge to accept the plan despite their objections.
- *Judgment proof.* If you do not have any means of repaying your debts—no source of income or liquidable assets—you are said to be judgment proof. This means you are not held responsible for your debts and they are discharged after seven years.
- *Sui generis.* From the Latin meaning "the only one of its kind." In the bankruptcy context, it describes how the court evaluates

which debts are dischargeable, and which assets are exempt—by looking at how the law applies to your particular case.

(*Note:* See also Chapter 21, Know Your Key Terms.)

## BASIC LEGAL RESEARCH

The following three legal texts (available at most libraries) are essential to basic legal research on bankruptcy (see Chapter 21, Basic Legal Research, for additional books):

- *Collier on Bankruptcy,* by Lawrence P. King et al. (Matthew Bender). This multivolume treatise is the most complete resource book available on bankruptcy statutes. Look up your topic of interest in the subject matter index, which will list the page numbers of the applicable statutes.
- *Bankruptcy Reports* (West Publishing). One of the best ways to get an understanding of bankruptcy law and how it applies to you is to review several cases with circumstances similar to your own. This publication, which consists of a number of volumes, is one of several that lists bankruptcy statutes, as well as case summaries that apply to the statutes. After you look up the statutes that apply to your situation, this is a good place to gain a better understanding of how these statutes work in real life.
- *The Commerce Clearing House Bankruptcy Law Reporter* (Commerce Clearing House). This is another extremely useful resource for deciphering bankruptcy statutes and rules, which also includes case summaries.

## KEY RESOURCES

- *Your local stationery store (for bankruptcy schedule forms).* These forms are not available from the bankruptcy court. Your attorney will probably be able to provide them but you may want to review these forms and start collecting data before visiting your attorney.
- *Bankruptcy petition preparers (BPPs).* If you are filing a simple Chapter 7 bankruptcy, you may not need to hire an attorney but may still need someone to assist with filling out the forms and other general aspects of the bankruptcy. BPPs aren't attorneys,

so they can't give legal advice or represent you in court. But they can type your forms, provide general information about bankruptcy requirements, and help you prepare for negotiations with creditors. BPPs usually advertise in the classified section of community newspapers, as well as the yellow pages, although a recommendation from a satisfied client is the best way to find one.

(*Note:* See also Key Resources, Chapter 21.)

## COURT COACH® SUGGESTS

1. *Be savvy when filing for bankruptcy with a BPP and without a lawyer.* You should be aware that many bar associations express concern about consumers working with those in a quasi-legal capacity with nonlawyers such as BPPs. There is a fine line between providing a customer with the facts of the law (which nonlawyers are allowed to do) and giving legal advice (strictly forbidden).

2. *When preparing your schedule of debt, be sure to list all your outstanding debts—from the phone company to your cousin Fred who loaned you $500 two years ago to start your company.* Only those debts that you list on your schedule can be discharged by your bankruptcy, so make sure this list is complete.

3. *Another tip for preparing your schedule of debt: Include not only people whom you currently owe money, but people who might have lost money due to doing business with you.* For example, let's say that six months ago you promised Joe's Factory a shipment of one million widgets to make electric potato peelers, to be paid for C.O.D. Due to the bankruptcy, you were unable to produce said widgets and Joe couldn't manufacture the electric potato peelers, which he had lined up a buyer for. Even though Joe never paid you any money, he lost a substantial amount because of the broken promise you made to deliver those widgets. Joe may very well sue you at some point, and unless he's listed as a creditor on your schedule of debt, you may be liable for damages.

4. *In the case of a Chapter 11 bankruptcy, if you object to a claim filed by a creditor, that creditor must respond or the claim will automatically be denied.* This leaves room for error on the part of the creditor—and a glimmer of hope for you, the debtor. If the creditor

is on the ball and responds, a hearing is held and the judge decides whether a claim is valid or not. Be aware that any claim you do not object to must be included in your reorganization plan.

5. *Only consider a cram-down, forcing your creditors to accept your Chapter 11 reorganization plan despite their objections, as a last resort.* This option not only can cause added delays and expenses but also may generate a great deal of animosity from creditors whom you may want or need to continue doing business with if your company is to survive. It's definitely not a good public relations move at a time when you may need all the friends you can get.

6. *While a Chapter 13 reorganization plan can be revised fairly easily after it has been accepted by the bankruptcy court, it is virtually impossible to make any revisions in a Chapter 11 plan after it has been accepted.* It's hard enough to get a reorganization plan past a committee of your creditors one time, let alone getting them to accept revisions if you find the plan isn't working out for you. Your only option at this point is converting your Chapter 11 reorganization to a Chapter 7 liquidation—in other words, shutting down your business.

7. *In the case of a Chapter 11 bankruptcy, you must group your creditors' claims according to prescribed classifications that determine how individual claims will be treated (how much money they're entitled to).* Creditors' claims are classified as "impaired" or "unimpaired." Impaired claims are not entitled to the full amount of money owed, and unimpaired claims will receive the full amount of money that you originally agreed to pay them. Your reorganization plan must classify each claim as impaired or unimpaired, as well as outline how each creditor will be paid.

8. *In the case of a Chapter 11 reorganization, the bankruptcy court can dismiss your bankruptcy at any point, so it's best to have an alternative plan for keeping your business afloat.* Dismissal may occur for the following reasons:

You fail to meet the deadline for preparing your reorganization plan and disclosure statement.

You fail to gain approval of your plan by the majority of your creditors.

You fail to pay the trustee all necessary administration fees.

You fail to meet the terms outlined in your reorganization plan after it is approved.

# 23

---

# RECLAIMING YOUR GOOD FINANCIAL NAME

## RECOVERING FROM FINANCIAL BLUNDERS, AND LIVING TO TELL ABOUT IT

Everybody makes mistakes, especially during their first go at setting up a business. The key to success is knowing how to recognize trouble and bounce back from it in a timely manner. This chapter will demonstrate different strategies for recovering from financial difficulties in two different categories:

1. Saving your credit rating by reorganizing your business without the help of the bankruptcy court.
2. Rebuilding your credit after bankruptcy or a financial pothole that doesn't result in bankruptcy but affects your credit rating negatively nonetheless.

## SAVING YOUR CREDIT RATING, AND YOUR BUSINESS, BY REORGANIZING YOUR BUSINESS WITHOUT THE HELP OF THE BANKRUPTCY COURT

As you can well imagine, bankruptcy is one of your creditors' biggest fears—especially unsecured creditors, such as credit cards and service providers, who have no collateral to collect from a failing business.

No matter what type of bankruptcy you, as the debtor, file, the unsecured creditors' chances of recouping 100 percent of the outstanding debts are pretty slim (see Chapter 22 for more information on unsecured creditors). Not to mention the time and expense involved in attending the creditors' meeting and bankruptcy hearing. Your creditors—whether a bank, credit card company, another business, or a person who has loaned money to you or your company—know this.

So, believe it or not, your creditors are realistic, and you do have options even if there are written formal agreements and contracts stating otherwise. The dollars that you pay to your creditors are worth more today than they will be tomorrow, given the inflation factor alone. Then too, a dollar earned not only can be saved but can be invested for growth. So, it is easy enough to see why a business owner wanting to negotiate payment on outstanding debts has a significant power base from which to operate.

### Creating a Self-Help Organization Plan without Filing for Bankruptcy

If you have a steady income, or some valuable assets you're willing to sell, you may be able to save your company by creating a repayment plan without the help of the bankruptcy court. In the process, you may also salvage your credit rating, and your relationship with suppliers and creditors.

This could turn out to be a good deal for both you and your creditors. Your creditors' get virtually the same benefits as a Chapter 11 or 13 reorganization plan (a schedule of when they'll see their money), without the hassles of dealing with the bankruptcy courts for months, or even years. You, on the other hand, can get back on your feet again, stabilize your profit and loss, or even go into growth mode and become more and more profitable.

In setting up a repayment plan without filing for bankruptcy, follow these three basic steps:

1. Set up a realistic monthly budget of your company's financial needs.

2. Determine how much money you can realistically afford to pay each creditor on a monthly basis.

3. Write a proposal and submit it to your creditors.

If you're already in a financial predicament, chances are that you'll need a pro to help you set up this repayment schedule and negotiate with creditors. Either a bankruptcy attorney or a trained credit negotiator fits this bill, although the latter will be much cheaper. The not-for-profit Consumer Credit Counseling Service (CCCS) can set you up with a trained financial counselor for as low as $10 to $20 per month (see Key Resources). The CCCS counselor will help you establish a budget and work out a plan to repay your creditors in full over three to five years, without filing for bankruptcy.

Although the CCCS restructuring plan appears on your credit report, it is by far less damaging than bankruptcy. Some businesses, including Sears and J.C. Penney, are willing to extend small, unsecured lines of credit to CCCS "graduates."

## Be a "Transformational Leader"

This is a slight detour off the beaten legal track into the realm of management, but it bears mentioning to get you thinking about shaking up your business organization and staff in time to avoid bankruptcy.

Noel M. Tichy, a professor at the University of Michigan's School of Business, uses this somber analogy for business owners who refuse to see when there's a problem: If a frog is put in a pan of warm water, he'll contentedly sit there while the heat is gradually turned higher and higher until the poor thing is literally boiled alive.

Tichy, who once headed General Electric's executive development center, says, "(Many failed business owners) stayed in place, doing the same things they had always done, while the environment around them gradually became more hostile" (*Entrepreneur*, March 1995). In Tichy's book, *Control Your Destiny or Someone Else Will: How Jack Welch Is Making General Electric the World's Most Competitive Company* (Doubleday Currency), he gives a remedy for becoming a "boiled frog": Learn to be a "transformational leader," who can destroy and remake a dysfunctional organization.

According to Tichy, the key to being a transformational leader is the ability to balance hope and fear. These are the two essential elements in change—the fear that something undesirable will happen (your business will fail) and hope for the future that leads to action. A transformational leader must be able to make the leap of faith from fear to hope, instead of staying paralyzed in a state of fear and being boiled.

After you've made that leap, you need to instill the same vision in your employees—yell "Fire!" and then show them the fire escape.

For our purposes, being a transformational small business owner entails being able to close the floodgates of debt before all your resources float away.

## A SHORT AND SWEET COURSE IN REBUILDING CREDIT

Thus far we've been discussing how to save your credit rating, and your business, by avoiding bankruptcy altogether. But there are situations when that's not financially possible and bankruptcy becomes a fact of life. Fear not, though, all is not lost and you will live to own major charge cards again!

In theory, filing for bankruptcy provides you with a clean financial slate; a second chance to get it right. Unfortunately, those who depend on your financial stability in carrying out business transactions, may not be of the mind to forgive and forget your past financial misdealings. Their acceptance that you have learned from your mistakes and developed a more prudent financial sensibility will most likely be along the lines of, "I'll believe it when I see it." This takes time, but not as long as you may think.

A bankruptcy filing remains on your credit record for up to 10 years from the date you filed your papers, but you can actually rebuild your credit to the extent that you won't be turned down for a major credit card or loan after about two years. And many creditors will completely disregard a bankruptcy after you've obtained a good credit rating for five years. But, how does one obtain this elusive "good credit rating" after emerging from financial turmoil? Consider the following steps.

### Step 1. Know Your Legal Rights against Postbankruptcy Discrimination

As you've probably gathered by now, whether you formally file for bankruptcy or settle accumulated debts out of court, you'll no doubt encounter some degree of discrimination in the aftermath. For example, although employers are legally prohibited from discriminating against you solely on the basis that you filed for bankruptcy, the reality is that you may experience difficulty in obtaining a job.

"All my job interviews started following a pattern; they'd go great until the interviewer found out I had filed for bankruptcy and then the discussion would abruptly end," recalls a former owner of a small advertising agency who applied for jobs with local advertising firms for two years until landing an account management position far below his level of skills. "It was like I was suddenly untrustworthy as an employee because my own business didn't succeed."

You may also have trouble renting an apartment or business space if your prospective landlord does a credit check. If you suspect that this is the problem, there are several ways you can reassure the landlord that you do, in fact, have the financial wherewithal to pay your rent in a timely fashion:

- Offer an unusually high security deposit to cover several months' rent.
- Offer to pay the rent on a weekly basis during a probationary period.
- If possible, supply at least one credit reference that you've maintained a good relationship with (paid your debts to).

The laws concerning discrimination because of a poor credit history are better defined for government agencies than for the private sector. Once a government-related debt has been discharged by a bankruptcy judge, all actions against you enacted by federal, state, and local government in an effort to recover that debt must cease. This means that you can't be denied the rights of any other citizen—from a driver's license to government contract—*solely* because you filed for bankruptcy. The government is not allowed to discriminate against you by denying or obstructing your pursuit of any of the following:

- Employment.
- A contract on a government project (for example, an engineering contract for a highway being constructed).
- A government-guaranteed student loan.
- A driver's license.
- Public benefits (such as welfare or Social Security).
- Public housing.
- Renewal of your state liquor license.
- Participation in a state home mortgage finance program.

## Step 2. Make Sure Your Credit Reports Are Accurate

Most lenders will check you out with one of the major credit reporting agencies: TRW, Equifax, and Trans Union. You can't count on these companies to update your files. But you can—and should—take on this responsibility yourself by calling the credit bureaus every six months and requesting a copy of your credit report (see section on Key Resources for phone numbers).

The credit bureaus are legally bound to supply you with exactly the same reports they send to lenders. If you've been denied credit within the previous 60 days, TRW, Equifax, and Trans Union will supply you with a copy of your credit report for free. Otherwise, Equifax and Trans Union charge an $8 fee.

We know of one entrepreneur who found several mistakes in his report after being rejected for a car loan. His file hadn't been updated for eight years and contained misinformation about his job status and income. Other common credit report mishaps include transposed Social Security numbers and failure to note when debts have been discharged either personally or by a bankruptcy court.

If you find a mistake on your credit report, challenge it in writing (see Figure 23–1). The bureau must then investigate the charge within 30 days. If the information is found to be incorrect, it must be corrected. If the information can't be verified, it must be removed from your credit report.

Then there's the case of legitimately negative information regarding your credit standing—your office furniture really was repossessed, or the outstanding phone bills you filed in the circular file cabinet (trash can) resulted in your phone being shut off. Another common situation is that joint debt in a divorce situation is disputed as to liability by one spouse or the other and left unpaid until the court decides an equitable distribution under the community property law of the state.

The best way to counteract authentic financial skeletons is to write a letter of explanation (less than 100 words) that is sent to lenders and potential lenders with your credit report (see Figure 23–2). On your request, this letter must also be sent to anyone who received your credit report within the past six months, and any employment-related parties who received the report within the past two years.

## Step 3. Rebuilding Your Credit Report

Now we get to the crux of the matter: making yourself look like a good credit risk on paper. The following activities are means to that end.

### Get a Job and Keep It

Steady employment is a big plus for creditors, so you may want to consider becoming employed elsewhere until you've built a nest egg

**Figure 23–1**     Letter to Credit Bureau Disputing Information

July 20, 1995

Joe Doe
Customer Service Manager
Credit Bureau X
10000 General Highway
Dallas, TX 45004

Dear Mr. Doe:

Upon reviewing a recent copy of my credit report, I have found an error that I would like to have corrected. As you'll see by the enclosed copy of my credit report, my monthly income is reported as $1,000.50. This report fails to note that I have received a raise three months ago, and my monthly income is now $1,120.40. Enclosed please find copies of my paycheck stubs for the last three months, as well as a letter from my supervisor to verify this information.

I will expect to hear from you about this matter within the 30 day period allotted by law for a credit bureau to investigate a charge of incorrect information. Please correct this information as soon as possible, so that my credit report accurately reflects my financial status.

Thank you for your prompt attention to this matter.

Sincerely,

Jan Smith

---

large enough and creditworthy enough to start your own business over again.

### Start Over at a New Bank

Open a new checking and savings account, and keep both in good standing—no bounced checks or overdraws. Zero!

### Develop a Budget and Build Up Your Savings Account

Sock away whatever you can, even if it's only $20 per week, with the goal of building up your savings account to about $1,000. This will give you $500 to obtain a secured credit card and $500 for peace of mind in case of emergency expenses.

**Figure 23-2** Letter of Explanation for Bad Credit

July 20, 1995

To Whom It May Concern:

This letter serves as an explanation for my current position of being in less than good standing as a credit risk.

Four months ago, I went through a divorce that left me responsible for $10,000 worth of medical bills that my ex-husband incurred for elective surgery last year. Since my ex-husband does not have a job and I do, I am responsible for paying his medical bills that were put on our Visa card. I am trying to pay off this debt as quickly as I can without neglecting my other living expenses.

Thank you for considering my predicament.

Sincerely,

## Obtain a Secured Credit Card

If you are in a postbankruptcy situation, credit will probably need to come through a bank that offers a limited line of credit secured by keeping a certain amount of money (usually a minimum of $500) on deposit with that bank. Your credit line is usually equal to the amount of your account.

On the downside, secured credit cards often come with interest rates as high as 20 percent. On the upside, now you can rent a car or make a hotel room reservation over the phone. Also, after a few years of faithfully paying your secured credit card bills, other large creditors will be more likely to grant you an unsecured line of credit.

## Get a Small Secured Loan from Your Bank ($500–$1,000)

You may want to do this in addition to, or instead of, a secured credit card. Make sure you pay back the loan on time, or even before the due date each month. After you pay off the loan, take out a slightly larger loan at a different bank to gain another credit reference.

After several years of sticking to a budget, and following the preceding plan, you should be able to get unsecured credit or a loan with many major financial institutions. Caveat: Be aware, though, that bankruptcy can still stick like glue long past the 10-year limit on bankruptcy showing up on your credit report. Any financial institution lending you money can still legally require you to fill in the blank on a loan application asking whether or not you have ever filed for bankruptcy. (And they can check it out for themselves if they care to.)

## KNOW YOUR KEY TERMS

- *Secured credit or debt.* A line of credit, usually offered by a bank, that is guaranteed by a savings account with a minimum balance equal to the amount of the credit limit. The savings account acts as insurance for the bank against your debt.
- *Unsecured credit or debt.* Credit or a loan given without security in the form of collateral.

(*Note:* See also Chapters 21 and 22, Know Your Key Terms.)

## BASIC LEGAL RESEARCH

- *Money Troubles: Legal Strategies to Cope with Your Debts,* by Robin Leonard (Nolo Press). Tells you how to negotiate with creditors, and save your credit rating.
- *The Credit Repair Kit,* by John Ventura (Dearborn Financial Publishing). Some good tips for rebuilding your credit rating.
- *Nolo's Law Form Kit: Rebuild Your Credit,* by Robin Leonard (Nolo Press). A step-by-step plan for rebuilding your credit, as well as tear-out forms you'll need along the way.

## KEY RESOURCES

- *Consumer Credit Counseling Services.* This is a nationwide business that can hook you up with a credit counselor who can negotiate a payment schedule with your creditors. For a local chapter, call (800) 388-2227.
- *Debtors Anonymous.* Habitual overspending can be an addiction as hard to kick as drugs or gambling. This 12-step support program can help you gain control of your finances. To find a local chapter, call (212) 642-8220.
- *Credit Bureaus.* The three major credit bureaus are Equifax Information Service Center, (800) 685-1111; TRW Consumer Assistance Center, (800) 682-7654; and Trans Union Consumer Relations, (800) 851-2674.
- *Bankcard Holders of America.* This source can provide you with information on where to obtain a secured credit card. Send a SASE to them at 560 Herndon Parkway, Suite 120, Herndon, VA 22070.

## COURT COACH® SUGGESTS

1. *Don't rely on agencies that claim they can "fix your credit."* After reading this chapter, it should be clear to you that there's no magic formula for fixing your credit. Credit repair agencies that claim to have the cure for your financial ailments may just go through the same steps outlined in this chapter to make sure that your credit rating is correct and up to date, and get you a secured credit card—and charge a service fee for doing the same work you could have done yourself.

2. *Beware of secured-credit scams.* These outfits usually demand an outrageously high up-front fee in exchange for getting you credit. What you'll probably wind up with is a list of lenders or applications for secured credit cards, with no guarantees of acceptance. Again, there's no magic formula for fixing your credit.

3. *Note that all your creditors need to agree to go along with an out-of-court repayment plan for it to work smoothly.* If you've got even one creditor who simply refuses to rectify your debt via an out-of-court repayment plan, this could prove to be a major chink in your armor protecting you from bankruptcy. Whatever you do, never pay off some creditors and try to work out a repayment deal with others. This is considered preferential treatment of creditors and is strictly forbidden. Perhaps a third party, such as your attorney or accountant, could reason with the uncooperative creditor.

# Appendix A

# STATE BAR ASSOCIATIONS

ALABAMA STATE BAR
P.O. Box 671
Montgomery, AL 36101
(205) 269-1515

ALASKA BAR ASSOCIATION
510 L Street, Suite 602
Anchorage, AK 99501
(907) 272-7469

STATE BAR OF ARIZONA
111 West Monroe, 19th Floor
Phoenix, AZ 85003-1742
(602) 252-4804

ARKANSAS BAR ASSOCIATION
400 West Markham, Suite 401
Little Rock, AR 72201-1408
(501) 375-4605

STATE BAR OF CALIFORNIA
855 Franklin Street
San Francisco, CA 94102-4498
(415) 561-8200

COLORADO BAR ASSOCIATION
1900 Grant Street, Suite 950
Denver, CO 80203
(303) 860-1115

CONNECTICUT BAR ASSOCIATION
101 Corporate Place
Rocky Hill, CT 06067-1894
(203) 721-0025

DELAWARE STATE BAR ASSOCIATION
1225 King Street
Wilmington, DE 19801-3233
(302) 658-5279

DISTRICT OF COLUMBIA BAR
1250 H Street NW, 6th Floor
Washington, DC 20005-3908
(202) 737-4700

FLORIDA BAR
650 Apalachee Parkway
Tallahassee, FL 32399-2200
(904) 561-5600

STATE BAR OF GEORGIA
800 The Hurt Building
50 Hurt Plaza
Atlanta, GA 30303
(404) 527-8700

HAWAII STATE BAR ASSOCIATION
1136 Union Mall, Penthouse One
Honolulu, HI 96813
(808) 537-1868

IDAHO STATE BAR
P.O. Box 895
Boise, ID 83701-0895
(208) 342-8958

ILLINOIS STATE BAR ASSOCIATION
Illinois Bar Center
Springfield, IL 62701
(210) 525-1760

INDIANA STATE BAR ASSOCIATION
230 East Ohio Street, 4th Floor
Indianapolis, IN 46204-2199
(317) 639-5465

IOWA STATE BAR ASSOCIATION
521 East Locust Street
Des Moines, IA 50309
(515) 243-3179

KANSAS BAR ASSOCIATION
P.O. Box 1037
Topeka, KS 66601-1037
(913) 234-5696

KENTUCKY BAR ASSOCIATION
514 West Main Street
Frankfort, KY 40601-1883
(502) 564-3795

LOUISIANA STATE BAR ASSOCIATION
601 St. Charles Avenue
New Orleans, LA 70130
(504) 566-1600

MAINE STATE BAR ASSOCIATION
P.O. Box 788
Augusta, ME 04332-0788
(207) 622-7523

MARYLAND STATE BAR ASSOCIATION
520 West Fayette Street
Baltimore, MD 21201
(410) 685-7878

MASSACHUSETTS BAR ASSOCIATION
20 West Street
Boston, MA 02111
(617) 542-3602

STATE BAR OF MICHIGAN
306 Townsend Street
Lansing, MI 48933-2083
(517) 372-9030

MINNESOTA STATE BAR
    ASSOCIATION
514 Nicolet Mall, Suite 300
Minneapolis, MN 55402
(612) 333-1183

MISSISSIPPI BAR
P.O. Box 2168
Jackson, MS 39225-2168
(314) 635-4128

MISSOURI BAR
P.O. Box 119
Jefferson City, MO 65102
(314) 635-4128

STATE BAR OF MONTANA
46 North Main Street
P.O. Box 577
Helena, MT 59601
(406) 442-7660

NEBRASKA STATE BAR ASSOCIATION
P.O. Box 81809
Lincoln, NE 68501-1809
(402) 475-7091

STATE BAR OF NEVADA
201 Las Vegas Boulevard South
Las Vegas, NV 89101
(702) 382-2200

NEW HAMPSHIRE BAR ASSOCIATION
112 Pleasant Street
Concord, NH 03301
(603) 224-6942

NEW JERSEY STATE BAR
    ASSOCIATION
One Constitution Square
New Brunswick, NJ 08901-1500
(908) 249-5000

STATE BAR OF NEW MEXICO
P.O. Box 25883
Albuquerque, NM 87125
(505) 842-6132

NEW YORK STATE BAR ASSOCIATION
One Elk Street
Albany, NY 12207
(518) 463-3200

NORTH CAROLINA STATE BAR
P.O. Box 25908
Raleigh, NC 28711
(919) 828-4620

STATE BAR ASSOCIATION OF NORTH
 DAKOTA
P.O. Box 2136
Bismarck, ND 58502-2136
(701) 255-1404

OHIO STATE BAR ASSOCIATION
P.O. Box 16562
Columbus, OH 43216-6562
(614) 487-2050

OKLAHOMA BAR ASSOCIATION
P.O. Box 53036
Oklahoma City, OK 73152-3036
(405) 524-2365

OREGON STATE BAR
P.O. Box 1689
Las Oswego, OR 97035-0889
(503) 620-0222

PENNSYLVANIA BAR ASSOCIATION
100 South Street
P.O. Box 186
Harrisburg, PA 17108-0186
(717) 238-6715

BAR ASSOCIATION OF PUERTO RICO
P.O. Box 1900
San Juan, PR 00902
(809) 721-3358

RHODE ISLAND BAR ASSOCIATION
115 Cedar Street
Providence, RI 02903
(401) 421-5740

SOUTH CAROLINA BAR
P.O. Box 608
Columbia, SC 29202
(803) 799-6653

STATE BAR OF SOUTH DAKOTA
222 East Capitol
Pierre, SD 57501-2596
(605) 224-7554

TENNESSEE BAR ASSOCIATION
3622 West End Avenue
Nashville, TN 37205-2403
(615) 383-7421

STATE BAR OF TEXAS
P.O. Box 1287
Austin, TX 78711-2487
(512) 463-1463

UTAH STATE BAR
645 South 200 East, Room 310
Salt Lake City, UT 84111
(801) 531-9077

VERMONT BAR ASSOCIATION
P.O. Box 100
Montpelier, VT 05601
(802) 233-2020

VIRGINIA STATE BAR
707 East Main Street, Suite 1500
Richmond, VA 23219-2803
(804) 755-0500

WASHINGTON STATE BAR
 ASSOCIATION
2001 Sixth Avenue, Suite 500
Seattle, WA 98121-2599
(206) 727-8200

WEST VIRGINIA STATE BAR
2006 Kanawha Boulevard
E. Charleston, WV 25311
(304) 342-1474

STATE BAR OF WISCONSIN
402 West Wilson Street
Madison, WI 53703
(608) 257-3838

WYOMING STATE BAR
P.O. Box 109
Cheyenne, WY 82001
(307) 632-9061

# Appendix B

# FIRST-RATE BUSINESS SCHOOLS THAT OFFER ENTREPRENEUR PROGRAMS OR CLASSES

University of Arizona
Karl Eller Graduate School of
    Management
Tucson, AZ 85721
(602) 621-2566

Babson College
Graduate School of Business
Babson Park, MA 02157
(617) 239-4317
(Of special interest: Entrepreneurial
    management)

Brigham Young University
Marriott School of Management
640 North Eldon Tanner Building
Provo, UT 84602
(801) 378-3500
(Of special interest: Entrepreneurship
    lecture series)

University of California-Berkeley
Walter A. Haas School of Business
350 Barrows Hall
Berkeley, CA 94720
(510) 642-1405
(Of special interest: Innovation and
    entrepreneurship)

University of California-Los Angeles
John E. Anderson Graduate School of
    Management
405 Hilgard Avenue
Los Angeles, CA 90024
(310) 825-6944

Carnegie Mellon University
Graduate School of Industrial
    Administration
Schenley Park
Pittsburgh, PA 15213-3890
(412) 268-2272

Case Western Reserve
Weatherhead School of Management
10900 Euclid Avenue
Enterprise Hall, Room 310
Cleveland, OH 44106
(800) 723-0203

University of Maryland
College of Business and Management
Management and Business Affairs
    Building, Room 2308
College Park, MD 20742
(301) 405-2278

Northwest University
J.L. Kellogg Graduate School of
    Management
Leverone Hall, Room 2-104
2001 Sheridan Road
Evanston, IL 602008
(708) 491-3308

University of Pennsylvania
The Wharton School Graduate Division
102 Vance Hall
Philadelphia, PA 19104
(215) 898-3430
(Of special interest: Wharton's Sol C.
    Snider Entrepreneurial Center)

Rensselaer Polytechnic Institute
School of Management
Lally Management Center
Troy, NY 12180-3590
(518) 276-6789
(Of special interest: Technological
    entrepreneurship)

Rice University
Jesse H. Jones Graduate School of
    Administration
P.O. Box 1892
Houston, TX 77251
(713) 527-4918

University of Southern California
Graduate School of Business
Briage Hall, 101 MC 1421
Los Angeles, CA 90089-1421
(213) 740-7846

University of Texas at Austin
Graduate School of Business
P.O. Box 7999
Austin, TX 78713
(512) 471-7612

University of Washington
Graduate School of Business
    Administration
110 MacKenzie Hall, DJ-10
Seattle, WA 98195
(206) 453-4660

# Appendix C

# STATE OFFICES OF CORPORATION ADMINISTRATION*

ALABAMA
Office of the Secretary of State
Business Division
11 South Union Street, Room 208
P.O. Box 5616
Montgomery, AL 36103-5616
(205) 242-7200


ALASKA
Department of Commerce and Economic
    Development
Division of Banking Securities and
    Corporations
P.O. Box 11807
Juneau, AK 99881-0807
(907) 465-2321


ARIZONA
Arizona Corporation Commission
Corporations Division
1200 West Washington
Phoenix, AZ 86007
(602) 542-3521

ARKANSAS
Department of State
Corporations Division
State Capitol
Little Rock, AR 72201
(501) 682-3404

CALIFORNIA
Department of State
Division of Corporations
1230 J Street
Sacramento, CA 95814
(916) 455-0620

COLORADO
Department of State
Division of Commercial Recordings
1560 Broadway, Suite 200
Denver, CO 80202
(303) 894-2200

CONNECTICUT
Department of State
30 Trinity Street
Hartford, CT 06106
(203) 566-6192

---

*Source:* International Association of Corporation Administrators

DELAWARE
Division of Corporations
John G. Townsend Building
P.O. Box 898
Dover, DE 19903
(302) 739-4279


DISTRICT OF COLUMBIA
Department of Consumer and
      Regulatory Affairs
614 H Street NW, Suite 1120
Washington, DC 20001
(202) 727-7120


FLORIDA
Division of Corporations
P.O. Box 6327
Tallahassee, FL 32314
(904) 487-6000


GEORGIA
Business Services and Regulation
2 Martin Luther King, Jr. Drive
West Tower, Room 315
Atlanta, GA 30334-1530
(404) 656-6478


HAWAII
Department of Commerce and
      Consumer Affairs
P.O. Box 40
Honolulu, HI 96810
(808) 586-2744


IDAHO
Department of State
Office of Commercial Affairs
State House
Boise, ID 83720
(208) 334-2300


ILLINOIS
Department of Business Services
330 Centennial Building
Springfield, IL 62756
(217) 524-1159


INDIANA
Department of State
Corporations Division
303 West Washington Street, Room E111
Indianapolis, IN 46204
(317) 232-6587


IOWA
Department of State
Corporations Division
Hoover Building
Des Moines, IA 50319
(515) 281-5204


KANSAS
Department of State
Corporations Office
Capitol Building, 2nd Floor
Topeka, KS 66612-1594
(913) 296-4565


KENTUCKY
Corporations Office
P.O. Box 718
Frankfort, KY 40602-0718
(502) 564-2848


LOUISIANA
Department of State
Commercial Division
P.O. Box 94125
Baton Rouge, LA 70804-9125
(504) 925-4716


MAINE
Department of State
Bureau of Corporations, Elections and
      Commissions
State House, Station 101, Room 221
Augusta, ME 04333
(207) 287-4190


MARYLAND
State Department of Assessments and
      Taxation
301 West Preston Street, Room 809
Baltimore, MD 21201
(410) 255-1330


MASSACHUSETTS
Department of State
Corporations Office
One Ashburton Place, Room 1710
Boston, MA 02108
(617) 727-2853


MICHIGAN
Michigan Department of Commerce
Corporation Division
6546 Mercantile Way
P.O. Box 30054
Lansing, MI 48909
(517) 334-6327

MINNESOTA
Department of State
Business Services Division
180 State Office Building
St. Paul, MN 55155
(612) 296-9215

MISSISSIPPI
Department of State
Business Services Division
202 North Congress, Room 601
P.O. Box 136
Jackson, MS 39205-0136
(601) 359-1604

MISSOURI
Department of State
Business Services
P.O. Box 1159
Jefferson City, MO 65102
(314) 751-4153

MONTANA
Business Services Bureau
State Capitol, Room 244
Helena, MT 59620
(406) 444-3665

NEBRASKA
Corporation Division
State Capitol, Room 1301
Lincoln, NE 68509
(402) 471-2554

NEVADA
Department of State
Corporations Division
Capitol Complex
Carson City, NV 89710
(702) 687-5203

NEW HAMPSHIRE
Department of State
State House, Room 204
107 North Main Street
Concord, NH 03301-4989
(603) 271-3242

NEW JERSEY
Department of State
Division of Commercial Recording,
    CN 308
Trenton, NJ 08625
(609) 530-6412

NEW MEXICO
Department of State
State Corporation Commission
P.O. Drawer 1269
Santa Fe, NM 87504-1269
(505) 827-4502

NEW YORK
Department of State
Division of Corporations
162 Washington Avenue
Albany, NY 12231
(518) 473-2492

NORTH CAROLINA
Department of State
Corporations Division
Legislative Office Building
300 North Salisbury Street, Room 302
Raleigh, NC 27603-5909
(919) 733-4201

NORTH DAKOTA
Department of State
Main Capitol Building, 1st Floor
600 East Boulevard Avenue
Bismarck, ND 58505-0500
(701) 224-2939

OHIO
Corporations Office
30 East Broad Street, 14th Floor
Columbus, OH 43266-0418
(614) 466-1145

OKLAHOMA
Department of State
Corporations Department
State Capitol Building, Room 101
Oklahoma City, OK 73105
(405) 521-3911

OREGON
Department of State
Corporation and UCC Division
158 12th Street, NE
Salem, OR 97310-4166
(503) 378-4166

PENNSYLVANIA
Corporation Bureau
P.O. Box 8722
Harrisburg, PA 17105-8722
(717) 787-1057

PUERTO RICO
Department of State
Corporation and Trademark Division
San Francisco Street
P.O. Box 3271
Old San Juan Station
San Juan, PR 00902-3271
(809) 722-2121, Ext. 320

RHODE ISLAND
Corporations Office
100 North Main Street
Providence, RI 02903
(401) 277-1309

SOUTH CAROLINA
Department of State
Corporation Department
P.O. Box 11350
Columbia, SC 29211
(803) 734-2170

SOUTH DAKOTA
Department of State
Corporations and UCC Central Filings
500 East Capitol
Pierre, SD 57501-5077
(605) 773-4845

TENNESSEE
Department of State
Corporation Section
James K. Polk Building, 18th Floor
Nashville, TN 37243-0306
(615) 741-0584

TEXAS
Department of State
Statutory Filings Division
P.O. Box 13697
Austin, TX 78711-3697
(512) 463-5586

UTAH
Utah Division of Corporations and UCC
160 East 300 South, 2nd Floor
P.O. Box 45801
Salt Lake City, UT 84145-0801
(801) 530-6438

VERMONT
Corporations/UCC Office
109 State Street
Montpelier, VT 05609-1104
(802) 828-2371

VIRGINIA
State Corporation Commission
Jefferson Building
1220 Bank Street
P.O. Box 1197
Richmond, VA 23209
(804) 786-3672

WASHINGTON
Department of State Corporations
     Division
505 East Union, 2nd Floor
P.O. Box 40234
Olympia, WA 98504-0234

WEST VIRGINIA
Department of State
Corporations/UCC Division
Capitol Building, Room W-139
Charleston, WV 25305-0776
(304) 558-8000

WISCONSIN
Department of State
Corporations Division
30 West Mifflin Street
P.O. Box 7846
Madison, WI 53707
(608) 266-3590

WYOMING
Department of State
Corporation and UCC Department
110 Capitol Building
Cheyenne, WY 82002-0020
(307) 777-5339

# Appendix D

# STATE LAWS REGARDING DAMAGE LIMITS ON BAD CHECKS*

| State | Limit on Damages |
|---|---|
| ALABAMA | Amount of check, attorney fees, plus punitive damages determined by court. |
| ARIZONA | Twice the amount of the check, or $50, plus attorney fees. |
| CALIFORNIA | Triple the amount of the check, not less than $100 or more than $500, plus attorney fees. |
| COLORADO | Triple the amount of the check, not less than $100 or more than $500, plus attorney fees. |
| CONNECTICUT | If a bad check is written on an account with insufficient funds, damages can't exceed the amount of the check or $400. If a bad check is written on a nonexistent account, the amount of damages is boosted to $750. |
| DISTRICT OF COLUMBIA | |
| FLORIDA | Triple the amount of the check, or $50, plus attorney fees. |
| GEORGIA | Twice the amount of the check, not to exceed $500. |
| HAWAII | Triple the amount of the check, not to be less than $100 or greater than $500. |
| ILLINOIS | Triple the amount of the check, not to be less than $100 or greater than $500. |
| INDIANA | Triple the amount of the check, not to be less than $100 or greater than $500. |
| IOWA | Triple the amount of the check, not to be greater than $500. |

*Note: "Attorney fees" refers to a reasonable amount as determined by the court. If a damage amount is listed as an alternative to the face amount of the check, the greater amount is charged the defendant.

326

| State | Limit on Damages |
| --- | --- |
| KANSAS | Triple the amount of the check, not to be less than $100 or greater than $500. |
| LOUISIANA | Twice the amount of the check or $100, plus attorney fees. |
| MAINE | Face value of the check, or the cumulative costs of court fees, collection, and processing expenses not to exceed $40, whichever is less, plus interest at 12% per year. |
| MARYLAND | Twice the amount of the check, not to exceed $1,000. |
| MASSACHUSETTS | The court sets the damages, not less than $100 or more than $500. |
| MINNESOTA | $100 plus market rate interest and attorney fees. |
| MISSISSIPPI | If the check is less than $26, the amount of the check. If the check is $26–$200, 50% of the face value. If the check is more than $200, 25% of the face value. |
| MISSOURI | Triple the amount of the check, not to be less than $100 or more than $500. |
| MONTANA | Triple the amount of the check, not to be less than $100 or more than $500. |
| NEVADA | Triple the amount of the check, not to be less than $100 or more than $500, plus expenses. |
| NEW HAMPSHIRE | Amount of check plus court and collection fees. Upon failure to pay judgment, the debtor is subject to a fine of $10 per business day up to $500 from the date of judgment until the debt is paid. |
| NEW JERSEY | |
| NEW MEXICO | Triple the amount of the check, not to be less than $100 or more than $500. |
| NEW YORK | If a bad check is written on an account with insufficient funds, twice the amount of the check or $750, whichever is less. If a bad check is written on a nonexistent account, twice the amount of the check or $400, whichever is less. |
| NORTH CAROLINA | Triple the amount of the check or $500, whichever is less, but at least $100. |
| NORTH DAKOTA | Triple the amount of the check or $100, whichever is less. |
| OREGON | Triple the amount of the check, not to be less than $100 or more than $500, plus attorney fees. |
| PENNSYLVANIA | Triple the amount of the check, not to be less than $100 or more than $500. |
| RHODE ISLAND | Triple the amount of the check, not to be less than $200 or more than $1,000. |
| TENNESSEE | Triple the amount of the check, not to exceed $500. |
| VERMONT | Amount of the check, plus expenses, not to exceed $50. |
| VIRGINIA | The amount of the check, plus expenses, not to exceed $250. |
| WASHINGTON | Triple the amount of the check or $100. |
| WEST VIRGINIA | |
| WISCONSIN | Triple the amount of the check, attorney fees, and damages not to exceed $300. |
| WYOMING | Twice the amount of the check, not to be less than $50, plus interest, costs, and attorney fees. |

# Appendix E

# MEDIATION SOURCES

The National Institute for Dispute
    Resolution
1726 M Street NW
Washington, DC 20036
(202) 466-4764

ALABAMA
Birmingham Dispute Settlement System
City Hall, Room 100
710 North 20th Street
Birmingham, AL 35203
(205) 254-2011

ALASKA
PACT
2nd Judicial District
P.O. Box 749
Barrow, AK 99723
(907) 852-7228

ARIZONA
Conciliation
County Courthouse
Flagstaff, AZ 86001
(602) 779-6598

Community Mediation Program of
    Terros
301 East Bethany Home Road, Room A119
Phoenix, AZ 85012
(602) 230-2567

ARKANSAS
University of Arkansas at Little Rock-
    Pulaski County Mediation Program
College Arts, Humanities and Social
    Sciences
2801 South University
University of Arkansas at Little Rock
Little Rock, AR 72204
(501) 569-3234

CALIFORNIA
Claremont Dispute Resolution Center
333 West Foothill Boulevard
Glendora, CA 91740
(818) 963-3969

M.L.K. Dispute Resolution Center
4182 South Western Avenue
Los Angeles, CA 90062
(213) 295-8582

Los Angeles County Dispute Settlement
Services
500 West Temple Street, Room B-96
Los Angeles, CA 90012
(213) 974-0825

Los Angeles County Bar Association
Dispute Resolution Services
Box 55020
Los Angeles, CA 90055
(213) 627-2727

Community Mediation of San Diego
2150 West Washington Street, Suite 112
San Diego, CA 92110
(619) 238-1022

Early Settlement Program
Bar Association of San Francisco
685 Market Street, Suite 700
San Francisco, CA 94105
(415) 764-1600

COLORADO
Office of Dispute Resolution
County Judicial Department
1301 Pennsylvania Street, Suite 300
Denver, CO 80203
(303) 837-3672

DELAWARE
Superior Court Compulsory Arbitration
Program
The Public Building
11th and King Streets
Wilmington, DE 19801
(302) 571-2343

DISTRICT OF COLUMBIA
Multi-Door Dispute Resolution and
Arbitration
500 Indiana Avenue, Room 1235
Washington, DC 20001
(202) 879-1549

FLORIDA
Court Mediation and Arbitration
Program
Court Administrator's Office
516 SE Fifth Street
Ft. Lauderdale, FL 33301
(305) 765-4491

Circuit Civil Mediation
P.O. Box 1989
West Palm Beach, FL 33402-1989
(407) 686-1903

GEORGIA
Civil Arbitration Program
136 Pryor Street SW
Atlanta, GA 30303
(404) 730-4551

HAWAII
Court-Annexed Arbitration Program
777 Punchbowl Street, 4th Floor
Honolulu, HI 96813
(808) 548-4380

IDAHO
Conflict Resolution Center
410 Sherman Avenue, No. 216
Coeur d'Alene, ID 83814
(208) 664-9884

ILLINOIS
Endispute, Inc.
222 South Riverside Plaza, Suite 800
Chicago, IL 60606
(312) 684-4343

Resolve Dispute Management, Inc.
650 North Dearborn
Chicago, IL 60601-9038
(312) 943-7477

KANSAS
Court Services Mediation
P.O. Box 543
McPherson, KS 67460
(316) 241-3510

LOUISIANA
Small Claims Arbitration
P.O. Box 3438
Baton Rouge, LA 70821
(504) 389-5279

MAINE
ADR Pilot Project
P.O. Box 328-DTS
Portland, ME 04112

MARYLAND
aw Settlement
Circuit Court for Baltimore County
County Courts Building
401 Bosley Avenue
Towson, MD 21204
(301) 887-2920

Pre-Trial Settlement
Circuit Court for Carroll County
Courthouse
Westminster, MD 21157
(301) 857-2953

MASSACHUSETTS
Mediation Project
University of Massachusetts
425 Amity Street
Amherst, MA 01002
(413) 545-2462

Crime and Justice Foundation Mediation
    Program
20 West Street
Boston, MA 02111
(617) 426-9800

Brockton Mediation Program
Brockton Consumer Advisory
    Commission
50 Maple Avenue
Brockton, MA 02401
(508) 580-7184

MICHIGAN
Mediation Tribunal Association
340 East Congress, Suite 700
Detroit, MI 48226
(313) 245-5606

MISSOURI
Community Mediation Service
University of Missouri
Columbia School of Law,
    104 Law Building
Columbia, MO 65211
(314) 882-2052

Dispute Resolution Program
University of Missouri at St. Louis
7952 Natural Bridge Road
St. Louis, MO 63121-4499
(314) 553-6040

NEVADA
Mediation
Second Judicial District Court
75 Court Street
Reno, NV 89501
(702) 328-3119

NEW JERSEY
Early Settlement Program
Bergen County Courthouse, Room 222
Hackensack, NJ 07601
(201) 646-3553

Small Claims Mediation
Superior Court of New Jersey
595 Newark Avenue
Jersey City, NJ 07306
(201) 795-6142

Early Settlement Program
Superior Court of New Jersey
Court Street
Morristown, NJ 07960
(201) 285-6406

Arbitration and Mediation Program
Superior Court Law Division
465 Dr. Martin Luther King, Jr. Boulevard
Newark, NJ 07102
(201) 621-4225

Mercer County Mediation Unit
650 South Broad Street, 3rd Floor
Trenton, NJ 08611
(609) 989-6744

NEW YORK
Brooklyn Mediation Center
210 Joralemon Street, Room 618
Brooklyn, NY 11201
(718) 834-6675

Arbitration
Supreme Court
92 Franklin Street
Buffalo, NY 14202
(716) 852-1291

Center for Dispute Settlement, Inc.
87 North Clinton Avenue, Suite 510
Rochester, NY 14604
(716) 546-5110

Community Dispute Settlement Program
12 King Street
Troy, NY 12180
(518) 274-5920

OHIO
Center for Mediation of Disputes
325 Hamilton County Courthouse
1000 Main Street
Cincinnati, OH 45202
(513) 632-8963

Center for Mediation of Disputes, Inc.
Common Pleas Project
8 West Ninth Street
Cincinnati, OH 45202
(513) 721-4466

Mediation Division
City of Cleveland Municipal Court
1200 Ontario Street, 8th Floor
Cleveland, OH 44113
(216) 664-4800

OKLAHOMA
Northwest Conflict Resolution Services
P.O. Box 130
Fairview, OK 73737
(405) 227-2711

Oklahoma City Dispute Mediation
    Program
Municipal Court Building
700 Couch Drive
Oklahoma City, OK 73102
(405) 231-3844

Early Settlement Precourt Hearing
    Program
Police Courts Building
600 Civic Center, Room 234
Tulsa, OK 74103
(918) 596-7786

PENNSYLVANIA
Board of Arbitration
P.O. Box 217
Middleburg, PA 17842
(717) 837-4230

Judicate, Inc.
1608 Walnut Street, Suite 1200
Philadelphia, PA 19103
(215) 546-6200

Allegheny Service Institute (ASI)
P.O. Box 90026
Pittsburgh, PA 15224
(412) 355-5625

Conflict Resolution Center, Inc.
2205 East Carson Street
Pittsburgh, PA 15203-2107
(412) 481-5559

ADR
Berks County Courthouse
33 North 6th Street
Reading, PA 19601
(215) 378-8283

PUERTO RICO
Dispute Resolution Center
P.O. Box 887, Hato Rey Station
San Juan, PR 00919
(809) 763-4813

RHODE ISLAND
Court-Annexed Arbitration
Garrahy Judicial Complex, Room 309
One Dorrance Plaza
Providence, RI 02903
(401) 277-6147

SOUTH CAROLINA
Alternative Dispute Resolution Pilot
    Program
171 Ashley Avenue
Charleston, SC 29425
(803) 377-1141

Appeals Arbitration
Supreme Court or Court of Appeals
P.O. Box 728
Chester, SC 29706
(803) 377-1141

VICTOR of the Midlands, Inc.
P.O. Box 5755
Columbia, SC 29250
(803) 256-2351

SOUTH DAKOTA
Settlement Conference
Supreme Court, State Capital
Pierre, SD 57501
(605) 773-4869

TENNESSEE
Rent-a-Judge
422 Supreme Court Building
Nashville, TN 37219
(615) 741-4416

TEXAS
The Dispute Resolution Center
P.O. Box 9257
Amarillo, TX 79105-9257
(806) 372-3381

The Dispute Resolution Center
512 East Riverside, Suite 202
Austin, Texas 78704
(512) 443-5981

Dallas Bar Association
ADR Community Mediator Training
    Program
c/o Steve Brutsche
15303 Dallas Parkway, Suite 700, LB17
Dallas, TX 75248
(214) 701-7040

Dispute Resolution Center
1302 Preston Street, Room 100
Houston, TX 77002
(713) 221-8274

Bexar County Mediation Center
436 South Main, Heritage Plaza
San Antonio, TX 78204
(512) 220-2128

UTAH
Commissioner Program
District Court Committee
240 East 400 South
Salt Lake City, UT 84111
(801) 535-5210

VERMONT
Burlington Mediation Center
431 Pine Street
Burlington, VT 05401
(802) 860-1029

Lamoille Small Claims Mediation
     Program
Quest RD 1, No. 1440-10
Johnson, VT 05656
(802) 635-7349

WASHINGTON
Dispute Resolution Center
Snohomish County Courts
P.O. Box 839
Everett, WA 98206
(206) 339-1335

Thurston County Mandatory Mediation
     Program
200 Lakeridge Drive SW, Building 2
Mail Stop FQ-11
Olympia, WA 98502
(206) 786-5557

King County Superior Court
Mandatory Arbitration
King County Courthouse
516 Third Avenue, Room W855
Seattle, WA 98104
(206) 296-9365

Judicial Arbitration and Mediation
     Services
1420 Fifth Avenue, Suite 400
Seattle, WA 98101
(800) 352-5267

Spokane County
Mandatory Arbitration Program
West 1116 Broadway
Spokane, WA 99260
(509) 456-5790

WISCONSIN
Dane County Case Mediation Program
City County Building, Room 243
210 Martin Luther King Boulevard
Madison, WI 53709
(608) 267-2523

Milwaukee Mediation Center
Wisconsin Correctional Service
436 West Wisconsin Avenue
Milwaukee, WI 53203

# Appendix F

# MEMBERS OF THE AMERICAN ARBITRATION ASSOCIATION*

| State | City | Arbitrator | Phone Number |
|---|---|---|---|
| ARIZONA | Phoenix | Harry Kaminsky | (602) 234-0950 |
| CALIFORNIA | Irvine | Patricia Baker | (714) 474-5090 |
| | Los Angeles | Rocco M. Scanza | (213) 383-6516 |
| | San Diego | Dennis Sharp | (619) 239-3051 |
| | San Francisco | Stephen Van Liere | (415) 981-3901 |
| CONNECTICUT | East Hartford | Karen Jalkut | (203) 289-3993 |
| DISTRICT OF COLUMBIA | Washington | Steven Gallagher | (202) 296-8510 |
| FLORIDA | Miami | Rene Grafals | (305) 358-7777 |
| | Orlando | Mark Sholander | (407) 648-1185 |
| GEORGIA | Atlanta | India Johnson | (404) 325-0101 |
| HAWAII | Honolulu | Keith Hunter | (808) 531-0541 |
| ILLINOIS | Chicago | David Carfello | (312) 616-6560 |
| LOUISIANA | New Orleans | Deann Gladwell | (504) 522-8781 |
| MASSACHUSSETTS | Boston | Christine Newhall | (617) 451-6600 |
| MICHIGAN | Southfield | Mary Bedikian | (313) 352-5500 |
| MINNESOTA | Minneapolis | James Deye | (612) 332-6545 |
| MISSOURI | Kansas City | Lori Madden | (816) 221-6401 |
| | St. Louis | Neil Moldenhauer | (314) 621-7175 |
| NEVADA | Las Vegas | Kevin Chin | (702) 364-8009 |
| NEW JERSEY | Somerset | Gene Truncillito | (908) 560-9560 |
| NEW YORK | Garden City | Mark Resnick | (516) 222-1660 |
| | New York | Agnes Wilson | (212) 484-4000 |
| | Syracuse | Deborah Brown | (315) 472-5483 |
| | White Plains | Marion Zinman | (914) 946-1119 |
| OHIO | Cincinnati | Philip Thompson | (513) 241-8384 |
| PENNSYLVANIA | Philadelphia | Kenneth Egger | (215) 732-5260 |
| | Pittsburgh | John Schano | (412) 261-3617 |
| TENNESSEE | Nashville | Judy Johnson | (615) 256-5857 |
| TEXAS | Dallas | Helmut Wolff | (214) 702-8222 |
| UTAH | Salt Lake City | Diane Abegglen | (801) 531-9748 |
| WASHINGTON | Seattle | Patrick Mead | (206) 622-6435 |

*Source: American Arbitration Association

# Appendix G

# UNLAWFUL EMPLOYMENT PRACTICES COVERED UNDER TITLE VII OF THE CIVIL RIGHTS ACT OF 1964*

(*Note:* The following is an abbreviated version of the unlawful employment practices outlined in Title VII, Sec. 2000e-2 (Section 702). For a complete version, see the Equal Employment Opportunity Commission's pamphlet, "Laws Enforced by the U.S. Equal Employment Opportunity Commission.")

(a) It shall be an unlawful employment practice for an employer:

    (1) to fail or refuse to hire or to discharge any individual, or otherwise to discriminate against any individual with respect to his compensation, terms, conditions, or privileges of employment, because of race, color, religion, sex, or national origin; or

    (2) to limit, segregate, or classify his employees or applicants for employment in any discriminatory manner based on race, color, religion, sex, or national origin.

(b) The same provisions listed above also hold true for employment agencies in their endeavor to place individuals in positions of employment.

(c) It shall be unlawful for a labor organization to exclude individuals from membership; limit or classify its membership; or cause an employer to discriminate based on an individual's race, color, religion, sex, or national origin.

(d) It shall be unlawful for any employer, labor organization, or joint labor-management committee controlling any form of training program to discriminate based on an individual's race, color, religion, sex, or national origin.

(e) The exception to the above provisions is in certain instances where religion, sex, or national origin is a bona fide occupational qualification.

---

* *Source:* U.S. Equal Employment Opportunity Commission

(f) These employment laws do not cover individuals who are members of the Communist Party of the United States or any other organization required to register as a Communist-action or Communist-front organization by final order of the Subversive Activities Control Board pursuant to the Subversive Activities Control Act of 1950.

(g) Notwithstanding any other provision of this subchapter, it shall not be an unlawful employment practice for an employer to fail or refuse to hire and employ any individual for any position, for an employer to discharge any individual from any position, or for an employment agency to fail or refuse to refer any individual for employment in any position, or for a labor organization to fail or refuse to refer any individual for employment in any position, if national security is at stake.

(h) Notwithstanding any other provision of this subchapter, it shall not be an unlawful employment practice for an employer to apply different standards of compensation and other employment privileges based on employees' merit, seniority, or productivity.

(i) Nothing contained in this subchapter shall apply to a business on or near an Indian reservation with respect to any publicly announced employment practice of such business under which a preferential treatment is given to any individual because he is an Indian living on or near a reservation.

(j) Nothing contained in this subchapter shall be interpreted to mean that an individual should receive preferential treatment because of his race, color, religion, sex, or national origin.

(k) (A) An unlawful employment practice based on disparate impact is established under this title only if:
   (i) a complaining party demonstrates that a respondent uses a particular employment practice that causes a disparate impact on the basis of race, color, religion, sex, or national origin and the respondent fails to demonstrate that the challenged practice is job related for the position in question and consistent with business necessity; or
   (ii) the complaining party makes the demonstration described in subparagraph (c) with respect to an alternative employment practice and the respondent refuses to adopt such alternative employment practice.
   (B) (i) With respect to demonstrating that a particular employment practice causes a disparate impact as described in subparagraph (A)(i), the complaining party shall demonstrate that each particular challenged employment practice causes a disparate impact, except if the complaining party can prove to the court that the elements of the respondent's decision making process are not capable of separation for analysis, and should therefore be examined as a whole.
      (ii) If the respondent demonstrates that a specific employment practice does not cause the disparate impact, the respondent shall not be required to demonstrate that such practice is required by business necessity.

A demonstration that an employment practice is required by business necessity may not be used as a defense against a claim of intentional discrimination under this title.

Notwithstanding any other provision of this title, it is not considered unlawful to refuse to hire an individual who is using or in possession of any illegal controlled substance.

(l) It shall be an unlawful employment practice to use different testing standards for an individual because of race, color, religion, sex, or national origin.

(m) An unlawful employment practice is generally established when the complaining party demonstrates that race, color, religion, sex, or national origin was a motivating factor for any employment practice, even though other factors also may have motivated the practice.

# Appendix H

# STATE EXEMPTIONS FOR BANKRUPTCY OR FEDERAL EXEMPTIONS

| State | Exemption Requirement |
|---|---|
| Alabama | State exemptions |
| Alaska | State or federal exemptions |
| Arizona | State exemptions |
| Arkansas | State exemptions |
| California | State exemptions |
| Colorado | State exemptions |
| Connecticut | State or federal exemptions |
| Delaware | State exemptions |
| District of Columbia | State or federal exemptions |
| Florida | State exemptions |
| Georgia | State exemptions |
| Hawaii | State or federal exemptions |
| Idaho | State exemptions |
| Illinois | State exemptions |
| Indiana | State exemptions |
| Iowa | State exemptions |
| Kansas | State exemptions |
| Kentucky | State exemptions |

| State | Exemption Requirement |
|---|---|
| Louisiana | State exemptions |
| Maine | State exemptions |
| Maryland | State exemptions |
| Massachusetts | State or federal exemptions |
| Michigan | State or federal exemptions |
| Minnesota | State or federal exemptions |
| Mississippi | State exemptions |
| Missouri | State exemptions |
| Montana | State exemptions |
| Nebraska | State exemptions |
| Nevada | State exemptions |
| New Hampshire | State exemptions |
| New Jersey | State or federal exemptions |
| New Mexico | State or federal exemptions |
| New York | State exemptions |
| North Carolina | State exemptions |
| North Dakota | State exemptions |
| Ohio | State exemptions |
| Oklahoma | State exemptions |
| Oregon | State exemptions |
| Pennsylvania | State or federal exemptions |
| South Carolina | State exemptions |
| South Dakota | State exemptions |
| Tennessee | State exemptions |
| Texas | State or federal exemptions |
| Utah | State exemptions |
| Vermont | State or federal exemptions |
| Virginia | State exemptions |
| Washington | State or federal exemptions |
| West Virginia | State exemptions |
| Wisconsin | State or federal exemptions |
| Wyoming | State exemptions |

# Appendix I

# ALTERNATIVE
# LEGAL SERVICES
# RESOURCE LIST

Brian Hudson Burke, 15 East Camillo Street, Santa Barbara, CA 93101, (805) 965-2888

A Certified Family Law Specialist and former President of the Santa Barbara Bar Association, Brian Burke has retired from litigation and concentrates on consulting and mediation.

Michael Cain, Tele-Lawyer, 18377 Beach Street, No. 305, Huntington Beach, CA 92648, Newport Beach, CA, (900) 370-7000, (714) 536-2325

Using a 900-number in which charges are billed directly to the client's telephone, Tele-Lawyer offers legal advice by the minute but does not prepare documents.

Mosten & Wasserstrom, 10990 Wilshire Boulevard, Suite 940, Los Angeles, CA 90024, (310) 473-7611

This urban three-lawyer firm offers pro se coaching billable in six-minute segments, ranging from $175 to $350 per hour. The firm has set up a client library with client educational books, videos, and computer facilities. The library, named for Louis M. Brown, father of preventive law, is available free of charge to clients, opposing parties and counsel, and professional colleagues. Routine Preventive Legal Wellness checkups are utilized by clients in both unbundled and full-service representation.

Will Hornsby, American Bar Association, 750 North Lake Shore Drive, Chicago, IL 60611, (312) 988-5000

Will Hornsby has served as staff counsel in the American Bar Association's Legal Services Division since January 1990. He is responsible for the development of the ABA Commission on Advertising and the Standing Committee on the Delivery of Legal Services. These entities design, coordinate, and conduct research; identify exemplary and replicable models; disseminate information; and develop and advance policy recommendations toward achieving the goal of justice for all.

Noreen Sharp, O.P., Maricopa County Central Court Building, 4th Floor, Phoenix, AZ 92648, (602) 266-6311

Noreen Sharp is the Director of Access to Court Services Programs for the Arizona Superior Court in Maricopa County, Arizona. She is currently implementing the Court's Self-Service Center, a program designed to provide self-represented litigants with court information and firms, and with linkages to services in the community including attorney consultations, counseling, and other social services, and community dispute resolution.

Barbara Shea, Court Coach, 105 Rowayton Avenue, Rowayton, CT 06853, (203) 838-7001

Ed Sherman, Nolo Press, with Anne Lober, Peggy Williams, and Susan Cameron at Divorce Helpline (and other legal services), 2425 Porter Street, Suite 18, Soquel, CA 95073, (408) 464-1114

Ed Sherman is best known for making legal procedures understandable and useful for average people, and for introducing numerous innovations in legal service. In 1971, he founded Nolo Press—the originator and national leader in self-help legal products. He is a partner at Sherman, Williams and Lober and cofounder of Divorce Helpline, a legal/counseling/mediation service for people who prefer to handle their own divorces.

Vivian Lynn Holley, Law and Mediation Offices, One Daniel Burnham Ct., Suite 240 C, San Francisco, CA 94109, (415) 474-1011

As a Certified Specialist in Family Law, and a marriage and family counselor, this attorney mediates disputes, family, neighborhood, and those concerning real estate and partnerships. Vivian has been mediating since 1977.

Louis M. Brown, National Center for Preventive Law, University of Denver, Denver, CO

A past president of the Beverly Hills Bar Association who practiced law for nearly 30 years before becoming a law professor at the University of California Law Center, he is widely regarded as the inventor of the field of preventive law. He is the originator of the personal legal check-up for individuals, the corporate legal audit to help companies identify legal needs and prevent problems, and initiated the Client Counseling Competition held in law schools internationally.

Ken Blonsley, Family Mediation Center, 1308 Main Street, Suite 103, St. Helena, CA 94574, (707) 463-3161

Ken is a psychotherapist and attorney/mediator with a specialized practice in Napa Valley, California.

Judge Roderick Duncan, 1221 Oak Street, Oakland, CA 94612

Recently retired from the bench after 20 years, 8 as family law judge, he is in the process of creating an alternative practice founded on his judicial expertise and is a founding member of the Creative Law Practice Institute.

Lowell Halverson, 3035 Island Crest Way, Mercer Island, WA 98040, (206) 236-9000

A matrimonial attorney with a long-established practice, Lowell Halverson offers clients a library and copying facility and uniquely utilizes the Myer-Briggs Personality Test with clients to help facilitate the legal process.

Alan Kaplan & Victor Musy, 60 Bonifacio Plaza, Monterey, CA 93940, (408) 375-5100

Founded in 1993 and staffed by lawyers and paralegals, Lawyers on Duty offers clients a range of choices from the sale of "how to" books to the full services of a lawyer. Fees are paid at the time of service.

Wayne Moore, AARP, 601 E Street NW, Washington, DC 20049, (202) 434-2149

The originator of the AARP legal hotlines for older Americans and a pioneer of pro bono legal service programs, Wayne Moore is currently developing a discount legal services program for AARP members.

Bill van Zyverden, Holistic Justice Center, P.O. Box 753, Middlebury, VT 05753, (802) 388-7478

The title speaks for itself. Bill, also the founder of the International Alliance of Holistic Lawyers, adheres to certain principles: client introspection, responsibility and partnership; and, civility to adversaries.

# Appendix J

# SELECTED PUBLICATIONS FROM THE AMERICAN BAR ASSOCIATION

The American Bar Association is the world's largest legal publisher. They produce publications in a variety of formats. To order the complete Publications Catalog, call (312) 988-5555.

### Alternative Dispute Resolution

*Alternative Dispute Resolution: An ADR Primer.* A pamphlet designed to answer some basic questions lawyers and judges frequently ask about Alternative Dispute Resolution (ADR).

### Antitrust Law

*Antitrust Law Developments (Second).* A comprehensive review of federal antitrust law, with reports on current case law and administrative and legislative developments, current through November 1983.

### Bankruptcy

*A Desk-Side Guide to the Rules of Bankruptcy.* Details the rules of bankruptcy in a handy form.

### Construction Law

*Design and Construction Contracts: Representing the Owner.* A book for attorneys representing the owners of building projects. It will be helpful in understanding and providing counsel on the design agreement, the contract for general construction, and the construction management agreement. Numerous sample agreements and forms are included.

## Corporations

*Corporate Tax Reform: A Report of the Invitational Conference on Subchapter C.* Contains proceedings of the April 1987 invitational conference on the taxation of corporations and their shareholders, including papers on corporate acquisition, distribution, and entity classification, as well as excerpts and summaries of the discussions on these topics.

*Executive Compensation: A 1987 Road Map for the Corporate Advisor.* A general guide and research aid for the nonspecialist, the report describes the leading kinds of executive compensation arrangements and their principal legal and regulatory aspects including tax, securities, corporation law, and financial accounting.

*Strategic Planning for Corporate Counsel: Tactics and Techniques for the 1990s.* Helps corporate law departments understand and implement a long-range strategic plan. Includes goal setting, review and assessment, budgeting, use of outside counsel, recruiting, and training.

## Courts

*The Supreme Court and Its Justices.* Contains articles from the *ABA Journal* by and about members of the Supreme Court, the great issues of their times, and the unique role of the court in American society.

## Insurance

*Commercial Blanket Bond Annotated.* Analyzes and annotates separately every section of the standard dishonesty policies now in use. Also includes a brief history of bonding policies and sample policies.

### Property Insurance Law Package

*Business Interruption Coverage, Standard Mortgage Clause, and Pollution and Contamination.* A package combining three TIPS property insurance law publications.

### Intellectual Property Law

*Recent Developments in Patent, Trademark, and Copyright Law.* Yearly analysis of developments in intellectual property law, including legislative updates, administrative rules changes, and decisions of the court of appeals for federal circuit.

### International Law

*The Antidumping and Countervailing Duty Laws: Key Legal and Policy Issues.* Compilation of articles previously published in the *International Lawyer* that examine key and often critical policy issues.

*The Convention for the International Sale of Goods: A Handbook of Basic Materials.* A thorough and revealing examination of the history of the Convention, both in the United Nations and the U.S. Congress. Details about the parties, signatories, and accompanying reservations are discussed.

*Joint Venturing Abroad: A Case Study.* A step-by-step guide to forming a joint venture outside the United States. A complete set of hypothetical joint venture documents and contracts are included and systematically analyzed.

### Labor and Employment Law

*In Defense of the Public Employer: Case Law and Litigation Strategies for Discrimination Claims.* Focuses primarily on the public sector. The first part of this guide presents a complete overview of the case law. The second part discusses strategies for the defense of the suit, from the initial response to the settlement of a claim.

*Model Partnership Agreement: For the Small Law Firm.* Designed to encourage the adoption of a written partnership agreement by small law firms. Has sections on organization, administration, capital and drawing accounts, income determination, loss of a partner.

*Recommended Law Books (2nd ed.).* Guide to the best law books and reference materials available, focusing on quality, usefulness, and value. Covers all areas of law and includes current prices. Reflects the tremendous increase of materials and the emergences of new areas since the original 1969 edition.

*Two-Tier Partnerships and Other Alternatives: Five Approaches.* This monograph examines different partnership structures, including two-tier partnerships. Analyzes the pros and cons, key features, and strategic considerations for implementing a new structure.

*Withdrawal, Retirement, and Disputes: What You and Your Firm Need to Know.* Economics of Law Practice Sect. Discusses issues, considerations, and problems related to partner withdrawal, disability, and retirement.

## Legal Services

*A Report on Self-Help Law: Its Many Perspectives.* Analysis of comparative study of the use of attorney representation and self-representation in no-fault divorces and simple bankruptcy actions in Maricopa County, Arizona.

*A Survey of Lawyer Referral and Information Services.* Annual survey of national lawyer referral services, containing information about management, membership, volume, referral process, quality control, publicity, and finances.

## Real Property

*Real Property and the 1988 Tax Reform Act: What You and Your Clients Should Know.* This publication will provide lawyers and their clients with an overview of the 1986 Tax Reform Act's impact on real estate acquisition and development.

*Title Insurance: The Lawyer's Expanding Role.* Details the uses of title insurance, the nature and extent of its coverage, the rights and obligations of the buyer and seller, and the lawyer's role in dealing with its problems.

## Taxation

*ABA Sales and Use Tax Handbook.* Provides attorneys, tax managers, and accountants with an extensive treatment of the sales and use tax laws in all states and the District of Columbia.

*Understanding the Federal Income Tax: A Lawyer's Guide to the Code and Its Provisions.* Describes the tax in effect for 1988 and later years (as provided for by the 1986 Tax Reform Act). This book offers clear, concise explanations of the reasoning behind the federal income tax, its interpretations, and its application.

## Trial Practice

*McElhaney's Trial Notebook.* Offers sound practical advice oriented to actual courtroom practice. Techniques for achieving more effective advocacy are illustrated with numerous examples.

# Appendix K

# SMALL BUSINESS ASSOCIATION OFFICES

Alabama SBDC Consortium
University of Alabama at Birmingham
Medical Towers Building
1717 11th Avenue, Suite 419
Birmingham, AL 35294-4410
(205) 934-7260

Alaska SBD Center
University of Alaska Anchorage
430 West Seventh Avenue, Suite 110
Anchorage, AK 99501
(907) 274-7232

Arizona SBDC Network
2411 West 14th Street, Suite 132
Tempe, AZ 85281
(602) 731-8720

Arkansas SBDC
University of Arkansas at Little Rock
100 South Main, Suite 401
Little Rock, AR 72201
(501) 324-9043

California SBDC Program
Department of Commerce
801 K Street, Suite 1700
Sacramento, CA 95814
(916) 324-5068

Colorado SBDC
Office of Business Development
1625 Broadway, Suite 1710
Denver, CO 80202
(303) 892-3809

Connecticut SBDC
University of Connecticut
368 Fairfield Road, U-41, Room 422
Storrs, CT 06269-2041
(203) 486-4135

Delaware SBDC
University of Delaware
Purnell Hall, Suite 005
Newark, DE 19716-2711
(302) 831-2747

District of Columbia SBDC
Howard University
Sixth and Fairmont Streets NW,
    Room 128
Washington, DC 20059
(202) 806-1550

Florida SBDC
Network University of West Florida
19 West Garden Street, Suite 300
Pensacola, FL 32501
(904) 444-2060

Georgia SBDC
University of Georgia
Chicopee Complex, 1180 East Broad
    Street
Athens, GA 30602-5412
(706) 542-5760

Hawaii SBDC
Network University of Hawaii at Hilo
200 West Kiwih
Hilo, HI 96720
(808) 933-3515

Idaho SBDC
Boise State University
1910 University Drive
Boise, ID 83725
(208) 385-1640

Illinois SBDC
Department of Commerce and
    Community Affairs
620 East Adams Street, 6th Floor
Springfield, IL 62701
(217) 524-5856

Indiana SBDC
Economic Development Council
One North Capitol, Suite 420
Indianapolis, IN 46204
(317) 264-6871

Iowa SBDC
Iowa State University
137 Lynn Avenue
Ames, IA 50014
(515) 292-6351

Kansas SBDC
Wichita State University
1845 Fairmount
Wichita, KS 67260-0148
(316) 689-3193

Kentucky SBDC
University of Kentucky
Center for Business Development
225 Business and Economics Building
Lexington, KY 40506-0034
(606) 257-7668

Louisiana SBDC
Northeast Louisiana University, CBA
700 University Avenue
Monroe, LA 71209-6435
(318) 342-5506

Main SBDC
University of Southern Maine
96 Falmouth Street
Portland, ME 04103
(207) 780-4420

Maryland SBDC
Department of Economic and
    Employment Development
217 East Redwood Street, 10th Floor
Baltimore, MD 21202
(410) 333-6995

Massachusetts SBDC
University of Massachusetts-Amherst
Room 205, School of Management
Amherst, MA 01003
(413) 545-6301

Michigan SBDC
2727 Second Avenue
Detroit, MI 48201
(313) 964-1798

Mississippi SBDC
University of Mississippi
Old Chemistry Building, Suite 216
University, MS 38677
(601) 232-5001

Missouri SBDC
University of Missouri
300 University Place
Columbia, MO 65211
(314) 882-0344

Montana SBDC
Montana Department of Commerce
1424 9th Avenue
Helena, MT 59620
(406) 444-4780

Nebraska Business Development Center
University of Nebraska at Omaha
60th and Dodge Streets, CBA Room 407
Omaha, NE 68182
(402) 554-2521

Nevada SBDC
University of Nevada, Reno
College of Business Administration-032,
    Room 411
Reno, NV 89557-0100
(702) 784-1717

New Hampshire SBDC
University of New Hampshire
108 McConnell Hall
Durham, NH 03824
(603) 862-2200

New Jersey SBDC
Rutgers University Graduate School of
    Management
180 University Avenue
Newark, NJ 07102
(201) 648-5950

New Mexico SBDC
Santa Fe Community College
P.O. Box 4187
Sante Fe, NM 87502-4187
(505) 438-1362

New York State SBDC
State University of New York
SUNY Central Plaza, S-523
Albany, NY 12246
(518) 443-5398

North Carolina SBDC
University of North Carolina
4509 Creedmoor Road, Suite 201
Raleigh, NC 27612
(919) 571-4154

North Dakota SBDC
University of North Dakota
118 Gamble Hall, UND, Box 7308
Grand Fork, ND 58202
(701) 777-3700

Ohio SBDC
77 South High Street
P.O. Box 1001
Columbus, OH 43266-0101
(614) 466-2711

Oklahoma SBDC
Southeastern Oklahoma State University
P.O. Box 2584, Station A
Durant, OK 74701
(405) 924-0277

Oregon SBDC
Lane Community College
44 West Broadway, Suite 501
Eugene, OR 97401-3021
(503) 726-2250

Pennsylvania SBDC
The Wharton School, University of
    Pennsylvania
444 Vance Hall, 3733 Spruce Street
Philadelphia, PA 19104-6374
(215) 898-1219

Puerto Rico SBDC
University of Puerto Rico
P.O. Box 5253, College Station
Mayaguez, PR 00681
(809) 834-3590

Rhode Island SBDC
Bryant College
1150 Douglas Pike
Smithfield, RI 02917
(401) 232-6111

SBDC
University of South Carolina
College of Business Administration
Columbia, SC 29201-9980
(803) 777-4907

South Dakota SBDC
University of South Dakota
414 East Clark
Vermillion, SD 57069
(605) 677-5279

Tennessee SBDC
Memphis State University
Building 1, South Campus
Memphis, TN 38152
(901) 678-2500

North Texas-Dallas SBDC
Institute for Economic Development
1402 Corinth Street
Dallas, TX 75215
(214) 565-5833

Texas-Houston SBDC
University of Houston
1100 Louisiana, Suite 500
Houston, TX 77002
(713) 752-8444

Northwest Texas SBDC
Texas Tech University
2579 South Loop 289, Suite 114
Lubbock, TX 79423
(806) 745-3973

UTSA South Texas Border SBDC
UTSA Downtown Center
1222 North Main Street, Suite 450
San Antonio, TX 78212
(210) 224-0791

Utah SBDC
102 West 500 South, Suite 315
Salt Lake City, UT 84101
(801) 581-7905

Vermont SBDC
Vermont Technical College
P.O. Box 422
Randolph, VT 05060
(802) 728-9101

UVI SBDC
Sunshine Mall, Suite 104
St. Croix, USVI 00840
(809) 776-3206

Virginia SBDC
901 East Byrd Street, Suite 1800
Richmond, VA 23219
(904) 371-8253

Washington SBDC
Washington State University
Kruegel Hall, Suite 135
Pullman, WA 99164-4727
(509) 335-1576

West Virginia SBDC
GOCID
I 1 15 Virginia Street East
Charleston, WV 25301
(304) 558-2960

Wisconsin SBDC
University of Wisconsin
432 North Lake Street, Room 423
Madison, WI 53706
(608) 263-7794

WSBDC/State Network Office
P.O. Box 3275
Laramie, WY 82071-3275
(307) 766-3505

# Appendix L

# LEGAL PRIMER:
# THE LAW OF THE LAND
# AND HOW TO FIND IT

Before you delve into the deep and potentially murky waters of the law, and how it applies to you and your business, we hope to help you understand in simple lay terms exactly what "the law" is. It will also be helpful to learn a few basics about using the law library.

This legal primer will teach you in a few short pages what law students often take many months to understand: the basic substantive and procedural fundamentals of the law. Since you will have neither the time nor the inclination to learn more than you need to know (hence, your purchase of this book), we will limit ourselves to teaching you the basics.

Be of good cheer knowing that your exposure to the law is no more limited than that of most students in their first semester of law school. Definitions for the "terms of art" (what is sometimes referred to as legalese) are the first building blocks we will give you. Second, we will help you understand the law—statutes, regulations, and case law—and then teach you how to apply the "law" to the facts.

Once you have a working knowledge of legal definitions, and the substantive and procedural laws applicable to your situation, and once you practice thinking analytically, you will be 10 steps ahead of your competitors and well positioned to save legal dollars when working with your attorney.

## WHAT IS THE LAW?

Several different answers to this question leap to mind. According to *Black's Law Dictionary* the "law, in its generic sense, is a body of rules of action or conduct prescribed by controlling authority, (that) have binding legal force." Black goes on to define law as "that which must be obeyed and followed by citizens subject to sanctions or legal consequences. . . ."

Philosophically, the law is an expression of society's value system as a whole. When society reaches a point at which certain behaviors become intolerable or the converse, desirable, or certain beliefs become self-evident, these values are often expressed as law in law. So, for example, as we became a merchant society, laws developed to ensure that merchants could exchange, manage, and operate money transactions, goods, and services in a way that would be fair to all. And because we as a society believe that all humans are created equal, we instituted laws abolishing slavery, sexual harassment and ensuring equal rights in the voting process. (But sadly, we did not pass the ERA.) And, for example, because we believe that as citizens we have certain rights and entitlements, we enact laws against discrimination in the workplace and limit immigration.

## Fact, Law, and Theory

From a lawyer's point of view, a fact is an actual occurrence impacting one of the senses. If you can see it, smell it, touch it, taste it, or hear it, then it qualifies as an evidentiary fact. A law, by contrast, is a tangible codification of principle. *Black's Law Dictionary* makes several other distinctions between facts and law; law is a principle, whereas fact is an "event." Law is conceived; fact is actual. Law is a rule of duty; fact is that which has been learned. This distinction between law and fact is an important concept to understand because this is exactly what lawyers do for a living *i.e.*, apply law to facts, and this book is meant to get you on track to thinking like a lawyer.

The legal process is to gather the facts, sort out truth from fiction, and then, with an understanding of what the law is, apply the law to the facts and reach a conclusion. If you can catch the flavor of this, you will be able to start sorting out the legal problems that arise in running a small business analytically, like a lawyer.

The goal of this book is to teach you to think like a lawyer so that you can learn to apply the law to the facts to determine the probable result or outcome. In this process, you will be working in the realm of "probability,"—what will most likely occur and the probable result; your conclusions will be a best guesstimate.

For small business owners, it's the civil laws that most often apply, although, as you know, every now and then a white-collar *crime* is committed and a businessperson can and will be subjected to criminal punishment. The usual legal standard or basis for drawing a conclusion from the facts based on the law is called the "reasonable person" standard. In short, one queries: What would a reasonable person, given these facts and this law, conclude?

Consequently, the more facts you gather accurately, and the better you understand the law, the better your chances of reaching the right, the winning conclusion! If you are experiencing difficulty reaching a conclusion that feels "right," then in all likelihood, you do not have enough information, facts, at your fingertips. Pieces of the puzzle are missing. Once you have all the pieces or facts, the answer to the problem will come sharply into focus. A wonderful experience, the *Aha!* experience.

## Civil versus Criminal Law

Law can also be viewed from the perspective of falling into one of two categories: a crime for which punishment in the form of incarceration and fines is meted out; or a civil matter that gives a complainant an opportunity to obtain all kinds of relief, from money damages to injunctions.

Anything not a crime falls into the category of civil. Civil law is concerned with our *private rights and remedies.* Criminal law is the province of the government and deals with *public rights and wrongs.* Consequently, the state and federal governments are charged with administering justice by prosecuting crimes and misdemeanors and having individuals sentenced to punishment for disobeying the law or acquitted. In a civil matter, your lawsuit is called "a cause of action." You, as the plaintiff, give your adversary notice by serving a "writ," "summons," and "complaint." In these papers, you as the plaintiff advise the defendant about what you are complaining about and set forth the "relief" you desire. It sounds simple and it is.

## State versus Federal Law

Quite simply, state laws are those that apply only in a given state, and vary from state to state. That is the reason an attorney must hold a license in each state of practice, ensuring that the attorney has the requisite expertise in your state's law. If you have a problem interstate, it is wise to seek out an attorney with multiple licenses or a larger firm with offices in the state where your legal problem arises.

Many of the midsize and large law firms have offices and attorneys in distant states, even other countries around the world. Also, you can ask your local attorney for a referral to an attorney in another state specializing in the area of law you need.

When bringing a dispute to court, you need to zero in on your state's statutory and case law. If there is no law on the specific subject or similar facts, look to neighboring state law. It will not be binding in your state but can show trends to the court in your state where the issue has not been litigated.

## Statutory Law versus Case Law

State and federal laws (as well as municipal laws) are further divided into two "kinds" of law: statutory, the statutes or laws passed by a legislative body; and case law, or the law developed by the courts. Case law flows from both private disputes between individuals and/or business entities in the civil courts, and from public disputes in the criminal courts.

Statutory law on a state level refers to the statutes, or the laws, that your elected representatives vote on and pass into law in the state legislature in your state capitol. Statutory law on a federal level refers to the laws passed in Congress, and also to federal regulations.

Each state develops its own system of courts. Basically the lowest courts, hearing the smallest matters, are generally the municipal courts (if any); state trial courts located in judicial districts around the state are usually called superior courts and hear civil or criminal matters. Appellate courts hear cases in which the disputants disagree with the results reached in the lower courts for either a civil or criminal action and "appeal" to the higher level appellate court.

In the state of Connecticut, and others, an intermediate appellate level court has been added to review appeals not handled by the highest court in the state, the supreme court. As an interesting aside, New York State, ever the maverick, has named its state trial court the "supreme court."

The case law is developed in the courts on a state and federal level in the following manner. If there is a dispute that cannot be settled by negotiation, it will go to trial. When the results, the judge's or jury's decision, are written down in the form of an opinion (a verdict), it becomes case law under the name of the plaintiffs and defendants. For example, *Sullivan v. The New York Times* is a famous libel case that is still a legal precedent.

The case law "reporters" record these decisions. These reporters start with the earliest reported case, either in federal volumes or in individual state volumes. Later in this chapter, we will explain how the federal and state citation systems work so that you can actually find the cases that apply to your situation.

## Constitutional Law

The Constitution of the United States is the framework upon which all of our laws are based. No law—case or statutory, state or federal, substantive or procedural—can be enacted or allowed to stand if it is in contravention of any of the Constitution.

Each state has a State Constitution that is the source of fundamental rights within the state; just as the U.S. Constitution, the Bill of Rights, and Amendments to the Constitution set forth rights for the nation.

## Regulations and Administrative Law

Congress empowers different administrative agencies to make rules and regulations. These regulatory bodies, like the Internal Revenue Service on a federal level, establish rules ("regs" or regulations) implementing congressional legislation that citizens and businesses are obliged to follow. When these private parties appear before an administrative body, administrative law is applied.

## Procedural and Substantive Law

Yet another way of looking at the law is to divide it into procedural law and substantive law. The procedural law constitutes the step-by-step "rules of the road" that need to be followed when taking a legal action. Hence, if you are incorporating, organizing, and running a partnership; filing a lawsuit; or dissolving your business, you need to understand and observe court rules and state and federal procedures (all codified as procedural law) to do it right and not be foreclosed from the protection, rights, and remedies, of the substantive law. You will find more on how to research and discover the applicable procedural law later in this chapter.

Then there's the substantive law, the body of law that developed from disputes between private parties (civil law), and between the government and its citizens (criminal and administrative law).

An easy way to differentiate between procedural and substantive law follows: Procedural law sets up the rules; substantive law describes what has happened in an individual situation—the decision and how it was reached. For example, there are rules about capitalizing your company and having a corporate structure. If you don't set up your corporation according to the law, you will be subject to the substantive law called "piercing the corporate veil," a legal concept holding a principal in a corporation personally liable for actions of the corporation if the corporation is, for example, a sham or shell.

Cases are really little vignettes, or novellas. Law libraries are filled with volumes of such vignettes describing what happens to an individual who is involved in an application of the law to certain circumstances. The "caption" of the case includes the name of the plaintiff, the person bringing the suit, and the name of the defendant, the person being sued, as for example (and only an example) *Barbara Shea v. John D. Doe.* Many different categories of substantive law impact a small business: commercial law, consumer law, tort law, international law, to name a few.

Other specific areas of law that might apply to your business, depending on its nature, are admiralty law, environmental law, commodities law, and securities law.

Should you fail as a small business owner, you might very well become familiar with bankruptcy law. You might also be affected by your city or town's laws and ordinances, known as municipal statutes.

## Statute of Limitations

A very important concept in the law is called the *statute of limitations*. Most people have at least a passing familiarity with this concept. Because of its importance to any entrepreneur, we will delve a little further into it. When something happens, for example, the town's snowplow hits and destroys your truck, you are a potential plaintiff. The statute of limitations means that you will be allowed a certain amount of time within which to seek legal redress.

The limitation of time by statute exists because the law does not want you to "sleep on your rights." People and business entities can stay in business and keep producing because the law encourages swift resolution and gives peace of mind by not allowing potential threats of liability to remain outstanding for many years. The statute of limitations varies for different kinds of lawsuits, called causes of action (see Table L–1).

Ordinarily, when you sue a municipality or government body there are additional requirements or limitations. Thus, if an accident happens, as with the snowplow, and

**Table L–1**   Connecticut Statute of Limitations

| Cause of Action | Time Limitation |
|---|---|
| • Enforce recorded restrictions on maps | 3 years |
| • Action on account | 6 years |
| • Balance book account | 6 years |
| • Adverse possession | 15 years |
| • Simple or implied contracts | 6 years (except U.S. court judgment) |
| • Tort (other than otherwise listed) | 3 years |
| • Highway—Change in grade of | 6 years |
| • Bond—Probate suit on | 6 years |
| • Contract—Oral | 3 years |
| • Sheriff or constable action against | 2 years |
| • Negligence, reckless or wanton misconduct or malpractice | 2 years |
| • Counterclaim | Anytime before pleadings close |
| • Forfeiture on penal statute | 1 year |
| • Bond or recognizance for costs—suit on | 1 year |
| • Note obtained by fraud | 1 year after notice, 6 months after due |
| • Forcible entry and detainer | 6 months after entry |
| • Time excluded while out of state | Shall not exceed 7 years |
| • Executor, on action that survives | 1 year from death |
| • Fraudulent concealment of cause of action | Time commences to run when cause discovered |
| • Remuneration for employment | 2 years |
| • Defamation | 2 years |
| • New Action, accidental failure | 1 year |
| • New Action, after reversal | 1 year |
| • New Action, wrong defendant | 1 year |

a local government agency is responsible, you may have a very short statute of limitation, perhaps just a month, to let the "powers that be" know that you intend to sue the town to recover damages for your truck so you can stay in business.

The most common statute of limitations is two years from the date of occurrence, but the statute of limitations in a breach of contract action is usually seven years. So, fair warning: *Do not sleep on your rights.* The statute of limitations is almost the very first thing a lawyer considers when a client comes into the office and says, "I have a legal problem."

The smart thing to do when you are involved in an incident with potential legal liability is to determine your time limits under the relevant statute of limitations for this kind of action. Since you will be foreclosed from going to court if you delay in filing suit until after the statute of limitations has elapsed. More than one entrepreneur with a very good case has lost a right to relief or recovery because of a failure to get into court in a timely fashion. Don't let it be you!

## WHERE TO FIND THE LAW: THE LAW LIBRARY

Now that you know what the law is, you need to know where to find it. Reading this book is a great way to whet your appetite to learn more on your own—primarily at the law library.

## Where to Find the Law Library and What You'll Find There

Obviously enough, your main source for the law is the law library. Generally, your local courthouse will have a law library (or, in the worst-case scenario, somewhere in your state, in some courthouse, there *will* be a law library). And many law firms also have law libraries, as well as on-line computerized research facilities. Don't be shy about asking your attorney to let you use their library, and check out any local law schools' libraries.

When you walk into the law library as a novice legal researcher, the first item to locate is, believe it or not, the law librarian or a law clerk. This is "the" person best equipped to help you find what you're looking for. The reception you receive depends, of course, on the person and your state's commitment to providing citizens with free legal services. Do not be daunted if the clerk informs you that legal "advice" is not available. Simply reply that you are not seeking advice but "information."

Inquire at your local courthouse about legal services such as mediation services, accelerated trial systems, alternative dispute resolution (ADR), and other alternatives to trial (master's programs, hearings by retired judges) that are being developed to deal with court overload and judicial logjams. Do not be afraid to ask questions. The law librarian in a state courthouse is a state employee, and your tax dollars are paying that salary.

On your law library shelves, you'll find bound volumes setting forth your state's laws, the amendments to and the repeals of those laws, and a handy index to those statutes. Federal law is also there, bound separately, and is referred to as the United States Code (USC).

If you are looking for a state statute, which is what is most likely, take these steps: (1) Find the index; (2) find the section number where, for example, the Business Law section is indexed. Under the Business Law Index, you can look up various major topics (e.g., corporations, partnership, sole proprietorship). Once you familiarize yourself with the index and start looking through the book, you will soon get the gist of how it works.

If you are looking for a case, take these steps: (1) Find the pertinent "court reporter," which is the set of casebooks with the abbreviation contained in your case cite (e.g., U.S. stands for United States and indicates reports for the Supreme Court of the United States); (2) note the first number in the cite—it is the volume number—go to that volume in the court reporter; (3) find the second number in your cite, which is the page number; (4) simply turn to that page and the decision for the case that you are looking for will begin there. After you've located the cases that apply to your situation, your next step is to find the copy machine, as these volumes of state statutes are reference books that are not allowed to wander far from the library.

It's a good idea to organize your case file from the outset as follows:

- One section for the statutory or regulatory law.
- One section for the state or federal case law applicable. Subdivide under issues, which can be more simply stated as cases supporting each of the arguments you want to make.
- If there are no cases on point (that is, having the same or similar facts and problems that you are facing), look at cases in neighboring states.

## Additional Sources for Federal Statutes

In the small business arena, you need to be mainly concerned about the following federal laws:

- Internal Revenue Code.
- Family and Medical Leave Act.
- Title VII.
- Americans with Disabilities Act.
- Occupational Safety and Health Administration (OSHA).
- Employment Retirement Income Security Act of 1974 (ERISA).
- Federal labor laws.
- Environmental Protection Act.

There are more, and federal law is more fully discussed in Chapter 18. These laws are available on your law library shelves and in bound volumes in bookstores as well. The U.S. Department of Labor can provide materials, including large posters with relevant information on federal law and also labor laws for all your employees gathered around the coffeepot to read. Also, the IRS will send you all necessary tax forms *and* provide you with a multitude of pamphlets and resources if you know what to ask for.

## Your Local Bar Association

Most state and local bar associations offer seminars on different aspects of business law—from franchising to bankruptcy—and print and bind these presentations for the local bar members and for the public to purchase (usually, at a rather hefty price). Call your state bar association and inquire into the materials they offer on a given subject. These presentations are usually available in audiocassette as well, but the printed materials have the bonus of being something you can underline, copy, fax, and mail. These are usually state-of-the-art and the latest word.

You could also ask for a schedule of upcoming presentations at your local bar association and inquire if you would be eligible to attend any of the seminars and be placed on a mailing list. Also some seminars are managed by independent companies such as the Practicing Law Institute (PLI), through the bar association. Your local bar association can tell you all about how to contact these companies on your own.

## Computerized Libraries

State and federal laws may be accessed by various means. On-line services can be accessed by a computer and a modem. The leading on-line networks are LEXIS and WESTLAW. Lots of individual companies are springing up (e.g., Casebase) that offer state law. Check your local phone directories for numbers to call for these services. In addition, various legal publishing companies have published state and federal material on CD-ROM, the current state-of-the-art technology for electronic libraries.

---

### BASIC LEGAL RESEARCH

- *Legal encyclopedias.* These provide brief overviews of all sorts of legal topics compiled by various legal publishers, such as American Law Reports and West Publishing.
- *Pocket parts.* These updates are found in the back of all legal statute books and case reports. They give you the most recent cases and statutes or amendments to statutes.
- *Horn books.* Various authors, top legal experts in the various fields of law, pen these series of books. Each of these substantive books covers a given topic.
- *Law digests.* These topical digests allow you to turn to a subject and, starting from the subject matter as a base, find any court cases in your state or region that talk about that issue. Example: Callimari and Perillo on Contracts.
- *Outline/Review books.* The "Cliffs Notes of law," these books cover individual topics in outline form. They are wonderful. Law students rely on them to consolidate their thinking and you will, too. Look to series by Legallines, Smith's Review, Emanuel and Gilbert Law Summaries.

---

### COURT COACH® SUGGESTS

1. *Research the law and apply it to your situation.*
2. *Don't "sleep on your rights."* Talk to an attorney at the outset for guidance.
3. *Protect your right to a legal remedy:* File a lawsuit promptly.
4. *Inquire at your local courthouse about alternative free legal services.*
5. *Organize your case file from the outset:*
   One section for the statutory or regulatory law.
   One section for the state or federal case law applicable. Subdivide under issues, which can be more simply stated as cases supporting each argument you want to make.
   If there are no cases on point (have the same facts and problems you are facing), look at cases in neighboring states.
6. *Organize your "Pro se attorney file" from the outset, too:* Notes, Pleadings, Documents.
7. *Always, we repeat, always check the Pocket Parts!*
8. *Know that you can find and have access to all cases heard in a particular "trial level" court in the courthouse under Plaintiff-Defendant name and docket number.*
9. *Rent the wonderful old Paul Newman movie,* The Verdict. You will watch a most entertaining example of how lawyers think, how to prepare your case for trial, and how important research and preparing your facts and presentation can be. And, in our opinion, it's vintage Newman, one of his best.

# INDEX